Pra

BLOOD

"Guadalcanal was an epic battle that produced a large body of literature including a number of highly distinguished works. To that body is now added Michael S. Smith's excellent account. . . . It is founded on deep and sagacious research, both in American and Japanese sources."

—Richard B. Frank, author of *Guadalcanal: The Definitive Account of the Landmark Battle*

"[This] book delivers a fascinating analysis of the actions that led to the battle, as well as depicting the combat itself."

—*Journal Inquirer*

"One of the turning points of the Second World War is ably described."

—*Veterans Voice*

The Battle That Saved Guadalcanal

BLOODY RIDGE

Michael S. Smith

POCKET BOOKS

New York   London   Toronto   Sydney   Singapore

POCKET BOOKS, a division of Simon & Schuster, Inc.
1230 Avenue of the Americas, New York, NY 10020

Copyright © 2000 by Michael S. Smith

Published by arrangement with Presidio Press, Inc.

All rights reserved, including the right to reproduce this book or portions thereof in any form whatsoever. For information address Presidio Press, Inc., 505B San Marin Drive, Suite 160, Novato, CA 94945

ISBN: 0-7434-6321-8

First Pocket Books printing February 2003

10 9 8 7 6 5 4 3 2 1

POCKET and colophon are registered trademarks of Simon & Schuster, Inc.

For information regarding special discounts for bulk purchases, please contact Simon & Schuster Special Sales at 1-800-456-6798 or business@simonandschuster.com

Designed by Melissa Isriprashad

Front cover photo by Corbis

Printed in the U.S.A.

Contents

Foreword

"What Guadalcanal stood for to Americans in 1942–3 was a very special thing," wrote James Jones in the introduction to *The Thin Red Line*, his vivid autobiographical novel of fighting there. It was on this obscure island tucked against the equator in the South Pacific that a select band of Americans met the critical moment of their generation's rendezvous with destiny. Time has vindicated Jones's assessment. In the recently acclaimed installment of the Oxford History of the United States, *Freedom from Fear* (1999), David Kennedy sets out what was at stake on Guadalcanal: "On its outcome came to depend not only the military balance in the Pacific but the war morale of the American public. It was, as much as any single engagement could be, a decisive battle."

The struggle for Guadalcanal lasted almost exactly six months, from August 1942 to February 1943. It was marked by seven major naval battles, a score of engagements ashore of varying dimensions, and an almost daily cut and thrust of air clashes. From August to November 1942, the outcome very much hung in doubt. The audacious American offensive had been launched in tremendous haste. That haste gave it the potent ally of surprise, but also bedeviled the enterprise with a host of potentially fatal defects. American sea and air power was in no better than balance with Japan's capacities in those spheres. American command arrangements were deeply marred by self-inflicted wounds in organization and personalities. Logistics were so abysmal that one later analysis declared that, if anyone tutored by subsequent experience in the Pacific had examined the project, he would have declared it impossible.

And Americans faced a foe with formidable military virtues at the crest of their capabilities. Once Japan recoiled from the shock of the landing, its soldiers and sailors turned to converting American imprudence into catastrophe. The Imperial Navy gave painful lessons in its expertise in night surface combat, while an unbroken string of triumphs against Western armies had pumped the Imperial Army full of hubris. It was on Guadalcanal that Japanese stereotypes of effete Americans, hopelessly dependent upon amenities, would suffer a severe collision with reality. The Japanese never came closer to victory on the island itself than in September 1942, on a ridge thrusting up from the jungle just south of the critical airfield, best known ever after as Bloody Ridge.

Guadalcanal was an epic battle that produced a large body of literature, including a number of highly distinguished works. To that body now is added Michael S. Smith's excellent account of the first two months of the fighting ashore. It is founded on deep and sagacious research, both in American and Japanese sources. From this groundwork emerges a powerful driving narrative, integrating command decisions and personalities, radio intelligence, and an acute tactile sense of the "sharp end" where the warriors of Japan and the United States grappled in close-quarter combat. There are always informed and sometimes provocative judgments that can be pondered with profit by veterans, active duty personnel, and just those with interest in this great tale. This is a superb work of the highest achievement.

—Richard B. Frank

Acknowledgments

Many individuals helped make this book possible. Richard B. Frank, author of the distinguished work *Guadalcanal: The Definitive Account of the Landmark Battle* (1990), provided unfailing support throughout this project. Richard also provided me with copies of the Japanese Self Defense Agency history volumes pertaining to the Guadalcanal campaign, which greatly assisted in the completion of this work. Hats off also to Stanley Jersey, an Army Air Force veteran of the Solomons campaign and soon to be a published author himself. Stanley unselfishly shared the fruits of his many years of research and provided me with important documents and sources of information I otherwise would have overlooked. His close friend Edward Rasmussen provided expert translations of some of the Japanese documents used in writing this account.

This book would not have been possible without the help of many U.S. veterans. Only some are listed here. Gunnery Sergeant Harry R. Horsman, USMC (ret.), George Codrea, and John L. Joseph, all of whom fought on Guadalcanal with the 1st Marines, were most helpful in answering questions about the

Battle of the Tenaru and providing maps of the battle. Colonel John Sweeney, USMC (ret.), Capt. Frank Guidone, USMC (ret.), and James Childs of the 1st Raider Battalion also answered many questions and provided copies of the Edson Raiders Association newsletter, *The Dope Sheet*. Master Gunnery Sergeant Ore Marion, USMC (ret.), was the source of a great wealth of information on the 5th Marines and, in particular, his company's participation in the fighting. Outstanding assistance was also provided by the veterans Col. Robert Amery, USAF (ret.), Edward Fee, Joseph O. Gobel, George Haertlein, and Robert Shedd, all of whom are members of the fine organization the Guadalcanal Campaign Veterans Association. The organization's informative periodical, *Guadalcanal Echoes,* remains one of the best World War II veterans publications in existence. Thanks must also go to Jim Donahue and Jim Garrett, who graciously gave me permission to quote from their fathers' World War II diaries.

Two individuals from Japan helped make this work even more accurate and informative with regard to the Japanese side. Itirou Inui, whose father served on Guadalcanal with the 8th Independent Antitank Company, was a big help in answering questions about the campaign, obtaining names of Japanese officers, and translating Japanese documents. Akira Takizawa, a military enthusiast who maintains an excellent website on Imperial Japanese Army weapons and armor, also pointed out obscure sources of information and answered important questions about the Japanese forces that fought on Guadalcanal.

Many research hours were spent at the Marine

Corps Historical Center in Washington, D.C. Several members of the center's staff merit special recognition for their outstanding assistance. Richard Long of the Oral History Section helped me through that collection and pointed out important sources of information. Amy Cantin of the Personal Papers collection was always courteous and most helpful, as was Joyce Bonnett of the Archives Section. George McGillivray, a veteran of the 7th Marines and a volunteer map curator, was particularly helpful in providing information on the 7th Marines and copies of obscure maps and photographs. My hat is also off to the entire staff of the Reference Section and Evelyn A. Englander in the library.

Frequent visits to other archives and libraries in the Washington, D.C., and Norfolk, Virginia, areas were made as well. Archivist James W. Zobel and his assistants at the MacArthur Memorial Bureau of Archives in Norfolk were extremely helpful, as were Thaddeus Ohta and Yoko Akiba at the Library of Congress's Asian Section in Washington. I would also like to thank the staffs of the Naval Historical Center and the National Archives in Washington, the Marine Corps University at Quantico, Virginia, and the Armed Forces Staff College library in Norfolk.

Several people provided vital critiques on style and content. Luis Leme read later drafts of this work and offered many useful suggestions, especially on weapons data. Mark Stille provided constant encouragement and support throughout this project, reviewing many portions of this work. Mark Perry reviewed early drafts of this narrative and provided many helpful suggestions, especially on historical technique and style. My deepest gratitude must go to E. J. McCarthy at Presidio Press, who saw the potential of this book. Special thanks must also go to Craig Spiers and the staff at Softree.com, who provided the software program used in making the maps. Finally, I must thank my wife, Karen, and my children, Michael, Nathan, Ammon, and Daniel, who showed great patience while I worked on this project. Of course, responsibility for any mistakes or errors that appear in this work are mine and mine alone.

—Michael S. Smith

Introduction

In order to capitalize on the decisive American victory at the Battle of Midway in early June 1942, the U.S. Joint Chiefs of Staff issued a directive on 2 July for offensive operations in the South Pacific. It was an ambitious, well-conceived plan, ultimately aimed at denying the Japanese use of New Britain, New Ireland, and New Guinea. To this end, the Joint Chiefs directive outlined three objectives. The first, designated Task One, called for the seizure of "Tulagi and adjacent positions" in the southern Solomons. These adjacent positions included Florida Island, Makambo Island, and the twin islets of Gavutu-Tanambogo, which together served as an important seaplane base for the Japanese. An excellent deep-water harbor between Tulagi and neighboring Florida Island greatly enhanced the military value of the area. Overall command of Task One was given to VAdm. Robert L. Ghormley, the new commander of the South Pacific Area. The Joint Chiefs set D day for 1 August.

On 7 July the Joint Chiefs, in conjunction with Adm. Chester W. Nimitz, Commander-in-Chief Pacific Ocean Areas, changed the principal target of Task One to Guadalcanal, a large island twenty miles south

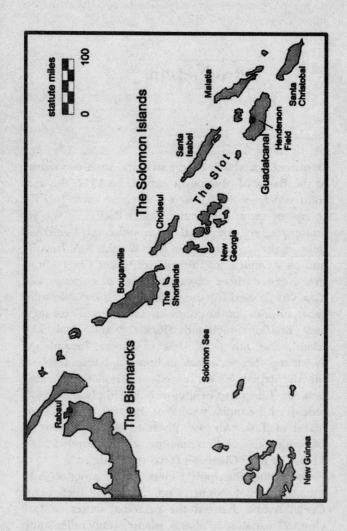

of Tulagi. There the Japanese had begun the construction of an airfield on the Lunga Plain capable of supporting bombers and fighters. The Allies needed to take this airstrip. If left unchecked, Japanese aircraft based on Guadalcanal could pose a serious threat to Allied bases in the Santa Cruz Islands and Espíritu Santo, vital strong points supporting Australia's lifeline to the United States. The airstrip needed to be taken before the Japanese put it into use. Thus, the timing of Operation Watchtower, the code name of the Guadalcanal-Tulagi operation, became even more problematic; the operation would have to begin as soon as practical.

The multiple objectives of Watchtower required at least a division of trained amphibious troops, and the only such unit immediately available was the 1st Marine Division, under Maj. Gen. Alexander A. Vandegrift. Word of the division's immediate employment came as a shock to Vandegrift. When he first learned that his division would take part in the Solomons operation, Vandegrift was still in the process of transferring his command from New River, North Carolina, to Wellington, New Zealand. Vandegrift's command post, the 5th Marines, part of the 11th Marine Artillery Regiment, and support elements were already at Wellington. But the rear echelon, composed of the 1st Marines, the rest of the 11th Marines, and the rest of the division, was still at sea and not due to arrive until 11 July, only three weeks before D day.

Gathering his far-flung command was only one of the many problems with which Vandegrift had to contend. Because of the rapid expansion of the Marine Corps, division training was sorely deficient. Since its inception in February 1941, the division had been subdivided numerous times, like an amoeba, to provide cadres for new divisional and nondivisional formations. For example, an entire battalion of the 5th Marines was permanently detached from the division to create the 1st Raider Battalion. Similar deprivations were imposed on the division's infantry regiments to man new divisional formations, such as the amphibious tractor, engineer, and pioneer battalions. Consequently, proficiency and unit cohesion suffered greatly. Moreover, too little time was available to effectively train the mass of new recruits filling out the division, some of whom were rushed through with only five weeks of basic training. Vandegrift hoped to remedy the division's state of training in New Zealand, but Operation Watchtower wrecked his plans.

The recent loss of one of Vandegrift's three infantry regiments, the 7th Marines, was another blow from which the general was still reeling. In April, the regiment and other divisional support units were detached by the Joint Chiefs to garrison Samoa, another vital link in the lifeline to Australia. Because he believed that this unit would see action first, Vandegrift gave the regiment some of his best officers, noncommissioned officers, and equipment. In a bit of irony, it was the division, not the 7th Marines, that was going to see action first. The loss of this regiment was a serious blow, but Vandegrift was not left wanting. In order to bring his division up to full strength, Vandegrift was temporarily assigned the 2d Marines of the 2d Marine Division. Vandegrift also learned that he would enjoy the services of the crack 1st Raider Battalion and the superb 3d Defense Battalion. Both would prove their worth in the months to come.

With less than a month before D day, time was a precious commodity for Vandegrift and his staff. Amphibious operations by their very nature are very complex and normally require months of painstaking preparation. Intelligence on the target areas must be gathered and communication, naval gunfire support, and landing plans must be drafted. Little was known about the Solomons, and most of the ships involved in the operation had not worked together before. And the time-consuming task of unloading and reloading his transports still needed to be done, since the transports used to move his supplies and equipment had been commercially loaded, not combat loaded. Thus, with so many important preliminaries remaining to be done, Vandegrift asked for and received a one-week postponement of D day to 7 August.

Faced with a lack of shipping, Vandegrift was also forced to make some tough decisions regarding the loading out of his division. Insufficient cargo space made it necessary to leave many of his vehicles and much of his equipment behind, including the powerful 155mm howitzers of the 4th Battalion, 11th Marines. Only a bare minimum of the items required to live and fight would be brought to the invasion. The haphazard nature of the planning and preparations, as well as the numerous obstacles, left few officers in Vandegrift's staff optimistic. As the official Marine Corps history dryly states, "Seldom has an operation been begun under more disadvantageous circumstances."

With the re-embarkation of the division complete, the convoy departed Wellington on 22 July and set sail for a rendezvous and rehearsal at Koro in the Fijis with the rest of the amphibious invasion fleet. The armada that gathered for Operation Watchtower was an impressive force, composed of more than eighty ships divided into two task forces. Designated Task Force 62, the invasion fleet, under the command of RAdm. Richmond K. Turner, consisted of eighteen transports and four destroyer-transports, six heavy and two light cruisers, and twenty destroyers. Air cover for the invasion was to be provided by the carriers *Enterprise, Saratoga,* and *Wasp* of Task Force 61, under the overall command of VAdm. Frank Jack Fletcher. The escorts and auxiliaries of Task Force 61 consisted of the battleship *North Carolina,* five heavy cruisers, one light cruiser, sixteen destroyers, and five oilers.

Operation Watchtower consisted of two separate landings, one to the south by some 11,000 troops of the division's main body near Lunga Point on Guadalcanal, and the other to the north by approximately 6,000 men on Tulagi and "adjacent positions." The landings in the north were comprised of two main assaults. Tulagi would be seized by the 1st Raider Battalion and the 2d Battalion, 5th Marines, while the 1st Parachute Battalion took Gavutu-Tanambogo. Although small elements of the 2d Marines would support the assaults against Tulagi and Gavutu-Tanambogo with landings on Florida Island, the bulk of the regiment would be placed on standby as a ready reserve. In the main landing to the south, the 1st Marine Division, consisting of only five rifle battalions (the 1st Marines and two battalions of the 5th Marines) and most of the division's support units, was given responsibility for seizing and holding the Lunga airfield on Guadalcanal.

The invasion began early on the morning of 7 August 1942. The landings came as a complete surprise to the Japanese garrisons, who were mostly still asleep. Taking advantage of bad weather, the invasion fleet arrived off Guadalcanal and Tulagi undetected by Japanese aircraft and ships. Indeed, the surprise was so complete that the Japanese garrison on Guadalcanal, comprised of about 490 naval troops and 2,200 Korean construction workers, was unaware of the fleet's presence until the ships had commenced their preinvasion bombardment. Panic-stricken by the suddenness and ferocity of the bombardment, the Japanese ignominiously retreated to the hills, resulting in the seizure of the airstrip on the following day without a single loss of life in combat. Never before had such an important objective been taken so effortlessly. It was a stunning achievement for General Vandegrift and his marines.

In contrast with Guadalcanal, the battles for Tulagi and Gavutu-Tanambogo were bloody hammer-and-tongs slugfests, lasting nearly three days. The Japanese defenders—approximately 400 naval troops and 550 naval aviation personnel and construction workers—fought from caves and pillboxes until the bitter end. Everything from tank-infantry attacks and short-range naval gunfire to grenades, explosives, and small-arms assaults were used to finish the job. Casualties on both sides were heavy, with few Japanese prisoners taken. About 120 American sailors and marines died to secure the islands of Tulagi and Gavutu-Tanambogo.

On 7 and 8 August, the Japanese 11th Air Fleet at

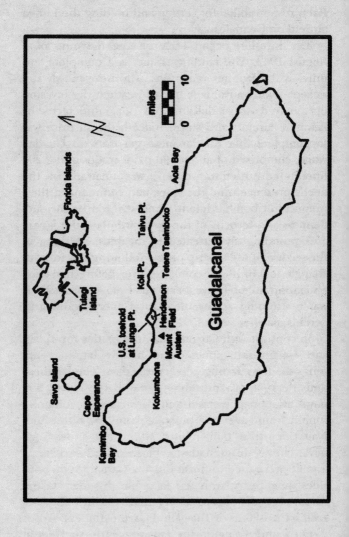

Rabaul responded to the invasion with fierce air attacks. On the 7th, twenty-seven Mitsubishi "Betty" bombers and escorting fighters bombed the invasion fleet, but heavy cloud cover disrupted their aim and only one minor hit was scored on a destroyer. The next day, twenty-three torpedo-laden Bettys and fighters launched another attack but sank only one of Admiral Turner's transports, the *George F. Elliot*. The Japanese lost thirty-two aircraft in these two raids, while the Americans lost nineteen to combat and operations. American aviators had proven, as they had at the Battles of the Coral Sea and Midway, that they were more than a match for the elite Japanese aviators.

Then, the operation that began so favorably for the Americans went terribly wrong. On the night of 8 August, a Japanese naval surface force, under the command of VAdm. Gunichi Mikawa, which had been dispatched to destroy the invasion fleet, completely surprised two of Admiral Turner's cruiser forces protecting the landing area. In the ensuing "battle," the Japanese sank the Australian heavy cruiser *Canberra* and the American heavy cruisers *Quincy, Astoria,* and *Vincennes* in a stunning, one-sided victory. This engagement, known as the Battle of Savo Island, was a humiliating defeat, the worst ever suffered by the U.S. Navy in wartime.

As bad as this defeat was, however, the worst news was yet to come for the marines on Guadalcanal. Because of American fighter plane losses and the threat posed by Japanese land-based air attacks, Admiral Fletcher decided to withdraw the carriers, which were providing air support for the invasion. Faced with the prospect of no air cover and additional enemy air and surface attacks, Admiral Turner rightfully decided to follow suit with his transports. Unfortunately for Vandegrift's marines, Turner's transports still had most of their supplies and equipment aboard—only a small fraction of what the marines needed had been put ashore.

Vandegrift received the shocking news of the imminent withdrawal on the evening of 8 August, during a conference on Admiral Turner's flagship, the transport *McCauley*. Faced with the prospect of being undersupplied and unsupported, one can imagine how Vandegrift felt as he returned to the island by small boat. Guadalcanal was only 600 miles from Rabaul in New Britain, the bastion of the Imperial Japanese Army and Navy in the South Pacific. Rabaul housed a magnificent harbor, where Admiral Mikawa's Eighth Fleet rode at anchor, and airfields where the Imperial Navy's Eleventh Air Fleet was based. The Japanese Seventeenth Army, a corps-size command, was also at Rabaul, overseeing the ground campaign in New Guinea. And the distance between Rabaul and Guadalcanal was a pittance—"a stone's throw" by Pacific standards. Thus, if the Japanese wanted to bomb from the air, or shell and land troops from the sea, there was very little that Vandegrift could do to stop them.

1 Marooned on Cactus

"We Are All Well and Happy"

A warm rain fell intermittently on Guadalcanal Island throughout the night of 8 August 1942. Restful sleep came to few Americans of the newly landed 1st Marine Division amidst the naval gunfire, mosquitoes, and moisture of the night. Soon after daybreak on the 9th, key officers of the division began to assemble at the division command post nestled along the shore near Block Four River. They were a "sorry-looking lot," with bloodshot eyes, unshaven faces, and dirty fatigues. They huddled under coconut trees and around a small fire and sipped hot coffee from hash tins to keep warm. A heavy mist obscured their seaward view, where sporadic firing from a large-caliber naval gun could be heard (this was an American warship finishing off the Australian heavy cruiser *Canberra*, one of four cruisers that fell victim to the Japanese navy the night before). The concussion of each blast shook the leaves in the trees overhead, showering the marines below with dislodged water droplets.[1]

The division commander, Maj. Gen. Alexander A.

Vandegrift, had summoned these officers to his command post for an important meeting. To the casual observer, Vandegrift's looks were deceiving. The balding, fifty-five-year-old Virginian resembled a schoolteacher more than a Marine Corps general. His personality did not fit the stereotypical mold of a marine general, but Vandegrift was a tough and gifted leader who knew how to get the most out of his men. The soft-spoken commander possessed a quiet, gentlemanly demeanor that radiated both optimism and determination. On Guadalcanal, he would need both. But Vandegrift's previous assignments had prepared him for the trials that lay ahead. He already had a taste of jungle warfare, having fought in the tropics of Central America and the Caribbean during the so-called "banana wars." In the 1930s Vandegrift helped develop the Marine Corps's amphibious warfare doctrine. Now, he was leading ground forces in this, the nation's first offensive and first amphibious operation of the war.[2]

In the moist and misty setting at his command post, Vandegrift described the general situation to his officers. He candidly told them what little he knew about the naval battle, but the scores of wounded sailors on the beach and the faint outline of the heavy cruiser *Chicago* with its bow blown off provided unsettling evidence of a defeat. He also explained that the carriers providing air cover for the landing had withdrawn, and that the transports with most of the division's supplies and equipment would follow by day's end. In a reassuring yet firm tone, Vandegrift told his deputies that as long as he could help it, Guadalcanal would not be remembered as another Wake Island or

Bataan. He also explained that the task of holding the beachhead depended on three urgent tasks: fortification of the beaches to repel enemy attacks, dispersal of the division's cargo piled up on the beach, and completion and repair of the newly captured airstrip. Although the airstrip was nearly completed by the Japanese, a 200-foot gap and depression in the center needed filling and leveling.[3]

The operations officer (D-3) and "spark plug" of the division, Lt. Col. Gerald C. Thomas, then stood up to issue the basic defense order. He announced that, according to naval intelligence, the Japanese were massing ships and assault troops at Rabaul and that an enemy counterattack was possible within ninety-six hours. With this threat from the sea in mind, Thomas explained that the division would defend their toehold at the Lunga beaches. The frontage would consist of two regimental sectors with the Lunga River forming a natural boundary: Col. Leroy Hunt's 5th Marine Regiment (less one battalion, which was on Tulagi) would defend the left or western sector, while Col. Clifton Cates's 1st Marine Regiment (less one battalion, which was held in division reserve) would defend the right or eastern sector. The three artillery battalions of Col. Pedro Del Valle's 11th Marines would support each sector from central firing positions near the airstrip. Glancing momentarily at Vandegrift, then back at the assembled officers, Colonel Thomas emphatically stated that no ground be given up without the express permission of the division commander.[4]

With a Japanese counterattack imminent, fortification of the beaches began immediately after Vande-

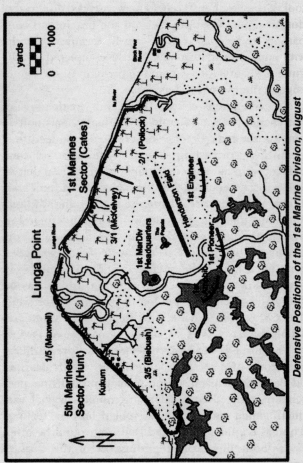

Defensive Positions of the 1st Marine Division, August

grift's order. Although all units were in place before dusk on the 9th, completion of the field fortifications took longer. The main effort focused on the construction of defensive strong points, composed of a company of tanks, which were dug in and camouflaged with palm fronds, and two batteries of 37mm antitank guns of the 1st Special Weapons Battalion. The lack of engineering equipment, shovels, and barbed wire (only eighteen spools were on hand) hampered the entrenching effort and made the task difficult and time-consuming.[5]

Hugging the Lunga Point coastline, the beach defenses stretched a length of 9,600 yards. The left or western flank was anchored on a high ridge about 1,000 yards southwest of a small village called Kukum, and extended eastward around Lunga Point to the western bank of the Ilu River. The long, unobstructed shoreline with clear lanes of fire presented what one marine officer called "a machine gunner's dream." Vandegrift's reserve consisted of only one company of tanks, four 75mm self-propelled howitzers, and a single rifle battalion—the 1st Battalion, 1st Marines.[6]

The small portion of beach defended by Sgt. Ben Selvitelle's light machine gun section of Company L, 3d Battalion, 5th Marines, was typical of Vandegrift's scheme. Flanked by a coconut grove on one side and thick jungle on the other, Selvitelle's sector was fronted by a thin strand of barbed wire, behind which sat two .30-caliber machine guns and a dozen marines armed with rifles. But that wasn't all. The line was bolstered by two 60mm mortars and a 37mm antitank gun, capable of wreaking havoc on enemy landing boats. The battalion's four 81mm mortars and a battery of 75mm howitzers of the 11th Marines were capable of rendering additional support. A regimental half-track mounting a 75mm gun was also available on call.[7]

A vital component of the Lunga defenses was the thirty-two howitzers of Colonel Del Valle's 11th Marines. Sited in central positions around the airfield, these howitzers could hit any threatened point in the Lunga defense. The most common weapon of the artillery regiment's inventory was the M8A1 75mm pack howitzer. Weighing 1,269 pounds, it fired a 13.7-pound shell up to 9,750 yards. The pack howitzer, however, was hardly more effective than the 81mm mortar and was considered too light for general support. In contrast, the M2A1 105mm howitzer was the most celebrated U.S. artillery piece in the war and would remain in service until the Vietnam War. Operated by a nine-man crew, the "105" could fire a thirty-three-pound shell 12,200 yards. The impact of each shell was 50 percent lethal within a radius of twenty meters. The gun weighed 4,980 pounds, and had a maximum elevation of 65 degrees.[8]

One risky element of Vandegrift's defensive scheme was the heavily jungled inland flank. Lacking rifle battalions, Vandegrift ordered support battalions to bivouac south of the airstrip to provide some kind of deterrent. Particularly worrisome was a narrow, grassy ridge only 1,700 yards south of the airfield. Like a dagger, it pointed at the airfield—the division's future lifeline. Vandegrift countered this danger by placing the 1st Engineer Battalion near the ridge and assigning the battalion a security mission to patrol it during the night. Another avenue of possible enemy exploitation was down the Lunga River, fordable throughout its upper reaches. The division countered this threat by posting elements of the 1st Pioneer Battalion on each bank of the river.[9]

More than ninety miles long and twenty-five miles wide, Guadalcanal Island—code-named "Cactus" by the Americans—was large, but the territory occupied by Vandegrift's division was tiny. Indeed, the division's toehold was no larger than twelve miles square. Until reinforced, prudence dictated confinement to this toehold. But the general had one thing in his favor and that was Guadalcanal's hellish terrain. Jagged ridges, impenetrable swamps, and thick jungle encroached upon the division's toehold at Lunga Point from the south, east, and west. Unless the Japanese chose to make a forced landing at Lunga Point, they would have to traverse this inhospitable terrain in the agonizing heat and humidity—no easy task for even the battle-hardened Japanese.[10]

Late in the afternoon of 9 August, General Vandegrift watched Admiral Turner's transports sail away, wildly maneuvering at high speed. These vessels departed with such haste that many left with their boats still ashore. The marines were rightfully concerned and disgusted with the withdrawal. While gazing at the spectacle, Vandegrift turned to Lt. Col. Bill Twining, the assistant D-3, and asked, "Bill, what has happened to your navy?" Twining answered, "I don't believe the first team is on the field yet, general." The 10,819 marines on Guadalcanal were on their own (see Table 1).[11]

Table 1
Unit Strength of the 1st Marine Division
Arrayed for the Landing on Guadalcanal

1st Marine Division Headquarters	371
1st Special Weapons Battalion	
(two 37mm antitank gun batteries,	
one 75mm self-propelled battery, and	
one 40mm antiaircraft battery)	498
1st Tank Battalion (less two companies)	346
H&S Company (2)	
Scout Company (64)	
Company A (eighteen M3A1 Stuart light tanks) (142)	
Company B (eighteen M3A1 Stuart light tanks) (138)	
1st Service Battalion	367
1st Medical Battalion	327
1st Amphibian Tractor Battalion	452
1st Engineer Battalion	586
1st Pioneer Battalion	703
11th Marine Artillery Regiment	1,947
H&S Battery (144)	
Special Weapons Battery (168)	
2d Battalion (eight 75mm Howitzers) (411)	
3d Battalion (twelve 75mm Howitzers) (585)	
5th Battalion (twelve 105mm Howitzers) (639)	
1st Marine Regiment	3,130
H&S Company (157)	
Weapons Company (195)	
1st Battalion (922)	
2d Battalion (929)	

3d Battalion (927)

5th Marine Regiment	2,142

    H&S Company (147)

    Weapons Company (197)

    1st Battalion (893)

    3d Battalion (905)

Attached: 3d Defense Battalion	480
Total:	11,349*

* Approximately 500 marines, retained for stevedore duty on the transports, never landed because of the hasty withdrawal of the navy on 9 August.

Source: *Final Report, I, Annex K.*

————————————

As Vandegrift watched Admiral Turner's transports precipitously sail off, the division staff relocated his command post from the beach to a permanent, inland position. Vandegrift chose a wooded site northwest of the airfield and next to a small coral ridge. The command post was, by any account, primitive. Lacking permanent structures, the division staff salvaged a couple of Japanese tarpaulins—one for Vandegrift and the other for the headquarters office. Inside the latter were two telephones, a desk, and a small safe for securing classified documents. Vandegrift's tent had few amenities but included a few pieces of furniture salvaged from the home of a deposed plantation owner. Due to its proximity to the airfield, the command post soon acquired the name "impact center."[12]

While Vandegrift's staff established some degree of

permanency, work began on the most important and most difficult job facing the division—completion and repair of the Lunga airstrip. Vandegrift assigned the task to Maj. Jim Frazer's excellent 1st Engineer Battalion. It was a big job, requiring heavy earth-moving machines, but none of that equipment had been landed. The marines overcame this obstacle by employing the captured Japanese equipment that had not been damaged by the pre-invasion bombardment. Although the 3,778-foot runway lacked taxiways, revetments, and an adequate drainage system, the engineers declared the airfield usable on 16 August.[13]

Vandegrift christened the airstrip Henderson Field in honor of Maj. Lofton R. Henderson, a marine squadron commander who gave his life at the Battle of Midway. The occasion was marked by a brief ceremony on Pagoda Hill, which included the raising of a tiny ensign removed from a disabled Higgins boat. On the 12th, the first American aircraft, a PBY Catalina, touched down on Henderson Field. The pilot of the aircraft, Lt. W. S. Simpson, deemed the airfield suitable for fighter aircraft only. Before he departed, Vandegrift handed Simpson a letter addressed to his immediate superior, Rear Admiral Turner. In it Vandegrift told Turner, "We are all well and happy," but warned "that if we are to hold this place that the 7th [Marines] be sent up."[14]

While work progressed on the airfield, the 1st Pioneer Battalion performed the backbreaking task of dispersing supplies. Although Turner left with most of Vandegrift's supplies and equipment, dispersing what was ashore was difficult and time-consuming. Mounds of boxes and crates lined the shore from Block Four

River to Beach Red where the initial landing had taken place. Every available vehicle, including the amphibious tractors, was used to transport supplies to inland dumps. The amphibious tractor, with its large cargo capacity and ability to travel practically anywhere except in the thick jungle, was especially valuable. The job was completed on the 11th. Until then, the supplies were extremely vulnerable to enemy air or sea attack. Fortunately for the marines, the Japanese failed to capitalize on this excellent opportunity to deal the Yankee invaders a serious blow.[15]

One of Vandegrift's many concerns was the division's supply of food. The navy's pullout left the 1st Marine Division with just a small fraction of what it needed for a sustained period of occupation. Vandegrift ordered the division quartermaster, Lt. Col. Ray Coffman, to provide an accurate count of the food on hand. After tallying the figures, Coffman returned with a disturbing report that Turner had landed no more than five days' worth of rations. Including captured stocks, this meant that the division on 9 August had enough food for only fourteen days. It was an alarming situation requiring drastic action. Because of the shortage, Vandegrift immediately placed the division on half-rations at two meals per day.[16]

Unfortunately, Vandegrift could tell no one about the supply problem, because he had no radio transmitter capable of reaching New Zealand, where his superior, Vice Admiral Ghormley, was located. (The radios the division possessed, such as the TBX, had a range of only twenty miles.) Marine ingenuity, however, overcame this obstacle. Before the marines landed, the Japanese had nearly completed the installation of a powerful short-wave radio station. Even though he did not know how to read Japanese, Master Sergeant Ferranto of the 1st Signal Company started tinkering with the transmitter and, after three sleepless nights, got it working with about 500 watts of power.[17]

Admiral Ghormley's staff looked upon Radio Guadalcanal's attempt to raise them with some degree of skepticism. Ghormley replied by asking Vandegrift to report his situation briefly and to authenticate the response by giving the names of the ships on which Vandegrift last saw RAdm. Daniel Callaghan. In his first radio message to Admiral Turner on the 13th, Vandegrift reported that he had only ten days of rations on hand (including captured stocks). Turner obstinately answered that he had put ashore more than fifty days' worth, a figure with which Vandegrift violently disagreed. Turner later acknowledged his error but did so secretly—by letter.[18]

Life on Guadalcanal

As the marines worked at strengthening their toehold on Guadalcanal Island, they encountered myriad problems acclimating themselves to their new tropical surroundings. Although coconut groves lined the north coast of the island, inhospitable jungle covered most of Guadalcanal. Sanitation and the living conditions for the Americans were primitive. Making life on this strange island even more difficult for the newcomers was the climate. The heat and humidity were unbearable. Diseases, such as dysentery, malaria, and a host of other ailments, were rife. The island was home to centipedes, bush rats, and tarantulas, as well as land crabs, iguanas, and fiery red ants. For city dwellers who had little experience in the wild, let alone the tropics, pests such as these (which had a penchant for crawling over the unwary at night) were troublesome and unnerving.[19]

Private First Class Edward Fee of the 1st Pioneer Battalion recalled one such encounter on a rainy night shortly after the invasion. Exposed to the elements, Fee propped his head up on a small, innocent looking dirt mound in order to keep his head off the wet ground. When he awoke the next morning, Fee was horrified to discover that the mound was the home of biting red ants. Hundreds of the tiny insects had burrowed into his scalp, leaving it raw and bloodied. During the day, a friend who helped pick the tiny critters out of his scalp told Fee he felt like a preening zoo monkey.[20]

Fee's encounter made light of the division's sleeping arrangements. "We slept on the ground," recalled Pfc. Robert Amery, a member of Company A, 5th Marines. "We each had a rubber poncho and we slept on that. If it rained, we put the poncho, or half of it, over us to keep us as dry as we could. We slept beside our foxholes. Everyone had his own foxhole, except for some high-ranking officers, who had sandbagged dugouts." These sleeping arrangements were obviously unsatisfactory, and within a few weeks, the marines began constructing small shelters or lean-tos out of scraps of wood or anything else they could get their hands on.[21]

Private Amery also recalled another fact of life on Guadalcanal: "You had your rifle or other weapon beside you at all times. You never went anywhere without your rifle," he stressed. "Very soon it became automatic, you just always picked it up and carried it on your shoulder no matter where you went, and if you found yourself without it you felt naked."[22]

The nights during the first week on the island were extremely unsettling for jittery eighteen-, nineteen-, and twenty-year-old marine sentries expecting a face-to-face encounter with the Japanese at any moment. The wildlife and the domesticated horses and bovines set loose after the landing did little to alleviate the tension. "Get used to the weird noises. This jungle is not still at night," complained Cpl. E. J. Byrne of Company L, 5th Marines. "The land crabs and lizards make a hell of a noise rustling on leaves. And there is a bird here that sounds like a man banging two blocks of wood together. There is another bird that makes a noise like a dog barking." These sounds, which seemed amplified in the stillness of the night, not only made nights tense for sentries but also made sleep difficult, because it was hard to distinguish between animal, friend, and foe.[23]

This inability to differentiate between animal, friend, and foe in the night brought on unfortunate cases of friendly fire. A few nights after the invasion, a nervous sentry took a shot at Colonels Cates and Leroy Hunt after a late-night meeting, but, in the words of Cates, "luckily he was an artilleryman and made a clean miss." On 10 August trigger-happy sentries of the 1st Marines fired at each other in the dark, creating pandemonium and quite a few casualties, though no one was killed. Two other marines, however, were not so fortunate. On the 10th, a leatherneck of the 1st

Marines was shot dead in his tracks by his startled tent-mate, a navy corpsman, after the leatherneck made a late-night nature call. A similar incident occurred the following night, when an officer of the 11th Marines accidentally shot and killed one of his sergeants with a .45-caliber pistol.[24]

As tragic and uncertain as the nights were on this strange, new island, one incident at a two-man marine listening post afforded comic relief. A few nights after arriving, Pvt. George Haertlein was awakened by his partner, Pvt. Gene Bentley.

"There's something out there," Bentley, whispered.

"Where?" Haertlein asked. "I don't see anything."

"A little to the left, looks like eyes."

"Jap eyes glow in the dark?" Haertlein asked.

"No one said," answered Bentley.

"You go, you saw it first."

"You go, you're older," charged Bentley.

Haertlein volunteered to attack the intruder. Adhering to strict instructions to shoot only as a last resort, Haertlein got up on one knee and charged the "eyes" at full-speed with his bayonet. After four or five full strides, Haertlein come to an abrupt stop after impaling a tree. The "eyes" that Bentley saw were actually two spots of phosphorescent moss.[25]

As a further means of acclimating his men to their tropical environment, Vandegrift ordered the regiments (including the 11th Marines at Colonel Del Valle's insistence) to mount vigorous patrols into the jungle in search of the enemy. At first, the inexperienced, often sleepless, marines were overcautious. With time, however, as they pushed deeper into the bush, they became increasingly surer of themselves.

After a few days, these patrols began capturing Korean construction workers who had escaped from their Japanese taskmasters. The marines captured thirty-two prisoners on 12 August alone. This success greatly increased their confidence and aggressiveness. Nerves became calmer, the men became better rested and more alert, and nocturnal shootings of wildlife and other marines became less common.[26]

As the marines became steadier and surer of their new surroundings, another more acute problem began to afflict the division. Sanitary laxness promoted a severe strain of dysentery, which made men weak and took pounds off in a single day. Some of the more serious cases required sufferers to visit latrines up to thirty times a day. By mid-August, one man out of five was afflicted with the debilitating sickness. "Dysentery has swept the battalion," wrote Pfc. Jim Donahue of the 2d Battalion, 1st Marines, a few weeks after the landing. "I am very hard hit with dysentery, having had it now for fifteen days. My rectum is the most painful thing on me. I can't get to sleep to the wee hours of the morning. By the time I get to sleep, I am a nervous wreck." Vandegrift ordered medical personnel to establish better sanitation to halt the spread of the debilitating sickness, but it remained an ongoing, albeit lesser, problem for much of the campaign.[27]

Strict rationing and the poor quality of the division's food also took its toll on the health of the marines. The menu was monotonous and provided little nutritional value; they ate a scoop of rice or oatmeal in the morning and the same in the late afternoon. Forced to work and fight while subsisting on such a diet left many men weak and debilitated. "The food was terrible," recalled Edward Fee. "The rice had lots of protein, bugs and worms. We ate it but we did not look carefully. Sometimes they found some catsup or tomato-paste, but usually it was plain fried rice." For a little variety, the marines sometimes ate coconuts, but these contributed to the ever-present problem of what one marine called "the trots."[28]

Private John L. Joseph of the 2d Battalion, 1st Marines, also recalled the meals on Guadalcanal: "During the early days on the island, chow was scarce. The cooks and messmen took a beating whether they deserved it or not. Captured Jap rice was the filler, and not a hell of a lot of anything to dress it up. I remember one mess server who we called 'two prunes' because that's all he would give you, regardless of what you said." Sometimes, the marines got a treat. "At one time they butchered a cow," Joseph recalls, "and believe me it was tough as shoe leather. You chewed and chewed and it didn't taste like beef. It didn't taste like anything but you kept chewing, hoping that it would."[29]

As if to remind them of their isolation and desperation, Japanese aircraft and submarines contemptuously harassed the marooned Americans. On 11 August six Zero fighters roared over the airfield, viciously strafing it and the surrounding marine emplacements at low altitude. The next day, 90mm antiaircraft guns of the 3d Defense Battalion opened up on Japanese aircraft for the first time, surprising three Betty bombers. The unexpected antiaircraft fire compelled the trio to drop their payloads west of the airfield. During the next week, the daily routine on Guadalcanal included an air raid around noon, but the Japanese failed to inflict substantial damage on the airfield. In addition to attacks from the air, the Imperial Navy employed submarines to bombard and observe the American castaways. These aquatic pests, collectively nicknamed "Oscar" by the Americans, usually visited at night, but Oscar occasionally surfaced during the day and harassed the Americans. These daylight appearances normally provoked an angry and effective response from marine 75mm half-tracks on the beach.[30]

Despite their isolation and hardships, the marines on Guadalcanal found time to amuse themselves with diverse activities. As usual with Americans, many gave top priority to souvenir hunting, with inscribed Japanese flags and swords being the most highly coveted items (the ornamental swords carried by Japanese officers commanded top dollar). In what little spare time they had, the marines wrote letters to home, bathed in the Lunga River, or played cards. One gunnery sergeant conducted a class in Japanese flower arrangement, using a beautifully illustrated book he had liberated from the Japanese. The marines also engaged in spreading the latest scuttlebutt, with the most popular topics being their imminent relief by the army and the victor of the recent naval battle. Others preferred to talk of girlfriends or family or dream of succulent dishes, pastries, or candy.[31]

The Goettge Patrol

Next to completing the airfield, eradicating the Japanese on the island was Vandegrift's foremost concern. In view of the Japanese garrison's actual strength of about 2,800, such a concern may be difficult to fathom. But before the invasion the division believed that a large force of troops and laborers were on Guadalcanal, including a well-armed regiment of 3,100 men. Tackling such a force was beyond his means at the time, so Vandegrift settled on patrolling in an effort to locate the main Japanese force. It soon became apparent that Colonel Hunt's 5th Marines had located the main body of the Japanese west near the Matanikau, a small but deep river located five miles west of the airfield. On the 9th, one marine was killed and several wounded, after a small patrol tried to cross the sand spit at the river's mouth. The next day a platoon was repulsed at the same location. The leader of this platoon reported that the high ground on the west bank was heavily defended and that strong enemy positions dominated the sand spit, a natural crossing point.[32]

During these and other encounters, the marines captured a few seamen of the Japanese naval garrison. On 12 August a Japanese prisoner was brought in and interrogated. At first, interpreters had a great deal of difficulty getting information out of him, but he confessed that his comrades might be willing to surrender and agreed to help find them. This information, coupled with a patrol report of a large white flag seen in the high ground beyond the Matanikau, seemed to substantiate his claim. First Sergeant Stephen Custer of the division's intelligence section offered to organize and lead a patrol to the Matanikau to contact those Japanese willing to surrender, but Lt. Col. Frank Goettge, the division intelligence officer (D-2), decided to lead the humanitarian mission himself.

Taking several members of his section, Goettge fleshed out the patrol with personnel from the 5th Marines. The patrol consisted of twenty-five Americans and the Japanese prisoner.[33]

Shortly after nightfall, the Goettge patrol left Kukum by boat. Around midnight, sentries in the 5th Marines' sector reported seeing tracers from the direction of Point Cruz, where Goettge had landed. Near daybreak, one exhausted member of the patrol, Sgt. Charles "Monk" Arndt, returned to report that the patrol had come under fire immediately following the landing and that he had been sent back for help. Two others, Cpl. Joseph Spaulding and Sgt. Frank Few, also survived. Neither marine, however, had a coherent story about what had happened, except that Goettge had been shot first shortly after entering the brush. Few, who escaped at dawn, stated that he saw the Japanese butchering the dead on the beach as he swam away. Colonel Hunt immediately dispatched Company L to the area, but the expedition failed to locate any survivors.[34]

Much has been written about the Goettge patrol and who was to blame for the fiasco. Vandegrift must certainly shoulder some if not all of the blame. Authorizing an expedition of twenty-five men to coax a large enemy force into surrendering is puzzling. Indeed, the marines knew the Japanese existed in force in the Matanikau region; several patrols had already confirmed their presence. Goettge, however, must also share some of the criticism. He landed his patrol near Point Cruz, the area of the enemy's greatest strength, against orders. Why he ignored orders and decided to land there will never be known. It was a costly error resulting in the deaths of twenty-two men, including himself.[35]

The loss of the highly talented Goettge, who was also a football player of national renown, was a blow Vandegrift felt keenly. It is certain that Vandegrift blamed himself for the disaster. Although Goettge's replacement, Lt. Col. Edmund J. Buckley of the 11th Marines, performed well, his level of competence never matched that of Goettge. Fortunately, the division intelligence section received a valuable addition on the 15th, when Capt. Martin Clemens, an officer in the British Solomon Islands Protectorate Defense Force, arrived with his team of native scouts. Near starvation, Clemens and his scouts had left their secluded lookout near Aola Bay a week earlier, after the marines landed. Jacob Vouza, a retired member of the Solomon Islands constabulary, soon joined them. Clemens offered their services as intelligence collectors and as guides, a proposition that Vandegrift delightfully accepted.[36]

Before dusk on the 15th, four high-speed transports flying the U.S. flag dropped anchor in the placid waters off Lunga Point, the first American vessels to do so since Admiral Turner's transports departed nearly a week earlier. These were the APDs [37] *Gregory, Little, Colhoun,* and *McKean,* which had left Espíritu Santo the morning before, bearing much-needed cargo. They put ashore 123 men, drums of aviation gasoline and lubrication oil, bombs, belted ammunition, tools, and spare parts. Most of the newly arrived personnel were members of CUB-1, a naval air base maintenance unit. The others belonged to a marine air operations detachment. Late on 17 August two more APDs, *Manley* and

Stringham, reached Guadalcanal and deposited more equipment and supplies for CUB-1. The APDs also brought with them a letter for Vandegrift from RAdm. John S. McCain, commander of air forces in the South Pacific. McCain promised to send one squadron of SBD Dauntless dive-bombers and one squadron of F4F Grumman Wildcat fighters to Guadalcanal in three to four days.[38]

Despite their many difficulties—the lack of supplies, engineering equipment, and men; an abundance of sickness; enemy bombing and shelling; and bad food—the U.S. marines were firmly entrenched and firmly in control of the small piece of priceless real estate around Henderson Field. Moreover, with the recent arrival of the navy, the situation was beginning to brighten somewhat. But Vandegrift knew the Japanese would not be idle while he strengthened his grip on the island. He was right. Although caught napping, the Japanese would awaken like a sleeping giant to deal with the annoying Americans on this small, isolated outpost in the South Pacific.

2 Operation KA

"The Changed Situation"

Lieutenant General Harukichi Hyakutake, the fifty-four-year-old commanding general of the Japanese Seventeenth Army, was slender and frail, a little over five feet tall. As such, he did not fit the stereotypical mold of a general in Japan—or anywhere else for that matter. But the mild-mannered commander from the Saga prefecture was a tenacious, loyal, and dedicated officer who loved both the emperor and his country. Commissioned in 1909, the same year as General Vandegrift, Hyakutake's record was impressive, having served in various staff and field positions throughout his lengthy career. His resume included action in China commanding several field units, including the highly touted 18th Infantry Division. Hyakutake was inspector general of Army Signals Training when he received orders in April 1942 to take command of the new Seventeenth Army.[1]

Hyakutake's original task as commander of the Seventeenth Army was an ambitious plan of conquest in the South Pacific aimed at cutting off Australia's supply line to the United States. Christened Operation

FS, the targets of this grandiose scheme included New Caledonia, Fiji, and Samoa. After the Imperial Navy's staggering defeat at the Battle of Midway in June, however, Imperial General Headquarters in Tokyo quietly canceled Operation FS in favor of a less ambitious plan to take Port Moresby in eastern New Guinea. Port Moresby was not a new target. The previous effort in May, known as Operation MO, was a joint army-navy operation turned back by U.S. carriers at the Battle of the Coral Sea. However, unlike the previous effort, Seventeenth Army's offensive would be exclusively by land, over the Owen Stanley Mountains, the formidable backbone of the Papuan peninsula.[2]

The Port Moresby offensive began well for Hyakutake. Brushing aside light opposition, the Yokoyama Detachment, a tiny Japanese force of 1,800 men, took the airfield at Kokoda, a key strategic objective, on 29 July. But the fighting by the Yokoyama Detachment was only a preliminary jab. Plans were developed by Hyakutake's staff in early August to deliver the knockout punch with the main body of a brigade called the Nankai Detachment. In preparation to land this final blow, Hyakutake ordered senior officers of the detachment to his headquarters on the morning of 7 August to conduct a map maneuver wargame of the New Guinea campaign.[3]

Not surprisingly, word of the American landing in the Solomons compelled a change in Seventeenth Army's itinerary of 7 August. One message from Japanese pilots placed twenty-one warships and thirty transports off Guadalcanal, prompting the Imperial Navy to estimate that one division had been put ashore. Some members of Hyakutake's staff agreed with the estimate, but the operations officer Lt. Col. Hiroshi Matsumoto, insisted that only a regiment had been put ashore, because of the American reliance on "the amenities." Hyakutake's first message to Tokyo reduced the number of U.S. transports to twenty but added that the escort consisted of one carrier, one battleship, four cruisers, and fifteen destroyers. In a move probably aimed at appeasing his superiors, Hyakutake requested permission the following day to employ part of a brigade to counter the new threat in the Solomons.[4]

Admiral Gunichi Mikawa, commander of the Eighth Fleet at Rabaul, met briefly with Hyakutake on the day of the invasion. Mikawa wanted the army to dispatch troops to Guadalcanal at once, but Hyakutake reminded him that army troops could be sent only with authorization from Imperial General Headquarters. Undaunted, Mikawa took matters into his own hands by ordering an ad hoc force of 519 naval troops, drawn from the Sasebo 5th and the Kure 3d and 5th Special Naval Landing Forces, to depart for Guadalcanal immediately on two transports. But Mikawa recalled the convoy when he learned that a full division may have landed on the island. On its way back to Rabaul, one of the transports, the *Meiyo Maru*, was torpedoed and sunk by an American submarine, taking 373 men with it.[5]

The subject of the American invasion also dominated discussions at Imperial General Headquarters in Tokyo. On 8 August the Army and Navy Sections convened a special meeting chaired by Gen. Hajime Sugiyama, chief of the Army General Staff, and Adm. Osami Nagano, chief of the Navy General Staff. The initial consensus was that the invasion amounted to no more than "reconnaissance in force," because, as most

Japanese officers believed, the United States was incapable of launching a full-scale counteroffensive until late 1943. Greatly influencing this view were the exaggerated claims of American carrier losses by the Imperial Navy in recent battles. The navy also concealed from the army that they had lost four carriers at Midway.

Yet, Lt. Gen. Shinichi Tanaka, operations officer of the Army General Staff in Tokyo, did not agree with the reconnaissance-in-force supposition. He recalled Gen. Douglas MacArthur's recent move to Australia and appointment to lead a new command in the South Pacific. He also remembered a July intelligence report announcing the departure of a large convoy from San Francisco. These events suggested important preliminaries to a major offensive of which Guadalcanal and Tulagi were a part. Although no consensus on American intentions could be reached, Tokyo did agree that the invaders needed to be ejected before they completed the airfield. For this purpose, General Sugiyama hurriedly assigned a special shock unit, the Ichiki Detachment, to Seventeenth Army's order of battle.[6]

On 10 August, General Sugiyama and Admiral Nagano issued a new central agreement, outlining future operations in New Guinea and the Solomons "in accordance with the changed situation." While emphasizing the importance of the Seventeenth Army's mission to seize Port Moresby, the agreement directed Hyakutake to immediately recapture Tulagi and Guadalcanal with forces already assigned to him. These included the Ichiki, Kawaguchi, and Aoba Detachments. Although these were powerful forces indeed, many miles of ocean separated them from Rabaul. The Kawaguchi Detachment was in the Palaus, the Aoba Detachment was in the Philippines, and the Ichiki Detachment was at sea. The fact that the Ichiki Detachment was at sea, however, made it Hyakutake's most readily available asset.[7]

To Japan's detriment, subsequent intelligence reports heavily influenced a reduction in the estimated size of the American occupation force. On 11 August the Japanese military attaché in Moscow cabled Tokyo that the American force consisted of only several thousand panic-stricken troops, whose mission was to wreck the airstrip and withdraw. The accuracy of this cable appeared to be confirmed by destroyer sweeps on the 11th and 12th, which announced the departure of the Allied invasion force, and by a reconnaissance flight on the 12th that observed no significant enemy activity on the island. Thus, based on this collective intelligence, Nagano briefed the emperor that the size of the American occupation force was still not known, but it was believed to be small, because of the Allied defeat off Savo and the subsequent withdrawal of the invasion fleet.[8]

As a result of this downward revision of American strength on Guadalcanal, Lt. Gen. Moritake Tanabe, the newly appointed deputy chief of the Army General Staff, transmitted the following message to Hyakutake on 12 August:

> The scope of operations for the recapture of strategic points in the Solomon Islands will be decided by the Army Commander on the basis of his estimate of the enemy situation. General Headquarters believes that it is feasible to use the 35th Infantry Brigade [Kawa-

guchi Detachment] and the Aoba Detachment
if the situation demands. However, since tactical opportunity is the primary consideration
under existing conditions, it is considered
preferable, if possible, to recapture those areas
promptly, using the Ichiki Detachment and
Special Naval Landing Forces.[9]

Aside from being highly suggestive, Tanabe's message starkly reveals the prevailing overconfidence at
Imperial General Headquarters and confirms Tokyo's
belief that only a token garrison force occupied
Guadalcanal and Tulagi. Otherwise, why would they
consider using just the Ichiki Detachment and Special
Naval Landing Forces, consisting of approximately
2,300 and 1,000 troops, respectively? The message also
reveals Tokyo's propensity at that time to commit
forces unequal to the task. By any reckoning, 3,300
troops would have a tough time dislodging a defending
force of equal size. The fatal practice of committing
forces piecemeal would play a major role in Japan's
defeat in the campaign.

Nevertheless, some officers at Imperial General
Headquarters had serious doubts about employing just
the Ichiki Detachment. Col. Susumu Nishiura, chief of
the administrative section, remembered the Imperial
Army's defeats against the Russians in 1939 at Nomonhan and later against the Chinese, when inadequate
forces were committed time after time. Nishiura was so
disturbed by the decision to send the Ichiki alone that
he called upon a former colleague and friend, the premier and defense minister, Hideki Tojo. The premier
politely listened to Nishiura's pleadings, but he refused

to interfere, because the decision, he said, was Sugiyama's. Nishiura then went to Sugiyama, who replied, "The orders have been issued. They cannot now be rescinded." Nishiura later lamented that "nothing more could be done. Would it not have been better to wait a few days to collect a larger force, and thus not repeat our previous mistakes? Still, I could but hope for the success of Colonel Ichiki."[10]

Formed in May 1942 for the invasion of Midway, the Ichiki Detachment was an elite shock unit derived from Col. Kiyonao Ichiki's own 28th Infantry Regiment, 7th (Ashigawa) Division. A hybrid unit, the detachment was essentially an infantry regiment, minus two battalions, but was augmented by certain support units. These latter included the regimental headquarters, mountain gun and antitank companies, an independent antitank company, and two companies of engineers. The entire unit numbered 2,328 men. The detachment's unusual organization at the time was consistent with its purpose in the Midway campaign, when it was planned to assault the island's beaches in conjunction with 3,000 naval troops. Formed in 1875, the 28th Infantry was one of the oldest, most illustrious regiments in the Imperial Army. It was the first to take 203-Meter Height during the siege of Port Arthur in the Russo-Japanese War of 1904-1905, the "San Juan Hill" of the Imperial Japanese Army (see Table 2).[11]

Table 2
The Ichiki Detachment

28th Infantry Regiment	719
28th Infantry Headquarters (13)	

Regimental Color Platoon (48)

28th Regimental Gun Company (150) (four 75mm)

28th Regimental Antitank Company (140) (four 37mm)

Special Duty Unit (218)

Medical Unit (51)

Miscellaneous Units (99)

2d Battalion, 28th Infantry   1,101

2/28 Headquarters Company (147)

1st Company (177)

2d Company (177)

3d Company (177)

4th Company (177)

2/28 Machine Gun Company (188)

2/28 Battalion Gun Platoon (58)

Attached Units:

1st Company, 7th Engineer Regiment	227
8th Independent Antitank Company (six 37mm)	133
One Company 28th Independent Engineer Regiment	148

Detachment Total: 2,328

Source: *Organization of Two Japanese Army Combat Teams, Japanese Land Forces #6.*

On 12 and 13 August, the Seventeenth Army staff began to plan for Operation KA, the code name of the Tulagi and Guadalcanal operation. Major General Akisaburo Futami, Hyakutake's chief of staff, had serious misgivings about sending just the Ichiki Detachment to Guadalcanal. Futami was convinced that previous estimates were too low and that the American occupation force numbered between 7,000 and 8,000 men. Brasher spirits argued that the American force was much smaller than that figure, and that Ichiki should be sent to Guadalcanal at once to capitalize on American weaknesses there. At the very least, they believed, Ichiki and his infantry guns would be able to prevent completion of the airstrip. Still, Futami's opinion did not change. On the 13th, Maj. Gen. Kiyotake Kawaguchi was ordered to prepare his detachment to sail for Guadalcanal at once, but sailing times precluded it from arriving until late August. In the interim, Ichiki would be landed, as Tanabe's message suggested.[12]

On 14 August, Colonel Ichiki met with Colonel Matsumoto at Truk, where Ichiki was hand-delivered his orders. The directive advised Ichiki that the strength of the American force that had landed on Guadalcanal was not certain, but their activity had not been very vigorous. The orders correctly noted that as of the 13th, the airfield remained unused. In conjunction with Eighth Fleet, the mission of the Seventeenth Army was to "quickly attack and destroy the enemy in the Solomons." Ichiki's role in this attack was to retake the airfield on Guadalcanal if possible and if not, to occupy a position on the island and "await the arrival of troops" at the rear. For this purpose, a "spearhead unit" would be organized by Ichiki and loaded on six destroyers for transportation to Guadalcanal.[13]

Matsumoto then gave Ichiki a short briefing. He warned Ichiki to avoid frontal attacks, as there might be as many as 10,000 Americans on Guadalcanal. If the Americans repelled his initial assault, Ichiki was told to take up a position near the airfield to prevent its completion. Despite the license Hyakutake gave him, Ichiki told Matsumoto that he planned on conducting a night attack against the Americans on 20 August. Ichiki said that each soldier in the First Echelon would carry only a week's worth of rations and only 250 rounds of ammunition, not only because he expected little in the way of resistance, but also because of the cargo limitations imposed by using destroyers. Ichiki was so confident of success that he asked if he could also retake Tulagi, but Matsumoto denied his request and told him to wait for Kawaguchi. At the conclusion of their meeting, Ichiki thanked Matsumoto for the opportunity to annihilate the Americans after having been denied that opportunity at Midway.[14]

Brave and resolute and an expert tactician, Ichiki was an officer with an outstanding record. Born on 16 October 1892 in the Shizuoka prefecture, Ichiki entered the Imperial Army in 1916. As a junior officer, he had a typical career while attached to several staffs and infantry units. Ichiki served two tours as an instructor at the Imperial Army's Infantry School in Chiba, solidifying his reputation as one of the army's finest tacticians. In July 1937, as a battalion commander in the 1st Infantry Regiment, Ichiki played a key role in the fighting against Chinese forces during the famous "Marco Polo Bridge Incident" near Peking. In July 1941, Ichiki took command of the 28th Infantry Regiment.[15]

During their meeting, Ichiki handed Matsumoto a paper detailing the table of organization of his First Echelon. It was a small, heavily armed force built around an attenuated 2d Battalion, 28th Infantry, commanded by Maj. Nobuo Kuramoto, a superb officer handpicked by Ichiki himself. The First Echelon consisted of detachment and battalion headquarters personnel, two platoons from each of the battalion's four infantry companies, and most of the Battalion Gun Platoon. It also contained part of the 2d Machine Gun Company, armed with eight *juki* 7.7mm heavy machine guns, and most of the 1st Company, 7th Engineer Regiment. Even though the engineers were heavily armed with flamethrowers, antitank mines, and demolition equipment, this did not offset the fact that nearly all of Ichiki's artillery, including all of his antitank guns, were left behind with the Second Echelon. The only artillery Ichiki brought along were three 70mm battalion guns, one of which belonged to his regimental headquarters. The First Echelon's total complement, including Ichiki, was 917 men (see Table 3).[16]

Table 3
Ichiki's First Echelon

Detachment Headquarters (one 70mm gun)	164
2d Battalion, 28th Infantry	603
2/28 Headquarters (23)	
1st Company (105)	
2d Company (105)	
3d Company (105)	
4th Company (105)	
2/28 Machine Gun Company (110)	
2/28 Gun Platoon (50) (two 70mm guns)	
1st Company, 7th Engineer Regiment	150
First Echelon Total	917

Source: *Senshi Sosho,* 14:292.

On 14 August, RAdm. Raizo Tanaka, newly appointed commander of the Guadalcanal Reinforcement Force, was ordered to lift Ichiki's First Echelon from Truk to Guadalcanal. The destroyers *Kagero, Hagikaze, Arashi, Tanikaze, Hamakaze,* and *Urakaze* were chosen for the task. Each destroyer would carry approximately 150 soldiers and depart Truk on the 16th. In order to minimize exposure to enemy reconnaissance aircraft, the decision was made to have the destroyers sail directly from Truk to Guadalcanal, instead of from Rabaul. This inaugural landing of army troops by the "Cactus Express" [17] was to take place at Taivu Point, about twenty-five miles east of the airfield, on the evening of 18 August. Each destroyer, equipped with two motorboats, two cutters, and seven collapsible boats, except for the *Hamakaze* and *Urakaze,* which had only six, was responsible for landing its own assigned troops. Ichiki would go to Guadalcanal aboard the *Arashi* and personally command the First Echelon. [18]

The 1,411 soldiers of Ichiki's Second Echelon, led by Maj. Takeshi Mizuno, were to depart Truk in the transports *Daifuku Maru* and *Boston Maru* on 16 August. This force was ordered to land at Taivu Point on the night of the 23rd and "overtake the remainder of the detachment." It was to land by large and small motorboats under the protection of the First Echelon. If this was not possible, the Second Echelon was directed to make an independent landing. Escort was to be provided by the light cruiser *Jintsu* and *Patrol Boats 34* and *35.* A diversionary landing, involving a part of the Yokosuka 5th Special Naval Landing Force (the Yasuda Force), was planned to take place ten miles west of the airstrip near Kokumbona. [19]

The "Kokumbona Vagabonds"

While Tokyo and Rabaul made plans to land the Ichiki Detachment on Guadalcanal, the Japanese naval units on the island were struggling with the creature task of just staying alive. When Vandegrift's marines landed on 7 August, the Japanese forces on the island were a motley assortment of Japanese naval infantry and Korean laborers who were members of three units. In the 84th Guard Unit, under Lt. Akira Tanabe, were 151 seamen who were formerly part of the Kure 3d Special Naval Landing Force. And in the much larger 11th and 13th Construction Units, led by Comdr. Tokunaga Okamura and Capt. Kanae Kadomae, respectively, were 341 seaman and about 2,200 laborers (see Table 4). With the exception of lower leg wrappings, most of the Japanese seamen wore green fatigues similar in appearance to those worn by the marines.

Table 4
Organization of the Japanese Naval Forces on Guadalcanal 7 August 1942

13th Construction Unit (Capt. Kanae Kadomae)

    91 seamen (Ens. Seizo Fuze)

    28 engineering seamen (PO1 Akamine)

    1,141 laborers

11th Construction Unit (Comdr. Tokunaga Okamura)

    222 seamen (Lt. Inado Yasuda)

    1,128 laborers

84th Guard Unit (Lt. Akira Tanabe)

    151 seamen (three platoons)

Source: Japanese sources.

On the morning of 8 August, Captain Kadomae ordered the disorganized remnants of these units—called the "Kokumbona Vagabonds" by the marines—to withdraw to the hills west of the Matanikau River. When Kadomae withdrew, he took with him only 220 seamen and 130 laborers, though during the successive days both of these figures grew. Armed only with rifles and a few machine guns, Kadomae's men were greatly overmatched by Vandegrift's 10,800 powerfully armed marines.[20]

Aside from being overmatched by the American invaders, Captain Kadomae had other problems to contend with. Kadomae's men brought with them as much food as they could carry, but it was consumed in three days. Fortunately for the Japanese, August is the harvest time for the sweet potato, and the native sweet potato gardens were plentiful on the island. Kadomae organized the construction workers into groups to gather these potatoes. Some workers escaped to find refuge with the Americans but most remained loyal. Although a large number of potatoes were found, they only lasted about a week. Hence, Kadomae's men were compelled to subsist on coconuts. But if food was a problem, radio contact with Rabaul was not. Both Kadomae and another naval outpost at Taivu Point, some thirty-five miles to the east, were in contact with Rabaul on a daily basis.[21]

While the construction workers gathered food, Kadomae's seamen labored hard to fortify their defenses along the Matanikau. The river offered a natural defensive barrier, along which nearly all the naval troops were positioned. When Goettge made his noisy approach toward Point Cruz on the evening of 12

August, a platoon led by CPO Goro Sakurai struck out toward the shore and attacked them. At dawn, Sakurai's platoon massacred those few of the Goettge patrol that remained. The Japanese counted twenty-two dead Americans. Japanese losses are unknown but included Sakurai.[22]

On 15 August, six Bettys from Rabaul dropped baskets of food, ammunition, and medicine to Kadomae and his men, but the baskets were dropped well to the east and drifted over marine lines. In one of them a translated message read: "Help is on the way! *Banzai!*" Outnumbered and with very little food, Kadomae needed all the help he could get. The following day, Lt. Soichi Shindo, a member of the 11th Construction Unit, took pen to paper to write: "At 1000, the enemy began to bombard us for the first time. We recalled the guards sent to Cape Esperance because they had the only wireless radio. Our submarines with whom they were in contact assured us of reinforcements. They also told us that the Eighth Fleet achieved a great naval victory on the night of 8 August. All of us went wild with joy."[23]

Kadomae did not wait long for the promised reinforcements. In a brazen display later that day, the Japanese destroyer *Oite* dropped anchor off Tassafaronga Point in broad daylight, where it landed the first Japanese reinforcements of the campaign. The destroyer put ashore 113 men of the Yokosuka 5th Special Naval Landing Force, led by Lt. Tatsunosuke Takahashi. Bolstered by this reinforcement, Admiral Mikawa radioed Kadomae, urging him "to defend the Matanikau River to the death." Even the Imperial Navy, at this early stage in the campaign, recognized the strategic importance of the river.[24]

The First Battle of the Matanikau, 18–19 August

Following the disastrous Goettge patrol, General Vande-grift contemplated a retaliatory strike west of the Matanikau to eliminate the Japanese gathered in that region. Captured documents and interrogations of pris-oners revealed that the Japanese garrison was lightly armed and numbered only a few hundred men, much smaller than originally thought. Although the danger posed by such a small, pitifully armed force was mini-mal, the fact that it existed so close to the airfield was enough to warrant action. Accordingly, Vandegrift ordered the 5th Marines to launch a limited assault with the objective to "seek out and destroy the enemy."[25]

Colonel Leroy Hunt selected three rifle companies for the mission. Company L, under Capt. Lyman Spur-lock, was to march overland about 1,000 yards inland from the mouth of the Matanikau, cross the river, and advance northward along the west bank. Company B, commanded by Capt. William Hawkins, was to advance overland and engage any Japanese encountered before reaching the river and, if possible, cross the sand spit. Company I, led by Capt. Bert Hardy, Jr., was to proceed by Higgins boat and debark west of Kokumbona. It was hoped that Hardy's company would surprise the Japanese by attacking them from the rear (west). The operation was scheduled to begin on the morning of 19 August, after a preliminary artillery barrage by howitzers of the 11th Marines.[26]

At 0800 on 18 August, the marines of Company L proceeded as planned. Cradled in their arms or slung over their shoulders were an assortment of rifles, machine guns, and mortars of varying quality. Most

marines in the company and on Guadalcanal carried
the venerable M1903 Springfield rifle, a .30-06–caliber
(7.62mm) bolt-action design. Despite its age, the Springfield was an extremely accurate and reliable rifle. Nearly
as old but much more effective was another .30-06
weapon, the M1918A2 Browning automatic rifle (BAR).
Although it was capable of firing in either the semiauto-
matic or automatic mode, the BAR had drawbacks—it
was heavy (seventeen pounds) and had a violent recoil.
The Japanese would come to fear the BAR. Some
marines on Guadalcanal also carried .45-caliber submachine guns. The Thompson M1928A1 was a reliable and
effective weapon but was sometimes mistaken for enemy
fire, because it sounded very similar to Japanese automatics. On the other hand, most marines cursed the
Reising Model 50 or 55, a new closed-bolt design. The
Reising, issued before thorough testing, had an annoying, and sometimes deadly, tendency to jam or malfunc-
tion in battle. Some marines on Guadalcanal called it
the "Rusting Gun."[27]

The machine guns and mortars that the marines
brought with them on this first offensive were excellent weapons, light and mobile enough to employ rapidly in the rugged terrain. The air-cooled Browning
M1919A4 .30-caliber machine gun was a superb, lightweight weapon (thirty-one pounds) capable of firing
between 400 and 550 rounds per minute. A heavier,
water-cooled machine gun of the same caliber, the
Browning M1917A1, was also used on Guadalcanal
and was capable of a slightly higher rate of fire—
between 450 and 600 rounds per minute. The marines
used two models of mortars or "smokepoles" on
Guadalcanal, although only the M2 60mm mortar was

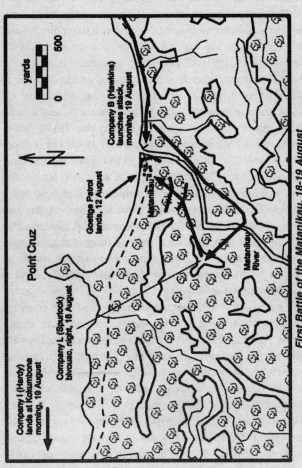

First Battle of the Matanikau, 18-19 August

brought on this mission. The 60mm mortar fired a 2.9-pound bomb nearly 2,000 yards and weighed just forty-three pounds. Carried by hand, the 60mm's light weight made it ideal for offensive missions. Much more effective was the M1 81mm, a 136-pound mortar. The 81mm fired a 10.6-pound shell up to 2,500 yards. Although it possessed both greater range and greater hitting power, the 81mm was better suited for defensive missions because of its excessive weight and size.[28]

By nightfall of 18 August, the marines were in place, with Company L securely bivouacked on a ridge on the west bank of the Matanikau River and Company B near the Matanikau. Company B began its march along the coastal trail at 1400, and as it came near the river, it encountered many Japanese lookouts and snipers who were flushed out from the underbrush. Most were Korean laborers forced into this activity by Captain Kadomae. Hawkins's men also discovered the bodies of several natives, most of whom had been savagely bayoneted by the Japanese. During the night, several Japanese vainly tried to penetrate Company B's perimeter, but all were killed in the attempt.[29]

At 0850 the following morning, the 11th Marines kicked off the offensive with a cannonade aided by forward observers perched in a Higgins boat lying offshore. The artillery barrage literally caught the Japanese napping, causing some to flee to the south. After the barrage lifted at 0945, Hawkins's Company B pressed toward the Matanikau sand spit, but was stopped by a whiplash of Japanese fire from a pair of 6.5mm (.256-caliber) Nambu machine guns, one sited on the west side of the river, the other from an abandoned Japanese barge on the beach. The initial burst of machine gun fire caught the marines out in the open, shattering the stock of Hawkins's submachine gun before he could take cover. Japanese snipers, armed with Arisaka rifles of the same caliber, also dogged the company.[30]

At 0430 Company I, accompanied by Lt. Col. William J. Whaling, the executive officer of the 5th Marines, left by Higgins boats toward Kokumbona. During the journey, the lumbering group attracted Japanese machine gun fire from the shore, but that was not all. At 0800 the two Japanese destroyers and a submarine spotted the Higgins boats and began lobbing shells at the now-fleeing boats. Despite numerous near misses from the Japanese vessels, Company I landed near Kokumbona at 0830, wet but unharmed. Almost immediately, Company I bumped into Lieutenant Takahashi's newly landed seamen. Although one marine was killed in the firefight, American fire proved more accurate, forcing Takahashi and his men to fall back into the hills. Takahashi later boasted of repelling the invading Yankees and capturing three boats and one machine gun.[31]

As a light rain gently fell on Guadalcanal, Company L ambled downhill at 0900 in single file from its bivouac in the jungle. About 1,000 yards of thick jungle and jagged coral ridges separated them from the village of Matanikau. Almost immediately, Japanese bullets pierced the moist air as Spurlock's company came under fire from a small ridge a few hundred yards to the west. Bullets hit 2d Lt. George Mead's platoon, killing Sgt. John Branic and wounding three others. The Japanese, who fought from several entrenched positions reinforced with logs, fiercely resisted the marine advance with machine guns, most of which were Nambus, except for one large piece the marines thought was a .60-caliber.[32]

One by one, Spurlock's company eliminated these deadly positions. Marine Gunner Edward Rust, temporarily attached to Company L headquarters, blasted one machine gun nest with grenades thrown from the incredibly short range of only a few yards. Despite the Japanese efforts to stop them, Spurlock's three platoons kept pressing toward the village, but soon after Mead's platoon entered it, Mead lost his life to an enemy bullet.[33]

A platoon of Japanese seamen, led by PO Norikiyo Sashihata, defended Matanikau village. Overpowered by the marine advance, Sashihata pulled his men back to the eastern side of the village and made a stand where the jungle begins. Facing the Japanese on the left closest to the beach was 1st Lt. John "Flash" Flaherty's platoon and on the right was Mead's platoon, now led by Gunner Rust. Soon after the arrival of a .30-caliber machine gun section, led by Sgt. Ben Selvitelle, Sashihata's seamen began chanting what one marine thought was some kind of ritual. Moments later, the Japanese came at the marines, three or four abreast, screaming and yelling with fixed bayonets in a banzai charge. Sashihata's attack, however, was initiated at long range and presented the marines "with a gratuitous opportunity for annihilation by fire." Rust answered by leading a bayonet charge of his own against the few Japanese who remained. Few Japanese escaped into the bush.[34]

At the beginning of the banzai attack, Platoon Sgt. "Wild" Bill Kulchycki whipped out his Reising to help cut down the charging Japanese who were only about forty yards away. But after three or four rounds, the submachine gun jammed. Kulchycki quickly dropped to one knee and loaded another magazine, and after another short burst, it jammed again. Frustrated, the sergeant angrily flung the gun like a boomerang at the screaming Japanese and unlimbered a .45-caliber pistol, dropping a few Japanese bearing down on him. "Lucky I didn't turn in my .45 like I was ordered to do when they issued me that damn piece of junk," Kulchycki later explained. "Holding that piece of junk in your hand was like holding a lot of hot air!"[35]

Although Sergeant Kulchycki's actions were humorous, the exploits of Pfc. Nicholas Sileo of Company L were extraordinary. Alone on one flank of his platoon, Sileo was advancing on the eastern edge of the village when six Japanese armed with rifles came at him. "I opened fire with my '03 [Springfield rifle] and got three of them," Sileo explained, "The other three took off. Then I saw twenty more coming at me." Greatly outnumbered, the young marine was in the act of rejoining his platoon when Japanese bullets hit him in the groin, chest, and arm. Sileo was lying on the ground in a daze when a Japanese sailor shoved a rifle into his face. Sileo put his hand up to ward off the shot, but lost a thumb and took a bayonet in the neck in the attempt. Despite severe blood loss, Sileo somehow survived the ordeal.[36]

Meanwhile, back at the sand spit, Company B was still encountering stiff resistance from the Japanese machine gun nest perched on the opposite side of the river. Colonel Whaling suggested that Hawkins try an inland flanking maneuver, but the Japanese crew, who relocated to another site to cover this move, repulsed this effort. Hawkins returned to the sand spit, where he called on his 60mm mortars to dislodge the stubborn Japanese gunners. Coordinating the mortar fire over telephone wires strung from Hawkins's forward point at the river back to the mortar position, the mortar crew went to work with ranging shots. After a series of adjustments, the seventh round scored a direct hit on the machine gun emplacement, leaving clumps of dirt and defenders sprawled around the nest. Having overcome this last bit of resistance, Company B then crossed the river and entered the village, where they met Company L around 1600. Company I, which had failed to take part in the Matanikau fighting, returned to Kukum by boat.[37]

Despite urgent calls from Colonel Hunt to return to Kukum, the marines quickly surveyed the battlefield around the village. The two companies counted some sixty-five Japanese, which included Petty Officer Sashihata. Marine losses in both companies were comparatively light, with only four killed and eleven wounded. Contrary to official accounts of the Guadalcanal campaign, remains of the Goettge patrol were found. The marines stumbled on the remains partially buried on Matanikau beach, a short distance west of the sand spit. Sergeant Ore Marion of Company L related, "I will always remember being with 'Monk' Arndt on the Matanikau beach, waiting to be evacuated to our perimeter, and Monk pointing to the Goettge patrol bodies and saying 'see that arm and leg sticking out? That's the colonel.'" (A football player in college, Goettge had very large physical features.) Many members of both companies, including Colonel Whaling and Gunner Rust, saw the shallow graves. But to this day, members of the Goettge patrol are still officially listed as missing in action.[38]

For Vandegrift's marines, the First Battle of the Matanikau was a minor tactical victory of little import to the campaign. But since Vandegrift's aim was to destroy the main Japanese body in the Matanikau area, the mission was a failure. Nevertheless, the battle bestowed one positive psychological effect, in that the marines avenged the Goettge patrol and finally fought and beat what had been an elusive enemy. The battle also provided lessons about command and control and terrain difficulties, as well as the perils of employing complex schemes of maneuver in unfamiliar terrain. At the unit level, only the performance of Spurlock's Company L was worthy of praise. Overcoming heavy resistance and rugged terrain, the company routed the Japanese and seized the village without substantial assistance from the other two companies.

3 Ichiki Moves Out

ULTRA

At 0700 on 16 August, six destroyers bearing Ichiki's First Echelon left Truk. Neither enemy submarines nor aircraft were encountered en route, thus enabling Ichiki's troops to make a bloodless landing at Taivu Point at 0100 on the 19th. Members of the Navy Surveillance Unit greeted them there and helped them to unload. Word of Ichiki's successful landing, coupled with news received later that day that the Nankai Detachment had landed at Buna, New Guinea, without loss, was received with joy at Seventeenth Army headquarters. General Futami said that the bloodless landings appeared to be a "good omen."[1]

Soon after landing, Ichiki eagerly ordered his men to move out. In order to secure the beachhead, the colonel left behind a token force of about 100 men. As Ichiki and his assault force—about 810 soldiers in all—marched westward along the coastal trail, they did so in high spirits, certain of a quick victory over the Americans. Proudly marching with them was the standard bearer of the 28th Infantry Regiment, 2d Lt. Ito Tomokazu. According to tradition, the regimental color was the symbol of honor and esprit de corps in the Imperial Japanese Army. Its capture was considered a disgrace. But Ichiki's regimental color had historical significance. It was the same flag that flew atop 203-Meter Height during the siege of Port Arthur, one of the grimmest, most decisive battles in the Russo-Japanese War of 1904-1905.[2]

Enjoying the cool ocean breeze as they confidently marched toward the airfield, Ichiki and his warriors made excellent progress. At 0200 Ichiki and his men crossed the Berande River, a swift and deep water course that came up to their chests. Before dawn, they halted to rest at Tetere, an abandoned native village about nine miles west of Taivu Point. Ichiki planned to stay there and rest during the day, in an effort to avoid enemy observation by air and sea, but an event later in the day scuttled that plan. After a hasty breakfast at daybreak, Ichiki ordered Capt. Yoshimi Shibuya, head of the regimental communication section, to form a patrol to reconnoiter the American positions around the airfield. If possible, he was to seize the former camp of the 11th Construction Unit, where Ichiki hoped to establish his headquarters. Shibuya assembled a patrol of thirty-eight men, including two navy guides. Marching in column, they struck out at 1100 along the coastal trail, without taking proper security measures. Shibuya, like Ichiki, did not expect to encounter any enemy until they reached the airfield.[3]

Unbeknownst to Colonel Ichiki and his superiors, the Americans were aware of the plan to land the Ichiki Detachment on Cactus, the Allied code word for Guadalcanal. The source of this intelligence was so secret that only a few Allied commanders and staff officers knew that it even existed. It was called ULTRA—the analysis or decoding of enemy message traffic. ULTRA helped the Americans stop the Japanese at the Coral Sea in May and Midway in June and confirmed the landings of Japanese naval construction units on Guadalcanal in early July. During the Guadalcanal campaign, teams of U.S. Navy "spooks" were at work in Washington, D.C., Hawaii, and Melbourne, Australia, trying to intercept, decode, and analyze the Imperial Navy's message traffic.[4]

In mid-1942, a sizable percentage of Imperial Navy messages were being intercepted and decoded. For example, on 26 May intelligence experts estimated that 60 percent of all Japanese navy radio messages were being intercepted and 40 percent of those were being read. The typical yield from the decoding of each intercepted message was between 10 to 15 percent. All of this abruptly changed two days later, when the Imperial Navy changed its code from what American cryptanalysts called JN-25b to JN-25c. Cryptanalysis became much more difficult from that point on and remained so for much of the Guadalcanal campaign. Nevertheless, periodic breakthroughs were made, revealing in detail the plans for a future offensive or for the landing of troops or supplies at some location on Guadalcanal.[5]

In contrast to the Imperial Navy code, American code breakers had no success in breaking the Imperial Army code in 1942. In fact, no intelligence was derived from the decoding of Japanese army communications traffic until June 1943. Why was the army's code so difficult to break and that of the navy compar-

atively easy? The primary reason lay with the sophisti-
cation of each service's cipher system. One Japanese
officer compared the navy's coding system to a sixth-
grade, middle-school level and the army's to a college-
level. As a result, army plans for joint operations with
the navy were often compromised by the navy's ele-
mentary radio codes.[6]

Aside from the difficulties of cryptanalysis, the
Japanese language itself bedeviled all but the most flu-
ent American radio analysts. Indeed, one wartime
American intelligence source characterized the complexities of the Japanese language as "amounting
almost to a cryptographic system." The Japanese, of
course, knew this and tended to place too much faith
in the security offered by their language. One aspect
that made the translation of characters difficult was
the prevalence of homonyms in the Japanese language. *Kaisen,* for example, could mean "decisive
engagement," "opening hostilities," "ghost ship,"
"barge," "rotation," or "itch." Because Romanji (the
method of using roman characters rather than Japanese ideographs) was employed during the translation
process, a little imagination was required by those who
translated the unique Japanese Morse code characters.
Key words might be recognized, but analysts sometimes encountered difficulties translating the message
into its original context.[7]

On 8 August, Station Hypo, the Hawaii processing
unit, reported that an urgent message had been transmitted from an unidentified unit associated with
Destroyer Division 4 to the commanding general of
the Seventeenth Army. The message revealed that the
destroyer division had been at Saipan on 7 August.

The contents of the rest of the message remained elusive, but the addressees clearly revealed that the two commands would be involved in a future operation. The destination of Destroyer Division 4 was established on the 15th, after partial decoding of a message sent on 8 August. The intercept disclosed that the destroyer division was in Guam and would leave for Rabaul. Sleuths were able to determine that the commander in chief, Eleventh Air Fleet, and the commander in chief, Eighth Fleet, were also addressees in this message.[8]

On 14 August, the Eighth Fleet transmitted an operations order to land the Ichiki Detachment on Guadalcanal. The directive outlined a two-part plan to recapture Guadalcanal and Tulagi. A portion of this partially decoded message, published on the 16th, read: "DesDiv 4 less second section, and DesDiv 17 less (blank) DD . . . Depart PT at (blank) hours on 15th, join (?) IKKI [ICHIKI] DETACHMENT and proceed to RXI, arriving off destination (?) on 18th. . . . "[9]

This same message also revealed that a naval "defense" force was to land on Guadalcanal. Intelligence officers in Hawaii believed that PT and RXI were the naval codes for Truk and Guadalcanal, respectively, and they were right. Although the destroyers were actually leaving Truk on 16 rather than 15 August, American cryptanalysts were able to nail down the precise date of the landing (18 August) and that is what really mattered. As a result of this coup, Admiral Nimitz's intelligence team issued a warning on 17 August that the Japanese intended to retake Tulagi and Guadalcanal with naval troops and a special army shock unit, the Ichiki Detachment. The date of the attack was estimated to be as early as 20 August.[10]

Vandegrift's communicators at the time did not possess the cryptographic aids needed to decrypt highly classified message traffic bearing ULTRA intelligence. Consequently, warnings and other critical information were delivered to Guadalcanal via other means. These included special air couriers, visiting flag officers, or visiting naval vessels equipped with high-grade cryptographic systems. This expedient was necessary until mid-September, when a U.S. Navy team arrived, equipped with the needed communications hardware. Vandegrift received Nimitz's 17 August warning from the APDs delivering supplies that day. The next day Vandegrift radioed Brig. Gen. William B. Rupertus at Tulagi with the following warning: "Information received from CTF 62 [Admiral Turner] indicates attack on CACTUS-RINGBOLT [Guadalcanal-Tulagi] Area possible within forty-eight hours."[11]

Brush versus Shibuya

On 12 August, a few marines of the 1st Engineer Battalion left the perimeter to survey the Koli Point area for a possible airfield site. A platoon under 2d Lt. Joseph Jachym was ordered to provide an escort. While the team was passing through the village of Tetere the following day, a Catholic priest warned them of a Japanese force farther east, ostensibly the Imperial Navy radio post at Taivu Point. Lieutenant Jachym wisely did an about-face to return to the perimeter with this important news. Supposedly under orders to destroy this detachment, Capt. Charles H.

Brush, a highly capable reservist, set out on the 19th with three native guides and sixty men from Company A, 1st Marines.[12]

As Brush's men were closing in on Tetere at noon, native guides returned warning them of a Japanese patrol—Shibuya's—heading toward them in the coconut grove between the coastal trail and the beach. Brush deployed his men immediately, placing five squads in front of the approaching enemy at a range of 100 yards. Not sure if the marines to his front were friendly, Captain Shibuya yelled the password, *"Yama"* ("mountain"), but his only response was gunfire. While Brush pinned down the Japanese with a frontal attack, Jachym sent one of his squads on an enveloping maneuver to the right to engage Shibuya's left rear. In a firefight that lasted less than an hour, the marines killed all but five Japanese, who escaped to warn Ichiki. In what would be a common occurrence during the war, as Brush approached one of the wounded Japanese officers, the officer put a pistol to his head and killed himself. This action shocked Captain Brush and the marines who were unaccustomed to such actions. Brush's losses totaled three killed and three wounded.[13]

Posting local security, Brush went to work at once examining the bodies of the four Japanese officers and twenty-nine men sprawled about the battle site. He noted that these troops, unlike those encountered in the past, were members of the Imperial Army. Furthermore, their fresh clothes indicated that they had been on the island only a short time. The high proportion of officers was unusual for a patrol of that size, as was the large amount of communications gear they carried. Brush rightly concluded that this patrol belonged to a larger force, and without delay started back for marine lines with the papers, diaries, and maps he had collected. The Japanese radio station at Taivu Point would have to wait.[14]

At 1630 breathless survivors returned to inform Ichiki that Shibuya's patrol had encountered an estimated company of American troops and were engaged in a battle to the death. Stunned by the news, Ichiki immediately ordered 1st Lt. Yusaku Higuchi's company forward to help Shibuya. Higuchi and his men ran for several miles past the battle site, but they found no sign of the enemy and returned to the site to begin the gruesome task of burials. By 1700 Ichiki learned from additional survivors that Shibuya and most of the men in his patrol had been killed and that some Americans were armed with light machine guns that could be used while standing (submachine guns). Ichiki and the rest of his command set out shortly thereafter, meeting Higuchi at the battle scene. Second Lieutenant Kiyoshi Sato's 1st Platoon, 4th Company, was ordered to continue burials while the rest of the detachment started out to the west. After crossing the Nalimbiu River, Ichiki halted at 0430 the following morning at the village of Rengo for a rest.[15]

Back at 1st Marine Division headquarters, Capt. Sherwood "Pappy" Moran, the fifty-six-year-old interpreter of the D-2 (intelligence) section, was hard at work translating the captured material. Moran, a Quaker, had lived in Japan for several years as the headmaster of a church school. The documents and diaries Moran translated confirmed that the dead

Japanese were members of a regiment hurriedly embarked at Truk and sent to Guadalcanal. None of the captured material, however, told Vandegrift what he needed to know: the strength, location, and intentions of the enemy force. The captured maps—one high-ranking staff officer said there were at least three—not only illustrated where the marine defensive positions were located, but also their state of development and whether or not they were actually manned. In addition, the maps pinpointed where the marine artillery positions were sited around the airfield. Colonel Gerald Thomas found the accuracy of their maps "chilling." According to Thomas's assistant, Lt. Col. Merrill Twining, the quality of the maps far surpassed what the marines possessed at any time during the campaign.[16]

Based on the available evidence, General Vandegrift and Thomas surmised that the Japanese might attack on the night of 20 August. Certain members of Vandegrift's staff urged him to use the division reserve, the 1st Battalion, 1st Marines, to engage the approaching Japanese force. But lacking intelligence on the enemy's strength and plan of attack, Vandegrift rightfully rejected such a move in favor of a more conservative option. Having taken the airfield, he would defend and hold it with the meager forces he possessed. As a precaution, Colonel Hunt placed a battalion of the 5th Marines on alert in the event that the division reserve was committed in battle. In addition, Thomas had Lt. Col. Leonard B. Cresswell, the commander of the division reserve, sleep in the operations shelter to shorten communications time and to expedite the battalion's deployment. Vandegrift also placed the Engineer and Pioneer Battalions on alert, both of which were well qualified to serve in an infantry support role. Finally, Vandegrift ordered Colonel Del Valle to register a battalion of 75mm howitzers on the eastern bank of the Ilu River.[17]

Meanwhile, Col. Clifton Cates, the slim and dapper commander of the 1st Marines and a highly decorated veteran of World War I, prepared his regiment for the expected attack. On the morning of 15 August, Vandegrift ordered Cates to prepare an inland extension of his position along the west bank of the Ilu River for a distance of 1,700 yards. Cates ordered Lt. Col. Edwin A. Pollock, commander of the 2d Battalion, 1st Marines, to prepare this extension. Pollock, like several other battalion commanders on Guadalcanal, was a grizzled veteran of the banana wars, having mounted several expeditions against rebel bandits in the jungles of Nicaragua. This was good experience to be sure, but the Japanese would bring a new set of challenges to the veteran marine officer.[18]

Edwin Pollock's battalion was responsible for defending a 2,700-yard front, which included about 1,000 yards on the Lunga coast and 1,700 yards on the west bank of the Ilu River. Two of the battalion's three rifle companies, E and F, led by Captains Martin Rockmore and John Howland, respectively, manned the front. Two platoons of Company E and most of the heavy weapons unit, Company H, commanded by Capt. James Ferguson, were dug in along the river. The battalion reserve was comprised of Capt. James F. Sherman's Company G. As Sherman pointed out to correspondent Richard Tregaskis, "lots of Boston boys [were] in the outfit." Company G's reserve was comprised of the 1st Platoon, led by 2d Lt. George Codrea. To the rear of the main line of resistance were Pollock's 60mm and 81mm mortars, standing by to rain down terror on any enemy.[19]

During the dry season, which included August, the Ilu was separated from the sea by a sand spit, which varied in width between twenty-five and fifty feet and rose about ten feet above the river. About thirty yards from the main line of resistance on the west bank of the spit, the marines of Company G erected a barbed wire barrier to keep out unwanted guests. Having no tools or special gloves to handle the wire, Lieutenant Codrea recalled that it was treacherous work. The area fronting the spit was defended by two platoons of Battery B, 1st Special Weapons Battalion, armed with two 37mm antitank guns, and a .50-caliber machine gun. Elements of Company H of Pollock's battalion also defended the sandbar. Some of the antitank and .30- and .50-caliber machine gun positions along the river were dug in and fortified with sand bags and logs.[20]

The Japanese Soldier

In the summer of 1942 the Japanese soldier was regarded by many in the West as a "superman" because of his uncanny ability to achieve victory against impossible odds. At Malaya and Singapore, for example, the Imperial Army defeated a British-led force more than three times its size. It was, according to British Prime Minister Winston Churchill, "the worst disaster and greatest capitulation of British history." Similar results were achieved by the Japanese against American-led forces in the Philippines. The Japanese fighting man was also somewhat of a mystery in the West. He was stereotyped as a rice-eating man-monkey who sniped from the top of coconut trees, grinned with heavy buckteeth, and wore thick "coke-bottle" glasses.[21]

At the Battle of the Tenaru River, Vandegrift's marines received a shocking introduction to this soldier. He was a tough and fanatical foe who often displayed a total disregard for his safety in battle. When defeat was certain and escape impossible, he invariably fought to the end, preferring death to surrender. Those few Japanese who did surrender did so because they were usually too weak or ill to resist capture or to commit suicide *(seppuku)*. The Japanese soldier also resorted to what the Americans thought was treachery. In the act of providing succor, Americans would sometimes be gunned down or blown up with a grenade by Japanese who were playing possum.

The Japanese soldier who fought on Guadalcanal was a product of his culture and military training. He was raised in a national environment where individualism was disdained and where teamwork, self-sacrifice, and obedience were emphasized. These teachings were taught throughout his life and encompassed all of Japanese society—families, neighborhood associations, schools, factories, and other large organizations. Equally important to the Japanese soldier were the ways of the old Samurai caste. These warriors extolled the virtues of courage, honor, and loyalty, of stoicism toward pain and suffering, and of a contempt for death. To become a prisoner of war was the ultimate disgrace; *seppuku* was always the preferred alternative.

The Samurai drew upon the doctrines of the Shinto religion as well. The emperor was worshiped as a divine being, and the heroic deeds of ancestors were extolled in Japan's mass media. Thus, the Japanese soldier sought to emulate acts of heroism that would earn him a hallowed place in the hearts of the Japanese people.[22]

In addition, the Japanese soldier's conduct was to be above reproach. He was expected to live according to the "Emperor's Rescript," issued by Emperor Meiji in 1882, which emphasized five principles of military ethics: loyalty, courtesy, valor, truthfulness, and frugality. Along with the values the Japanese soldier was taught throughout his life, the emperor's code imbued the soldier with a level of spirit and determination, which enabled him to endure the hardships of war. Consequently, a commander could count on a soldier's obedience regardless of the situation. This high level of obedience, however, was achieved at the expense of individual initiative. Thus, the typical Japanese enlisted men and noncommissioned officers (NCOs) did not think well on their own. "Their NCOs are poor," observed one marine officer. "If you shoot their officers, they mill around. You can tell they are officers by their sabers and leather puttees."[23]

The Japanese soldier's training was intense and thorough. He was taught not only how to fire his weapons and operate his equipment, but also why he should fight and not lose. Physical conditioning was also important. This training grew in intensity until it culminated in marches of twenty-five miles a day with full equipment. Many Japanese soldiers were farmers before conscription who were accustomed to long hours of work and physical hardships. Hence, man-handling heavy weapons and light artillery through jungles and along mountain trails was less of a problem for men who routinely carried 200-pound sacks of rice on their backs.[24]

Although the Japanese soldier was good, he was not super. Marksmanship was not stressed in training and the Japanese were the worst of the major armies when it came to the use of artillery, with the exception of the Italians. Another area in which the Japanese soldier was sorely deficient was security. When Japanese soldiers were captured, they talked freely (surrender was so foreign to the Japanese that instruction on personal conduct after capture was apparently never taught). Throughout the Guadalcanal campaign, the Americans also obtained a great deal of information from captured orders, maps, and diaries, which were carelessly carried to the front lines. The amount of captured intelligence was so prolific that one marine officer said, "it causes me to want to never write another order."[25]

Despite the flaws in his training, the Japanese soldier possessed definite strengths. He was the best in the world when it came to night combat, because more than one-quarter of his training was devoted to that area. He was also adept at exploiting the advantages of all types of terrain, including the jungle, and was a master in the use of camouflage, infiltration, and trickery. He used English phrases to confuse, taunt, and terrify. "The Japs yell at us," observed one marine colonel. "Malines, we're gonna keel you! More blood for the emperor."[26] Another marine once heard a Japanese soldier order his company forward in perfect English. Use of English by the Japanese was very common on Guadalcanal, but the Japanese employed other tricks as well. A Japanese soldier would sometimes work his rifle bolt back and forth or send soldier decoys out in the open or down rivers to draw fire or reveal American positions. At other times he would bang bamboo poles together or light firecrackers to simulate rifle fire. "They ain't supermen," summarized one marine corporal, "they're just tricky bastards."[27]

The Final Approach

About noon on 20 August, Ichiki gathered his commanders at the village of Rengo to issue the movement order and plan of attack. Commencing at 2000 that night the units would march in column with the 2d Company and Major Kuramoto's headquarters in the lead, followed by the 1st Company, the 4th Company, Colonel Ichiki's headquarters, and the Machine Gun Company. The Battalion Gun Platoon, the 3d Company, and the Engineer Company would take up the rear. Ignoring the intelligence and maps on the American positions provided to him by the navy, Ichiki for some unknown reason decided to advance westward down the coastal track. This route would expose his force to the strongest American positions. The former camp of the 11th Construction Unit would serve as Ichiki's initial objective, which he hoped to take by 0200 in a surprise night attack. From there, the battalion would split into two groups—one aimed at the airfield, the other at a nearby position on the Lunga. Like bloodhounds, teams of Ichiki's engineers—led by a few native guides-would sniff for obstacles and river crossing points before the main body.[28]

To maintain the element of surprise, Ichiki stressed the importance of remaining quiet before the attack. Taunts and screams and the loading of rifles, in order to avoid accidental discharges, were forbidden. Based on his orders, it was obvious that Ichiki expected little resistance from the 2,000 or so marines he expected to encounter. Indeed, his contempt for the American fighting man and belief in the night attack were so great that he said he would annihilate the Americans with "one brush of the armored sleeve."[29]

The night attack was successfully employed by the Japanese for centuries, including the Russo-Japanese War of 1904–1905, the China Incident of 1937–1945, and in the conquest of Hong Kong (1941), and Ichiki and the Imperial Army had great faith in it during the summer of 1942. Capitalizing on what they thought was the superior faith and fighting spirit of the Japanese soldier, the tactic was used by the Japanese as a means of neutralizing an enemy's superiority in heavy weapons, artillery, and aircraft. "The night is one million reinforcements," they taught. Indeed, the Japanese believed that enemy positions, no matter how heavily fortified, could be surprised and overwhelmed through speed, mobility, and stealth. In a pamphlet issued to their soldiers titled "Read This Alone—and the War Can Be Won," it said: "Westerners—being very haughty, effeminate, and cowardly—intensely dislike fighting in the rain or mist or in the dark. They cannot conceive night to be a proper time for battle—though it is excellent for dancing. In these weaknesses lie our great opportunity."[30]

The tactics employed by the Japanese in the night attack were time-tested and emphasized surprise. The basic formation for the night attack was the infantry company, with the objective of the assault being the seizure of either a hill or enemy strong point or a penetration in depth of an enemy's line. Their assault tactics were simple and emphasized positive control. Since coordinating the movement of large bodies of troops was difficult at night, especially in thick woods, the Japanese army preferred to attack in concentrated formations. An added benefit of attacking in such a formation was that it reduced the likelihood of cowardice because others would probably observe such actions. The Japanese also underscored the need for complete familiarity with the terrain and thorough preparation for the attack. According to Japanese army regulations, the company commander was required to lead the assault and was encouraged to defeat the enemy by suddenly engaging in hand-to-hand combat.[31]

The Imperial Army employed special equipment in the night attack. For maintaining direction, they used luminous compasses, route markers, lime, tape, ropes, and marker lights. For maintaining control, small white flags, luminous watches, whistles, contact ropes, luminous markers, white sashes, white belts, marker lights, and signal cartridges were used. In order to help maintain the element of surprise, special cloth was given to each soldier to deaden the sound of equipment and to remove the telltale glint of metallic objects.[32]

As for weapons, the Japanese carried rugged, quality designs, which were well-tested in battle. Most of Ichiki's soldiers were armed with the Model 38 (1905) Arisaka rifle. This crude yet highly reliable weapon was a bolt-action design like the Springfield. Unlike the marine rifle, the Arisaka was chambered for a 6.5mm (.256 inch) cartridge, though a 7.7mm version (the Model 99) was also available. At the tip of the Arisaka was what the Japanese considered the most important weapon in the night attack, the *juken* (bayonet). "Don't rely on your bullets, rely on your bayonet," said one of their training mottoes. The standard Japanese bayonet was a strong, mass-produced blade, slightly longer than fifteen inches. Most came with a hooked prong below the handle to catch an enemy blade in hand-to-hand combat.[33]

Ichiki's men also brought with them two models of machine gun. The most common was the Model 96 Nambu 6.5mm light machine gun. A copy of the Czech ZB series, the Nambu fired 550 rounds per minute and was magazine-fed and air-cooled. The Nambu had the distinction of inflicting perhaps more Allied casualties than any other Japanese infantry weapon in the war, and it would take its toll on Guadalcanal. The Imperial Army's heavy machine gun was the Model 92, a 7.7mm weapon. Called the *jukikanju* by the Japanese, it was an air-cooled, strip-fed weapon capable of firing 450 rounds per minute. Including the tripod, the *juki* weighed 122 pounds and could be carried either assembled using poles or disassembled. Muzzle flash suppressors, which kept the guns concealed during night combat, were carried for both models.[34]

Major Kuramoto's artillerymen hefted what was perhaps the most distinctive looking weapon in the Japanese inventory: the stocky Model 92, 70mm *daitaiho* (battalion gun). Versatile and easy to handle, the battalion gun had a maximum range of 3,075 yards, and, with a 50-degree elevation, it could be used like a mortar. The battalion gun weighed just 468 pounds and could be broken down into several smaller loads. Ichiki's First Echelon was armed with three 70mm guns, two of which belonged to 2d Lt. Tatsuharu Hanami's Battalion Gun Platoon. Another distinctive Japanese weapon was the ubiquitous Model 89, 50mm (1.97-inch) mortar. Popularly known as the "knee mortar" to the Americans, it was light (just 10.25 pounds), easy to employ, and fired a 1.75-pound projectile up to 700 yards. The mortar's nickname was derived from its distinctive concave-shaped base plate, enabling it to be mounted either in the ground, on a log, or on a fallen tree. It was not fired from the knee, as a marine on Guadalcanal painfully discovered after having his leg shattered.[35]

A Key Turning Point

The 20th of August was a red-letter day on Cactus. In the afternoon the marines heard the distant hum of approaching aircraft engines and prepared to take cover, for this sound had come to be associated with the enemy. This time, however, such thoughts were quickly dispelled as familiar aircraft came into view bearing the white star, not the dreaded "meatball" of the Japanese. Touching down on a dusty Henderson Field were ten SBD Dauntless dive-bombers, under the command of Maj. Richard C. Mangrum, and nineteen rotund Grumman Wildcat F4F fighters, led by Capt. John L. Smith. The pilots were surprised at the celebration and emotion of their new hosts, most of whom were cheering and throwing their helmets into the air as if they were at a ball game. Their joy was so great that many could not help but shed a tear or two. Colonel Twining called the arrival of these aircraft one of the turning points of the campaign.[36]

4 The Tenaru

Ichiki Attacks

At 2000 on 20 August, Ichiki's force struck out toward the Ilu River according to plan. It was a pitch-black night on Guadalcanal; only the pulsating lights of countless fireflies were visible. At about 2300, two marine sentries in the coconut grove east of the river fired a shot at trespassers who failed to answer their challenge. First one sentry and then the other withdrew to the west side of the river to make a report to the senior noncommissioned officer on watch, Sgt. Anthony Conti of the 1st Special Weapons Battalion. The first sentry told Conti that he had heard the sounds of walking in the bush, and the other said that he had heard voices—probably Ichiki's engineers. Concerned, the sergeant phoned and explained the situation to his captain, asking if the marines had lost a patrol out in the grove. The captain tersely answered "No!" told him that the fireflies were getting to him, and hung up. But Conti sensed something was brewing and explained to his men that "this may be it."[1]

Several hundred yards downstream, Pvt. John L. Joseph of Company G, 1st Marines, was standing watch

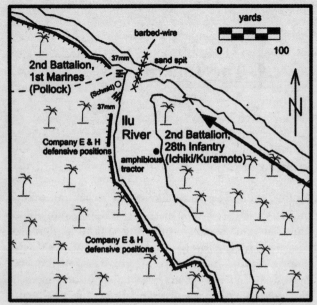

Battle of the Tenaru, Ichiki's Approach, 0030, 21 August

on the west bank of the Ilu River when he noticed a disturbance in the water. To his astonishment, the dark form of a helmeted soldier with a rifle strapped to his back silently rose up out of the river on his hands and knees and came toward him. Joseph, like all the other marines on sentry duty this night, was not expecting any visitors, so he struck the Japanese soldier in the face with the butt of his rifle. In the words of Joseph, the Japanese intruder "just slid out of sight." Joseph immediately woke up his partner, Pvt. Ed Fahey, to tell him what had happened. The two were about to make a report to the rear when a match or lighter suddenly lit up across the river. Both men fired their rifles at the flickering light, followed by bursts from a Company H .30-caliber water-cooled machine gun a few yards to their left.[2]

While Private Joseph was confronting this solitary enemy scout, Ichiki's main body was steadily closing in on the sand spit. At 0030 the van of Ichiki's column, Capt. Tetsuro Sawada's 2d Company, provoked angry machine gun and rifle fire as it was about to cross the sandbar. Colonel Ichiki was surprised to encounter American opposition so far from the airfield. Thus, the colonel ordered Major Kuramoto and Captain Sawada to destroy these positions in an improvised attack across the sand spit. Since the element of surprise was lost, Ichiki said that he would support the assault with mortar and machine gun fire.[3]

An atmosphere of tense expectation gripped the marines as they waited in foxholes for the anticipated attack. Peering out across the river, they watched and listened to the Japanese soldiers screeching and shooting their guns into the air, stirring themselves into a sharklike feeding frenzy. At about 0130, the marines fired a green parachute flare over the sand spit, illuminating a dark, bobbing mass of screaming Japanese steadily moving toward them. The marines on the west side of the river waited until Captain Sawada's helmeted soldiers were halfway across the sandbar before they opened fire in a sudden, deafening roar. Machine guns spewing out streams of bullets and tracers and antitank guns belching mouthfuls of ball bearings tore into Sawada's densely packed squads and platoons, invoking ghastly screams of pain. Supported only by Nambus with limited fields of fire and 50mm mortars, some of Sawada's crack warriors responded with rifle fire, but most answered with fixed bayonets as they pressed home the attack against the marines.[4]

In the face of the onslaught stood Pvt. Johnny Rivers of Company H, 1st Marines, manning a .30-caliber water-cooled machine gun in a log-and-earth emplacement only a few yards from the spit. Private Rivers fired hundreds of rounds into the Japanese before he took a bullet to the face. But even as Rivers took his last breath, he sent another 200 rounds into the onrushing Japanese before collapsing. Corporal Leroy Diamond then fired the gun until wounded in the arm. The third marine to appear behind the trigger was Pvt. Albert A. Schmid. Assisted by Corporal Diamond, Schmid continued his deadly work until a mortar shell exploded at the embrasure, blinding Schmid. Determined to fight on, Diamond, who still had his eyesight, and Schmid, who still had two good hands, resumed firing until they were relieved hours later. For their heroism, Schmid and Diamond subsequently received the Navy Cross.[5]

Marines like Al Schmid firing machine guns dropped many Japanese on the sand spit, but the two canister firing antitank guns proved decisive, cutting large swaths in the enemy ranks. The barrels of the two guns glowed red as the gunners pumped out round after round as fast as they could. But the gunners encountered unexpected problems. The gun blasts sucked sand into the guns, causing frequent jams. The resourceful gunners soon solved this problem by staking blankets underneath the muzzles of the guns. These stoppages, however, gave Japanese snipers and mortar-men sufficient time to zero in on the antitank gun crews. Several replacement crew members were needed to keep the guns in action against the Japanese.[6]

The barbed wire barrier, erected some thirty yards in front of the marine line just the day before, also played an important role in stopping and slowing the Japanese attack. Apparently, with so many of their comrades falling at or near the wire to American fire, some of Captain Sawada's men cautiously examined the wire believing it was electrified. But the barrier did not stop all of Sawada's crack soldiers. Vaulting or circumventing their way past the obstacle, small groups of Japanese engaged the marines in hand-to-hand combat. Some Japanese held their razor-sharp bayonets in their hands and used them like swords. Corporal John Shea was in the thick of the fight at the apex of the sand spit, dubbed Hell's Point, firing his Thompson until it jammed. Rolling over onto his back, Shea was tending to the faulty weapon when an enemy soldier jumped into his foxhole and began stabbing one of his legs with a bayonet. Astounded, Shea kicked and jammed the Japanese against the wall of the foxhole, freed the jammed bolt, and pumped five quick rounds into the attacker.[7]

Out of the darkness, three Japanese made for Cpl. Dean Wilson's foxhole at Hell's Point. Wilson pointed his BAR at the onrushing trio and pulled the trigger, but nothing happened. One Japanese yelled at Wilson, "Maline, you die!" and lunged at the corporal with his bayonet. Wilson quickly grabbed a razor-sharp machete and took a swipe at the enemy soldier, dropping him to the ground with his bloody entrails squirting out between his fingers. The other two unlucky Japanese suffered a similar fate from Wilson's machete.[8]

During the initial attacks, other groups of Japanese made it across, seizing a few marine positions at Hell's Point. Exhausted from digging and patrolling during the day, some marines were still asleep in their foxholes when the Japanese attacked. One marine corporal was stabbed through the face while he slept by a sword-waving Japanese officer. Another marine in the foxhole, Pvt. Eddie De Joinville, woke up in time to draw his gun, but the gun's safety was on. All that the frustrated private could do was parry the enemy officer's blow, in the process receiving a badly lacerated hand. The Japanese officer, who figured that the situation was getting a little too dangerous, started to back away from De Joinville when a shot rang out from another marine a short distance away, dropping the enemy officer. The next morning, the sharpshooting marine retrieved the dead officer's sword.[9]

In the meantime, at about 0145 Colonel Pollock ordered Company G's 1st Platoon, under Lieutenant Codrea, forward to stave off further breakthroughs and to retake those positions. Bivouacked some 300 yards in the rear, Codrea's platoon rapidly moved out along the coastal trail in a column of squads. About halfway to the spit, the platoon stopped and deployed after encountering the angry snapping of enemy bullets buzzing all around them. Codrea led one squad forward to Hell's Point, moving on hands and knees to avoid the enemy fire. Sergeant James Hancock led his squad to his right (south) toward the downstream 37mm gun position. Sergeant Charlie Spakes led the remaining squad forward to the sandbar to take up a rear position with orders to engage and stop any Japanese who broke through.[10]

As he approached the sand spit, Lieutenant Codrea was hit in the arm by red-hot fragments from either a hand grenade or mortar round. Two marines bandaged the six-foot, four-inch officer's wounded arm and applied a tourniquet. Later, a lone Japanese soldier lunged at Codrea with his bayonet, hoping to skewer the wounded lieutenant, but Codrea unlimbered his weapon in enough time to drill the enemy soldier through the nose at eight feet. Codrea also recalls seeing several Japanese on the west side of the river, moving south toward the upstream 37mm gun, but, according to Codrea, "they were quickly disposed of" by his men.[11]

Codrea deployed the squad he led forward to the sand spit. Since there were no foxholes or protective cover on the spit, the members of the squad burrowed themselves into the sand to avoid the enemy fire. Firing at anything on the sandbar that moved, the squad drew increasing retaliatory fire from enemy snipers and machine gunners. One burst from a Nambu sprayed the squad's position, hitting Pvt. James Wilson, who felt a tug at his helmet. A bullet had pierced the front of his helmet, parted his hair, and exited out the rear, spraying pieces of metal into Wilson's spine. Temporarily numb from the waist down, Wilson watched the rest of the battle from this prone position until after dawn, when a navy corpsman dragged him to safety.[12]

After the attack of Captain Sawada's 2d Company fizzled out, Ichiki ordered another attack across the sand spit, choosing 1st Lt. Yusaku Higuchi's 1st Company and 1st Lt. Toshiro Chiba's 4th Company. At about 0230, however, Colonel Pollock ordered his own reinforcements forward—the 2d and 3d Platoons of Company G. These platoons took up positions a short distance downstream from Hell's Point in time to help thwart the determined yet suicidal attack by all of Lieutenant Higuchi's company and part of Lieutenant Chiba's. The bolstered marine line not only stopped the Japanese attack, but also drove those who remained alive back across the sand spit. Colonel Cates recalls that the "din of battle was terrific."[13]

Meanwhile, back at division headquarters, Colonel Thomas was awakened by a report that the 1st Marines had encountered an enemy force east of the Ilu. Since minor nocturnal clashes were commonplace, Thomas dozed off, but he jumped to his feet about 0300 when the thunder of battle grew great. Moments later, Cates called Thomas on the field phone to tell him that the Japanese had attacked some time before, and that he wanted Cresswell's battalion to buttress his threatened position. Thomas told him to wait and "let the situation develop" until daybreak, when they could determine where the main Japanese effort would hit. Thomas spent the next three hours pacing outside the front of the operations shelter, watching the arching flares over the coconut trees to the east and listening to threatening sounds of battle. To Thomas, the waiting seemed to last an eternity.[14]

After the original crew of the downstream 37mm gun had fallen to Japanese snipers and grenades, three marines of Sergeant Hancock's squad—Pvt. Harry Horsman and two others—decided to try and fire the now-silent weapon. With no training or experience in artillery, the three fired by trial and error until Hancock, a former artilleryman, climbed into the gun pit to lead the impromptu crew against the Japanese. Within moments, the four began firing canister rounds with efficiency and precision. "Canister played hell, I can tell you," Horsman recalled. "They showered us with grenades, but we stood our ground." Horsman remembers one grenade in particular, which landed in the pit. "I picked it up and looked it over. I was mesmerized. I just kept staring at the strange writing on it until one of the other marines yelled for me to throw it away. It exploded a second or two later." Sergeant Hancock's crew, however, did not remain untouched this night. One explosion later engulfed the position, severely wounding Hancock.[15]

Some time after the slaughter of his company, Captain Sawada, bloodied and badly wounded, staggered back to where Ichiki was directing the battle. Sawada, a veteran of the Nomonhan debacle against the Russians in 1939, thought that this battle was even worse. Sawada begged Ichiki to withdraw or formulate plans for another attack, but Ichiki had no intentions of retreating. With his commanders huddled around him, Ichiki hatched another plan of attack. First, volunteers of a "forlorn hope" would swim across the river and destroy the American positions. Then, the 3d Company, led by 1st Lt. Magozo Maruyama, and the Engineer Company, commanded by 1st Lt. Hideo Goto, would outflank and strike the Americans about 100 meters upstream. The attack would occur about 0400. But as the volunteers were about to leave, Ichiki ordered them to stop. Why he changed his mind is not known. Instead, Ichiki decided to unlimber three 70mm battalion guns and the eight *jukis* of 1st Lt. Shigenao Komatsu's 2d Machine Gun Company, in an

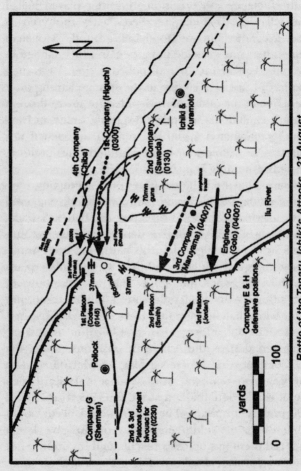

Battle of the Tenaru, Ichiki's Attacks, 21 August

effort to establish fire superiority over the marines.[16]

For a time Ichiki's heavy weapons commanded the battle area, especially the 70mm guns, which bucked and roared in preparation for the inland attack. Retaliatory marine artillery and mortar fire, however, silenced the heavy weapons one by one. Artillery fire also helped blunt the attack of Maruyama's 3d Company, but small groups of Japanese managed to gain a small foothold across the river and engage the marines in hand-to-hand combat. This enemy foothold, however, was quickly eliminated. In support of his company's attack, Maruyama ordered three Nambus forward. One of these was set up in an abandoned amphibious tractor about 100 meters upstream from the spit. The Japanese gunners exploited the tractor's dominant firing position for perhaps two hours, killing and wounding several leathernecks. Unable to silence the Japanese gunners in the tractor with small arms, Harry Horsman recalls his gun crew being asked to eliminate the enemy gunners at dawn. Although the gun had to be moved a bit because of the angle, a well-placed high-explosive round finally silenced the Japanese machine gun nest.[17]

After watching the destruction of three companies of Japan's finest, those Japanese who remained alive were still determined to destroy the Yank defenders. Attempts to overpower the now alert marines by rushing across the sand spit had all been fruitless. Perceiving the need to neutralize the stubborn Americans, the Japanese hatched another plan to outflank the marine positions. Using the remaining half of Lieutenant Chiba's 4th Company and small numbers of volunteers from other units, the improvised Japanese task force—christened the "Sea Raiding Unit"—hoped to outflank the marine left flank by wading in the ocean along the shore. At first, the effort met with some success, but the marines detected the Japanese about 0530 in the light of explosions and flares. With their rifles held high above their heads, and with no cover, the result was predictable for the Japanese. Enfilading weapons fire from marine gunnery Sgt. Red Smythe's light machine gun section turned the sea red with the blood of these brave and determined attackers. At dawn, droves of the unfortunate dead who had attempted this aquatic maneuver could be seen washed up on shore, partially buried in the sand.[18]

Shortly after daybreak, Capt. Martin Clemens was summoned to Pollock's command post, where he found Sgt. Maj. Jacob Vouza bleeding profusely and near death. Vouza recounted an amazing story of his capture by the Japanese while attempting to hide a small American flag given to him by the marines. When Vouza proved uncooperative during the interrogation, his captors tied him to a tree and searched him. They found the American flag. After Vouza refused to answer their questions, he was beaten with rifle butts, slashed with a sword, and made to lie on a nest of fiery red ants. The next morning the Japanese tied his wrists and took him with them toward the battle. At the approach, the guards were ordered to dispatch him as quietly as possible. They bayoneted him repeatedly, including a thrust to the neck. As the battle heated up, Vouza escaped and chewed through the cords that bound his wrists. Staggering and sometimes falling, Vouza made his way to the American lines, where Pvt. Wilbur Bewley of Company G, 2d Battalion, 1st Marines, challenged him. It did not take long for Bewley to realize he was not Japanese. Vouza thought he was going to die but made a miraculous recovery in a division hospital, where he received many pints of blood.[19]

21 August: The Destruction of Ichiki

As the sun rose over the horizon on the morning of 21 August, it was a brilliant red, as though reflecting the bloody carnage of the battlefield below. Although each of Ichiki's attacks had been defeated in detail, he showed no sign of retreating at daybreak. Hidden in the grove of trees, which stood like silent sentinels across the river, the Japanese received no respite as the marines inundated them with a constant barrage of rifle and machine gun fire. Under the circumstances, the Japanese found it impossible to escape, as they took refuge behind trees and in shallow pits. One survivor heard a Japanese sergeant exhorting his men, "We will go back after sunset. You must endure until dark." All who heard him knew that was their only option, because those who carelessly exposed themselves even for an instant were cut down by American fire.[20]

But the Americans were not about to let Ichiki's veterans "endure until dark." In a huddle at Cates's command post shortly after dawn, Gerald Thomas said, "We aren't about to let those people lay up there all day." Cates agreed, "We've got to get them out today." Joined by Cresswell, the three devised a plan to eliminate the Japanese holed up in the triangle of land near the sand spit. With his finger, Thomas traced the plan of attack on a map. Accompanied by a platoon of M3A1 Stuart light tanks from Company B, 1st Tank Battalion, Cresswell's battalion would cross the Ilu about a mile and a half inland and envelop the rear of Ichiki's force. Thomas told Cresswell to relentlessly drive home the attack as Captain Brush did two days prior. Upon receiving Vandegrift's authorization, both units were released from division reserve at 0800. Because of the difficulty in passing through the entangled jungle, the attack was nearly two hours late. The streambed also stopped the tanks from supporting Cresswell. According to Cates, an angry Vandegrift gave him "billy-hell" for the lengthy delay.[21]

At 0950 Cresswell's three rifle companies pivoted to the north, while Company D advanced northward along the east bank of the Ilu. The unit on the far right, Company C, led by Lt. Nick Stevenson, encountered the first sizable resistance in the vicinity of Block Four Village. There a platoon of Japanese armed with machine guns bickered with the marines. Stevenson countered with two platoons, while the third was sent around the left to isolate the Japanese force from the main body at the Ilu. The Japanese reacted to this move with "the customary bayonet charge," which was cut down by the marines. In the meantime, Company A on the right and Company B on the left pushed north then northwest without resistance. By 1230 both companies were marching westward, compressing the Japanese in the triangle of land on the east bank of the Ilu River.[22]

In mid-afternoon, Colonel Cates ordered a platoon of Stuart tanks, led by Lt. Leo Case, to patrol the beach on the east side of the Ilu. About 1500, four Stuarts plunged across the sand spit toward the Japanese. The M3A1 Stuart was ideally suited for this particular mission. Weighing 14.3 tons, it was light and nimble enough for use in lightly wooded coastal areas but not in Guadalcanal's rugged interior. Housed in its small turret was a single 37mm gun, capable of firing armor-piercing, general purpose, and canister rounds. The tank was also studded with five M37 Browning .30-caliber, air-cooled machine guns to mow down enemy troops. A maximum armor thickness of 51mm, however, did not offer much protection for its four-man crew.[23]

From the west bank, correspondent Richard Tregaskis and others watched in awe as the tanks entered the grove and went to work:

> It was fascinating to see them bustling amongst the trees, pivoting, turning, spitting sheets of yellow flame. It was like a comedy of toys, something unbelievable, to see them knocking over palm trees, which fell slowly, flushing the running figures of men from underneath their treads, following and firing at the fugitives. It was unbelievable to see men falling and being killed so close, to see the explosions of Jap grenades and mortars, black fountains and showers of dirt near the tanks, and see the flashes of explosions under their very treads. We had not realized there were so many Japs in the grove. Group after group was flushed out and shot down by the tanks' canister shells.[24]

Lacking the detachment's 37mm antitank guns, which were with the Second Echelon, Ichiki's veterans fought the steel beasts with magnetic antitank mines and grenades. Many Japanese were killed trying to stop them with these weapons. A sudden explosion on one tank broke a tread and stopped it dead in its tracks. The other tanks huddled around the disabled beast and rescued its crew, then resumed their deadly work. About this time, Colonel Cates radioed Case and ordered him to withdraw. But Case rebuked the colonel, saying, "Leave us alone. We are too busy killing Japs." The tanks flattened machine gun nests and cut down large numbers of Japanese with canister and machine gun fire.[25]

But Case's tanks did not kill all of the Japanese. One survivor, Sgt. Sadanobu Okada, of Ichiki's Regimental Headquarters unit, played dead as two tanks approached the area where he was lying. The first drove over his back, but the large root of a coconut tree protected his body from the tank's bone-crushing weight. Okada pulled the pin from a grenade as the second tank approached, but this tank did not drive over him. Another survivor, a Sergeant Kuragane, playing dead nearby, received only a slight bruise as this tank passed over him. The large, octopuslike tree roots also saved this sergeant's life. Others were not so fortunate. When Case's tanks later returned to the east bank, Vandegrift wrote, "the rear of the tanks looked like meat grinders."[26]

When the tanks left Okada's area to ravage other parts of the grove, Sergeant Okada noticed that it became deathly silent. Not even the groans of wounded countrymen could be heard. While Okada and Kuragane were discussing a plan of escape, a Japanese soldier cried, "Tanks coming!" Okada saw not only the three tanks returning, but also hundreds of Americans closing in from the rear (this was Cresswell's battalion conducting its enveloping maneuver).

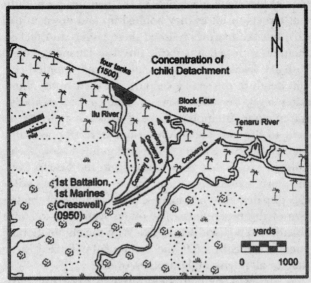

*Tenaru River, Counterattck of the 1st Battalion,
1st Marines, 21 August*

Cresswell's men showed no mercy as they ruthlessly drove forward. Private First Class Andy Poliny of Company A recalled that some of the marines in his unit cheered when they encountered the first bit of Japanese resistance, but their spirits were dampened when several were hit by Japanese bullets. Despite their best efforts, however, the Japanese were being pushed back toward the triangle of land at the sand spit. Correspondent Tregaskis was surprised by the large number of Japanese being ferreted out of the grove.[27]

Many Japanese ran for the sea toward their only avenue of escape, but most were felled by small arms fire before they reached the beach. Their heads, which

looked like small black dots to the marines, were difficult targets to hit as they bobbed up and down in the
surf, but the marines relished these targets and picked
them off with well-aimed rifle fire. Two Japanese, 1st Lt.
Yoshiaki Sakakibara and an enlisted man, avoided certain death in the sea by keeping just their noses above
water level. Very few, however, managed to escape in
this manner. Attempts by some of Ichiki's men to flee by
land to the east and to the south were stopped, and
Lieutenant Stevenson's company gunned down one
unlucky group that broke through to the beach. Even
the newly arrived aircraft got into the act. Strafing Wildcats dispatched some Japanese taking refuge on the lee
side of the beach and a few others who took to some
abandoned boats at Beach Red. With the elimination of
enemy targets by 1700, the Battle of the Tenaru River
was, for all intents and purposes, over.[28]

A survey of the battlefield revealed a horrific sight.
One of those who witnessed the grisly scene was
Richard Tregaskis. At the sand spit, he saw small and
large clusters of Japanese sprawled about in various
poses of death. Many of them, partially buried along
the water's edge, looked "puffed and glossy, like shiny
sausages." The carnage at the spit was not pleasant to
look at, but Tregaskis found the scene in the grove
even worse. He saw groups of Japanese whose remains had been blackened by artillery fire and others
who had been shredded by canister fire from the
tanks. Even more gruesome were the flattened bodies
of soldiers who had been run over by the tanks. Tregaskis saw one bucktoothed, bespectacled private
lying on his back, with his chest "a mess of ground
meat." The stench, a sickening sweet smell, was un-

bearable. Tregaskis tried to come to grips with what he saw: "There is no horror to these things. The first one you see is the only shock. The rest are simple repetition."[29]

As the marines moved about the battle site to collect souvenirs and tend to the wounded, the few Japanese who remained tried to exact a small measure of revenge. Feigning death, they shot and blew up a few marines who were in the act of providing relief. Pollock, Twining, and Cresswell were surprised when a Japanese soldier unleashed a pistol and tried to shoot the three in their faces. When the gun failed to discharge, the Japanese soldier turned the weapon on himself and blew the top of his head off. Such actions were a shock even to an experienced veteran like Vandegrift, who wrote to General Thomas Holcomb, the Marine Corps commandant: "These people refuse to surrender. The wounded wait until men come up to examine them . . . and blow themselves and the other fellow to pieces with a hand grenade. You can readily see the answer to that."[30]

Casualties in the Battle of Tenaru River were high, especially for the Japanese. Nearly 790 Japanese were killed. Only one Japanese soldier willingly surrendered, while another fourteen were taken captive, including Capt. Takao Tamioka. Of those captured, only two were not wounded. Marine casualties were thirty-eight dead and seventy-eight wounded. The marines found three 70mm battalion guns, ten *jukis*, twenty Nambu machine guns, twenty knee mortars, twelve flamethrowers, 700 rifles, as well as a large amount of demolition equipment, including prepared TNT charges, antitank mines, and bangalore torpedoes. The marines received an unexpected bonus from Ichiki's men in the form of more than 700 short-handled shovels, which were put to good use.[31]

The marines found that the backpack each Japanese soldier carried was scrupulously clean and contained a variety of items. Each contained a three-piece set of cooking utensils, two or three cans of food, small cakes, bread, and rice. In addition, each pack had camouflage nets for helmets and shoulders with foliage woven into them, as well as an extra pair of shoes, underwear, socks, and toilet items. Each Japanese soldier also carried a first-aid kit consisting of two large bandages and two picric acid gauzes for burn victims. Sometimes, Japanese flags with inscriptions were found in the backpacks and small quantities of opium.[32]

The exact cause of Ichiki's death is a mystery. The official Japanese history says that he committed *hara-kiri* in the grove after burning the regimental color. But Japanese survivors emphatically state that he was killed on the battlefield, probably near the sand spit. Another possibility was that he was killed during mop-up operations after the battle. A few feet from where Lieutenant Colonel Cresswell and six other marines stood near the spit were two Japanese bodies lying next to each other on their stomachs. One was a Japanese officer. While a marine was in the process of ensuring their death with his rifle, the Japanese officer rolled over and shot the marine in the face with a tiny pistol, the kind used by Japanese officers to commit *hara-kiri*. Witnessing this act, Pfc. Andy Poliny, ran forward and riddled the two Japanese soldiers with his BAR at close range. Poliny is certain that the Japanese officer whom he had shot was none other than Colonel Ichiki.[33]

The destruction of Ichiki and his First Echelon reveals much about the mind-set of the Imperial Army in the summer of 1942. It is true that Ichiki's intelligence on American strength was faulty, but Ichiki was also guilty of recklessness and foolishness. Not only did he choose to launch his attack after the destruction of Shibuya's patrol, but he also chose to enter the Lunga area along the coast, exactly where his maps indicated that the marines were the strongest. The reason for this decision appears to be the ailment with which the Japanese were sorely afflicted in the summer of 1942—victory disease. Given the outcome of the war up to that time, the Imperial Army regarded themselves as invincible. Ichiki simply did what his superiors expected of him. Even so, his actions are difficult to understand under scrutiny and resemble the actions of an amateur rather than one of Japan's foremost military tacticians.[34]

Colonel Cates provided an interesting analysis of the Battle of the Tenaru:

> This engagement has proved to my youngsters that the Jap is no super-fighter. He possesses plenty of animal courage, but it is of little value unless it is combined with intelligence. As far as training goes, the Japanese should be far superior to our Marines, as they have had approximately ten years of warfare in China, and . . . it takes actual battle to thoroughly train troops. There is one thing that may react against them; the fact that they have been fighting Chinese, who were poorly equipped. They will be sadly surprised when they run up against troops that have modern automatic weapons

with a terrific firepower, plus the courage and
intelligence needed to employ them.[35]

"I Think It's a False Report"

After the Battle of the Tenaru, survivors of Ichiki's
command drifted east toward Taivu Point, many of
them pillaging native gardens along the way. By 29
August, a total of 128 men had gathered there, including those who were left behind after the landing. The
trek of one seriously wounded survivor, Superior Private Isamu Mashiko of Ichiki's signal unit, was typical.
His plan was to sleep during the day and travel by
night to avoid American patrols, but an army of ants,
which swarmed on his wounds, forced a change in
plans. Enduring fierce pain and hunger, Mashiko
made his way east along the shore like a staggering
sleepwalker, lacking the strength to even fight off the
swarms of flies, which tried to suck his blood and lay
eggs on his wounds. Finally, on the fourth day jubilant
comrades at Taivu Point greeted him, where he was
treated and given food.[36]

While Ichiki's survivors migrated eastward, Imperial
Army and Navy officers at Rabaul struggled to obtain
information on the Ichiki Detachment's fate. On 21
August, Captain Kadomae, who just one day earlier
announced that thirty U.S. aircraft had landed on the
airfield at Lunga, sent several messages to his superiors at Rabaul. In the first, Kadomae reported that at
daybreak he could hear a furious battle taking place
near the airfield and that four or five American fighter
planes had taken off at that time. In the next, transmitted a short time later, he disclosed that the planes

had landed and that the battle was still raging. Later, Kadomae said that no more U.S. planes had taken off, and, based on this observation, he optimistically declared, "It appears that our attack on the airfield is proceeding favorably."[37]

These and other messages were received by the Imperial Navy commands at Rabaul and were in turn relayed to Adm. Isoroku Yamamoto's Combined Fleet staff. Kadomae's transmissions fueled an optimistic appraisal of the situation. Later that night, however, Seventeenth Army headquarters received a message that burst their bubble: "The First Echelon of the Ichiki Detachment was almost annihilated this morning at a point near the airfield." But this report was discounted for three days because the originator was unknown. Later that night, General Futami was asleep in his quarters when he was awakened by Colonel Matsumoto: "They tell me the navy received a wire reporting the Ichiki Detachment was annihilated." Matsumoto then smiled and added, "I think it's a false report. I didn't want to tell you about it, but . . ." When Futami heard this he felt his heart skip a beat, hoping that the report was false. But the possibility of its truth bothered him. Over the next two days, Futami's mind was filled with anxiety and uncertainty over the Ichiki Detachment's fate.[38]

On the 23rd, the Japanese navy analyzed all of the communiqués received during the last few days and concluded that the Ichiki Detachment's situation was not necessarily to be viewed with optimism. They pointed out that if Ichiki had indeed captured the airfield, as was hoped, it would have been reported by now. Even though they doubted that Ichiki had been "annihilated," they admitted it was apparent that Ichiki had been forced into a desperate battle. Additional confusion, however, occurred on the 24th, when another message from Kadomae came in: "Gunfire still heard near the airfield. Aircraft with lights are flying all over the place." Jubilantly, the navy phoned Futami and Imperial General Headquarters in Tokyo, reporting, "The Ichiki Detachment is still in good shape near the airfield. They are apparently still storming it." (It was later learned that this message was three days old and was delayed in transmission by the navy.)[39]

Then, on 25 August, the Japanese learned the truth. They found out that the originator of the 21 August message reporting Ichiki's annihilation was Lt. Yoshiaki Sakakibara, a signal officer in the Ichiki Detachment. After arriving at Taivu Point, he had the message radioed by the navy observation unit there—Sakakibara's transmitter was too weak to reach Rabaul without navy relay. Evidently, the confusion about who had sent Sakakibara's message was created during the relay process over navy channels, which involved an unidentified destroyer or submarine. At 1000, the Seventeenth Army received another message from Sakakibara: "The detachment's losses have been fairly large, but now we are holding firmly the area around Taivu Point, and we have some ammunition and foodstuffs." Sakakibara also reported that Colonel Ichiki had died in battle and that about 100 survivors were gathered at Taivu Point. News of the Ichiki Detachment's fate was a shock to the Imperial Navy, but no less shocking to them was the news that aircraft were now operating from their old airfield on Guadalcanal.[40]

5 Threat from the Sea

"The Men Are Fine and in Good Spirits"

The last ten days of August were relatively quiet for Vandegrift's marines, while the Japanese licked their wounds and geared up for another assault. One important development during this time was the U.S. Navy's increasing presence, which, in addition to the recent arrival of aircraft at Henderson Field, seemed to lessen the feeling of isolation for the Americans on Guadalcanal. On the afternoon of 21 August, the APDs *Manley, McKean, Stringham, Little, Gregory,* and *Colhoun* arrived again off Lunga Point bearing 240 tons of badly needed food. Although the marines remained on strict rations, the arrival was welcome. And these vessels performed another valuable service. Responding to Vandegrift's request, the ships ferried the 2d Battalion, 5th Marines Reinforced (Combat Team 2), from Tulagi to Guadalcanal (see Table 5). This augmentation now gave Vandegrift six rifle battalions and six batteries of 75mm pack howitzers—nearly 12,000 men—to defend Henderson Field.[1]

The day after the arrival of the 2d Battalion, 5th

Marines, Lieutenant Colonel Cresswell's 1st Battalion, 1st Marines, fresh from its enveloping maneuver against Ichiki, reconnoitered the area around the Tenaru River in search of Japanese stragglers. At 1300, Cresswell dispatched a company of marines with tanks across the river, where they encountered light sniper fire. In a short firefight, the marines killed four Japanese and wounded one. Off Koli Point, these marines also spotted a small boat, which was strafed and sunk by American planes later that afternoon. Cresswell's men encountered no other Japanese opposition, but two Japanese were captured by a 1st Marines patrol near Block Four River on the 25th.[2]

Table 5
Composition of Combat Team 2
(2d Battalion, 5th Marines)

2d Battalion, 5th Marines	853*
Battery E, 2d Battalion, 11th Marines	142
2d Platoon, Company A, 1st Engineer Battalion	27
2d Platoon, Company A, 1st Amphibian Tractor Battalion	29
Detachment, Company A, 1st Medical Battalion	49
Combat Team 2 Total	1,100

*Total excludes casualties of eight killed and sixteen wounded suffered in the assault on Tulagi.

Source: *Final Report, I, Annex I, 2.*

In the meantime, the American air detachment on Guadalcanal, now christened the Cactus Air Force, received a welcome shot in the arm. On the 22nd, five P-400 Aircobras of the 67th Fighter Squadron, commanded by Capt. Dale Brannon, landed at Henderson Field. They were the first U.S. Army aircraft to arrive on the island. Five days later, nine more Aircobras joined them. The Aircobra lacked superchargers and oxygen equipment sufficient for high-altitude air combat, but the Japanese soldier on the ground would soon dread these deadly flying machines. Heavily armored, each was also armed with one 20mm cannon and two .50-caliber and four .30-caliber machine guns. The Japanese would fearfully call them the "long nosed planes."[3]

As the first Aircobras touched down on Henderson Field, General Vandegrift found time to write a letter to Lt. Gen. Thomas Holcomb. In it he gave a brief description of the Tenaru River battle, calling the one-sided action initiated by the Japanese the "greatest boner" he had ever seen. In particular, Vandegrift cited the effectiveness of the 37mm canister and the tanks. He also wrote:

> We at last have planes on our field and now do not feel so helplessly blind. . . . They (the Japs) had intended this for a major air base and were going to make a good one. Power-houses in duplicate, underground wires, perfectly great radio receiving and sending sets (we are now using them). One runway paved with coral and gravel and another staked out. Plans for dispersal fields. . . . To go back to canister, we are putting in for more, that and hand grenades are the most effective weapons

for this type of jungle work. . . . The men are fine, in good spirits, and thank God still in good health. These youngsters are the darndest people when they get started you ever saw.[4]

On 23 August bad weather protected Guadalcanal from Japanese bombers, but word of an approaching Japanese convoy concerned many marines, including General Vandegrift, who expected a landing during the night (it was rumored that the Japanese had as many as 10,000 troops in the transports). This convoy was Admiral Tanaka's, bearing Ichiki's Second Echelon and the Yokosuka 5th Special Naval Landing Force. After carefully pondering the risks of committing his tiny air force to battle, Vandegrift ordered his flyers to attack the enemy convoy. At 1630 he watched as twenty-one planes lifted off the dusty airstrip, not knowing if he would ever see them again. But bad weather forced them to turn back. When the dejected airmen landed, they found Vandegrift pacing the wooden floor of the Pagoda, the structure built by the Japanese to conduct their own air operations. Vandegrift tried to console the marine aviators as best he could, despite the visible strain on his own worried face.[5]

The same day that Tanaka's convoy was first sighted, Vandegrift's marines received more visitors off Lunga Point flying the "Red, White, and Blue." These were the cargo ships *Formalhaut* and *Alhena* escorted by three destroyers. All hands on the ships and the beach detachment turned to discharging more than half the cargo—mostly food and ammunition—before dusk. At this time the ships upped anchor and departed. It was a good thing they did, because Admiral Tanaka dispatched a welcoming party of his own, a pair of destroyers, to sink the American vessels. Only one Japanese destroyer made it to Lunga Point, however, because of bad weather. With no nautical targets, the lone Japanese destroyer shelled the marines after midnight, wounding four near the 5th Marines command post.[6]

Unlike the previous day, on 24 August, Henderson Field came under attack from the air. Around 1400, the marines on Guadalcanal scurried for cover after the air raid siren sounded. Minutes later they watched as aircraft overhead became entangled in a furious dogfight. The marines saw nine aircraft fall, six sporting the red "meatball." Before the day ended, the Cactus Air Force received unexpected reinforcements in the form of eleven SBDs from the carrier *Enterprise*. These newcomers received a rude welcome around midnight, when four Japanese destroyers shelled Lunga Point, killing two marines and wounding six. While the bombardment was in progress, another Japanese destroyer landed food and ammunition for Kadomae's troops at Kokumbona.[7]

While the situation picked up on Guadalcanal, things were really heating up at sea. In support of Tanaka's convoy sailed the bulk of the Combined Fleet, including carriers and battleships. But an American carrier force was also at sea protecting Guadalcanal's lines of supply to Espíritu Santo. On the 24th these forces traded blows in what became known as the Battle of the Eastern Solomons, the first carrier battle of the campaign. The U.S. Navy scored better in the exchange, with the Japanese losing the small carrier *Ryujo*. The Americans lost no ships, although the carrier *Enterprise* suffered moderate damage. The day

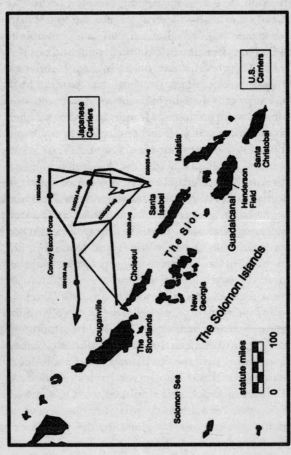

Track of Admiral Tanaka's Convoy, Battle of the Eastern Solomons, 23-25 August

ended with the opposing forces withdrawing from the battle area.[8]

Although the American carriers were departing the scene, Tanaka was not yet out of the woods. Shortly after midnight on the 25th, an American PBY patrol plane located Tanaka in the bright moonlight, only 180 miles north of Guadalcanal. This report was promptly relayed to Vandegrift, who ordered an attack as soon as possible. At daybreak, sixteen aircraft lifted off from Henderson Field to attempt another attack against Tanaka's convoy. Like birds of prey, they swooped down on the unsuspecting Japanese ships, scoring hits on Tanaka's flagship, the cruiser *Jintsu*, and the transport *Kinryu Maru*. The latter, carrying the Yokosuka 5th Special Naval Landing Force, was left burning and sinking. Adding salt to the wound, three American B-17 bombers sank one of Tanaka's destroyers later in the morning, while it was picking up survivors. It was a humiliating day for Tanaka and the Imperial Navy.[9]

In the meantime, Captain Kadomae's radio crackled with intelligence of mixed value. On 23 August, Kadomae provided Rabaul with a detailed but inaccurate report on American strength and activity. Kadomae estimated that the U.S. force on Guadalcanal numbered over 2,000 troops, armed with twenty pieces of artillery, ten tanks, and a "rather large number of machine guns." He admitted that the distribution of these guns was unknown, but said that "large concentrations were around the airfield and on the beach nearby." He also erroneously stated that American air activity at Henderson Field involved only fighters. He mentioned the 19 August attack against his forces at

Matanikau, and declared that since Ichiki's attack almost no gunfire had been heard. Another report transmitted the next day reported that American shipping activity off Lunga Point and Tulagi had increased over the past week.[10]

The Kawaguchi Detachment

Major General Kiyotake Kawaguchi, commanding general of a reinforced regiment called the Kawaguchi Detachment, was in the Palaus, preparing to ship out to New Guinea on 13 August, when he received orders to retake Guadalcanal. Since Pearl Harbor, his detachment had constantly been on the move, taking part in firestorm campaigns in Borneo and the Philippines. Having spent the last month or so preparing to campaign in New Guinea, Kawaguchi received the new assignment as somewhat of a shock. Reflecting on these new orders, the forty-nine-year-old general intuitively sensed the seriousness of the situation and predicted that Guadalcanal would be the focal point of the war.

In contrast with Ichiki, Kawaguchi brought patience, stubbornness, and complexity to the battlefield and would prove to be General Vandegrift's most worthy adversary. Born in the Kochi prefecture, Kawaguchi entered the Imperial Army in December 1914 at age twenty-two and served in a prisoner of war camp for German soldiers during World War I. Later in his career, he served mainly on staffs in Formosa and China, including assignments with the 4th Division and the Army General Staff. As a former instructor at the Heavy Artillery School at Uraga, Kawaguchi understood the value of artillery in an army that was generally considered weak in its use. With a powerful frame, piercing eyes, and Kaiser mustache, he was an impressive physical specimen. But many found him difficult to work with, and once Kawaguchi made up his mind, it was hard to change. Kawaguchi also was a controversial figure after his attempts to stop revenge killings of senior Philippine officials. For this, bloodthirsty radicals in the Imperial Army labeled Kawaguchi a "liberal."[11]

Consisting of 3,880 men, the Kawaguchi Detachment was a formidable, battle-hardened outfit. The core of the unit was formed around the 124th Infantry Regiment, which before the war had been part of the crack 35th Infantry Brigade, 18th (Kurame) Division. The 124th Infantry was made up of men who were rugged and tough, most having come from the Fukuoka prefecture in northern Kyushu, where many worked in coal mines before the war. But beneath the surface, problems were present. The leader of the regiment, Col. Akinosuke Oka was a mediocre battlefield commander and tactician. Moreover, the thin ranks of the regiment had been filled out with over 1,000 inexperienced replacements in the Palaus. The regiment also lacked discipline. According to one Japanese officer, the men of the Fukuoka prefecture "were fond of rough work, but were quarrelsome and apt to commit acts of violence and plunder."[12]

The organization of the 124th Infantry was standard, with few differences from other regiments in the Imperial Army. It consisted of three battalions of infantry; a regimental headquarters unit; and communications, machine gun, infantry gun (75mm), transportation, and antitank (37mm) companies. Each battalion, averaging about 830 men, had four infantry companies, a machine gun company, and a battalion gun platoon. Two 81mm mortars from the 3d Light Trench Mortar Battalion were attached to each battalion as well. Besides the 124th Infantry Regiment, the rest of the Kawaguchi Detachment was comprised of the 35th Brigade Headquarters, a shipping engineer regiment, a platoon of combat engineers, a radio platoon, a special radio squad, and a water purification unit (see Table 6).[13]

Table 6
The Kawaguchi Detachment (as of 24 August 1942)

Kawaguchi Detachment Headquarters	145
Brigade Guard Company	38
124th Infantry Regiment	
124th Regimental Headquarters	140
124th Communications Unit	120
124th Machine Gun Company	135
124th Regimental Gun Company	76
124th Regimental Antitank Company	79
124th Motor Transport Company	26
1st Battalion, 124th Infantry	872
1/124 Headquarters Company (75)	
1st Company (129)	
2d Company (137)	
3d Company (128)	
4th Company (143)	
1/124 Machine Gun Company (150)	
1/124 Battalion Gun Platoon (74)	
1/124 Trench Mortar Platoon (36)	

2d Battalion, 124th Infantry   842

    2/124 Headquarters Company (78)

    5th Company (127)

    6th Company (134)

    7th Company (131)

    8th Company (144)

    2/124 Machine Gun Company (124)

    2/124 Battalion Gun Platoon (64)

    2/124 Trench Mortar Platoon (40)

3d Battalion, 124th Infantry   796

    3/124 Headquarters Company (75)

    9th Company (123)

    10th Company (120)

    11th Company (120)

    12th Company (127)

    3/124 Machine Gun Company (131)

    3/124 Battalion Gun Platoon (58)

    3/124 Trench Mortar Platoon (42)

6th Independent Shipping Engineer Regiment   450

24th Water Purification Unit   55

One platoon from 15th Independent Engineer

    Regiment   64

6th Independent Radio Unit   30

Special Radio Squad   12

Kawaguchi Detachment Total: 3,880

Source: *Organization of Two Japanese Army Combat Teams, Japanese Land Forces #6.*

———

Discussions at Seventeenth Army Headquarters on 17 August focused on the employment of the Kawaguchi Detachment, which was expected at Truk on the 20th. Given the intensification of the Port Moresby operation, the staff grappled over how much of the Kawaguchi Detachment to use on Guadalcanal. Major General Tomitaro Horii's Nankai Detachment had already been sent to New Guinea, and the 41st Infantry Regiment was earmarked to join it, but the Seventeenth Army needed a reserve, prompting some members of Hyakutake's staff to consider using part of the Kawaguchi Detachment for this purpose. That day, General Futami met with an Eighth Fleet staff officer, who was overly optimistic about the situation on Guadalcanal and who believed that the American force on Guadalcanal was not very large. Since Kadomae's naval troops were already on the island fighting it out, he believed that only one of Kawaguchi's battalions was needed to deal with the marooned Americans. The ever-cautious Futami, however, did not share his level of optimism. Instead, Futami decided to send all but one battalion of the Kawaguchi Detachment to Guadalcanal.[14]

Having been summoned to Seventeenth Army Headquarters, Kawaguchi hitched a ride on a Kawanishi flying boat to Rabaul on 19 August, just two days before the destruction of Ichiki's First Echelon. Accompanying him were two staff officers: a Major Osonoe and a Second Lieutenant Takenaka, Kawaguchi's aide-de-camp. At Seventeenth Army headquarters, Kawaguchi sat down to read his new orders. The printed directive ordered the detachment, less one battalion of the 124th Infantry Regiment, to land at Taivu Point on 28 August to recapture both the Guadalcanal airfield and Tulagi. For the opera-

tion, the Kawaguchi Detachment would be brought up
to brigade strength, with Kadomae's naval troops and
the Ichiki Detachment also assigned to his command.[15]

After digesting the details of his orders, Kawaguchi
was handed another directive, starkly revealing the
Seventeenth Army's level of optimism. It ordered
Kawaguchi to provide a paper on the strategy of capturing Tulagi and the approximate force required for
safeguarding Guadalcanal once it was retaken. This
directive, Kawaguchi later wrote, was written under the
assumption that if his force went to Guadalcanal,
recapturing it would be a simple task, and that the
Ichiki Detachment would be waiting for him, with the
airfield already under Japanese control. This order
makes it abundantly clear that Ichiki was not the only
one supremely confident of success.[16]

On 20 August, Kawaguchi winged off to meet his
detachment at Truk, where it had just arrived in the
transports *Sado Maru* and *Asakayama Maru*. Three days
later, Kawaguchi met with RAdm. Shintaro Hashimoto,
the commander of Destroyer Squadron 3, and two officers from the Seventeenth Army and Eighth Fleet staffs
to discuss the transportation of his detachment to
Guadalcanal. The original agreement had the detachment sailing to the island in the two transports
escorted by Hashimoto's destroyers. But Kawaguchi
rightly questioned the wisdom of sailing in slow transports within range of enemy submarines and land-
based aircraft. Kawaguchi instead urged that the transports sail from Truk to Shortland, where the
detachment would embark in Daihatsu armored barges
and leapfrog at night along the Solomons chain to
Guadalcanal. Some found Kawaguchi's unorthodox

proposal disturbing. The Seventeenth Army representative pointed out that a landing on any island other than Guadalcanal had to be approved by higher authorities. The Eighth Fleet staff representative said that either method exposed the ships to enemy planes and submarines, but that escorting transports to Guadalcanal instead of barges involved less risk for the Imperial Navy. Unlike the others in attendance, however, Hashimoto was willing to try either plan.[17]

The Kawaguchi Detachment set sail at noon on the 24th on the transports *Sado Maru* and *Asakayama Maru*. The beating that Tanaka's convoy took on the 25th at the hands of the Cactus Air Force vindicated Kawaguchi's fears about the vulnerability of the transports and prompted a major revision in Seventeenth Army's landing plans. At 1100 on the 26th, Kawaguchi was ordered to immediately ship 600 soldiers to Guadalcanal aboard four destroyers for a night landing on 28 August and to take the rest of the detachment to Rabaul. Kawaguchi chose Maj. Etsuo Takamatsu's 2d Battalion, 124th Infantry (less the 6th Company and miscellaneous support troops), for the move. Smooth seas aided the mid-ocean transfer of Takamatsu's soldiers to the destroyers *Asagiri, Amagiri, Yugire,* and *Shirakumo,* and soon the four vessels were sailing at high speed for Guadalcanal.[18]

This diversion of 600 troops was part of the first installment of Seventeenth Army and Eighth Fleet's new plan to land reinforcements on Guadalcanal using destroyers. Finalized on 26 August, the plan called for the transportation of more than 4,700 troops in five separate landings at Taivu Point. The first landing, scheduled for the night of the 28th, would put ashore

1,000 men of Ichiki's Second Echelon and 600 men of the 124th Infantry. The second landing was set for the evening of the 29th and would bring in 450 men of the 124th Infantry on three destroyers. The third landing on the night of the 30th would disembark an assortment of 1,000 men from various units. On the final evening of the month, a fourth landing of 650 troops and two 75mm antiaircraft guns would be made. In the fifth and final run, set for the first night of September, 1,000 men would be put ashore. The plan looked good on paper, but the unknown factor in the whole operation was, of course, the Cactus Air Force.[19]

Meanwhile, the addition of the 2d (Sendai) Infantry Division to the Seventeenth Army's order of battle on 29 August provided badly needed muscle to Hyakutake's rapidly dwindling pool of units. Led by Lt. Gen. Masao Maruyama, the 2d Infantry Division was one of the most highly regarded units in the Imperial Army. The division had been a part of the Sixteenth Army and took part in the conquest of Java in the Dutch East Indies. It consisted of the 4th, 16th, and 29th Infantry Regiments. The Aoba Detachment, a brigade-size unit taken from the 2d Division, led by Maj. Gen. Yumio Nasu, would land on Guadalcanal first. The Aoba Detachment consisted of the 4th Infantry Regiment, the 1st Battalion, the 2d Artillery Regiment, and a host of support units, including a company of armored cars and a company of engineers.

The Kokumbona Raid

While the air and naval activity heated up around Guadalcanal, Vandegrift made preparations for

another strike against the Japanese in the Kokumbona-
Matanikau region. An attack was planned on the 23rd
of August, but the threat of Tanaka's convoy delayed
the strike. Vandegrift rescheduled the attack for the
morning of the 27th, using Lt. Col. William E. Maxwell's
1st Battalion, 5th Marines, a strange choice because
Maxwell had been in Vandegrift's "doghouse" since the
landing on 7 August, when Maxwell was too cautious. An
intelligent, hardworking twenty-two-year veteran of the
Marine Corps, Maxwell was also aloof, uncommuni-
cative, and arrogant. "A real gap in communication
existed between him and his four company commanders," wrote Capt. William Hawkins, commander of
Company B. "Action to correct this should have been
taken by Division, or by Regiment, long before the day
of the patrol."[20]

Colonel Maxwell's orders were simple: Land west of
Kokumbona, march eastward down the coast, and
return to Lunga Point before dusk. Supported by
artillery, an additional company from the 3d Battalion,
5th Marines, would cross the Matanikau River and
drive west and crush the enemy in a giant pincer.
Although timing for the operation was critically
important, success depended upon the rapid movement of Maxwell's battalion after the landing in order
to surprise the Japanese from the rear (west). Overlooked by Vandegrift and Gerald Thomas during planning, however, was the terrain. Along the coast to a
distance of between 200 and 300 yards inland lay
dense jungle flatlands, where the coastal trail ran parallel to the beach. Abruptly beyond this level ground
was a series of jagged coral ridges covered with tall
kunai grass, which provided excellent cover for the

enemy. Furthermore, the sunless ravines between these ridges were covered with thick jungle, making any type of movement difficult and time-consuming.[21]

The Kokumbona raid began with part of Maxwell's battalion still embarking at Kukum at dawn on the 27th—the same time the entire battalion was scheduled to arrive at Kokumbona. While the battalion made its approach, the 11th Marines fired some forty-five 75mm and thirty 105mm rounds at the village of Matanikau as a diversion. At 0700, the first of Maxwell's fifteen Higgins boats hit the beach west of Kokumbona, but the Japanese apparently thought that the marines were friendly, because several Japanese were gathered and waving on the beach. Captain Hawkins expected fire from the Japanese but none came—the Japanese instead vanished into the bush, some of them leaving behind meals.[22]

Leaving Company A at the landing point to provide rear flank protection, Maxwell advanced eastward along the track with Company B in the lead and with Company C guarding the exposed inland flank about 200 yards from the shore. His troops encountered no opposition in Kokumbona or nearby villages, but discovered evidence that the Japanese were bivouacked there. Based on prior orders, the marines began to burn some thatched huts housing small caches of ammunition, but Maxwell belayed the order, fearing the smoke might draw enemy aircraft. Maxwell's men captured one prisoner, a Korean construction worker.[23]

The subsequent drive eastward by Maxwell's men was slow. Not surprising, Company C was unable to keep pace with the rest of the battalion on the jagged high ground, so Maxwell replaced Company C with 2d Lt. Thomas Grady's 1st Platoon from Company B. This helped quicken the pace but not at the level expected by Vandegrift at headquarters. The advance along the coast proceeded slowly until 1140, when the Japanese, in the form of sniper, machine gun, and 50mm mortar fire, stopped the leading platoon of Company B. This occurred about 1,500 yards east of Kokumbona between the coast and a coral ridge 300 yards inland. Maxwell responded with his own 81mm and 60mm mortars and lifted another platoon from Hawkins's company (the 3d) to protect the battalion's seaward flank. Grady's platoon was in an excellent position to outflank Kadomae's men, but, lacking radios to coordinate the maneuver with the rest of the battalion and unable to obtain timely permission from Maxwell by runner, Grady was unable to execute this maneuver.[24]

With his advance stalled by the Japanese, Maxwell surmised that he could not both overcome the Japanese and return to the Kukum area by nightfall. Accordingly, at 1430 he asked for the boats to re-embark the battalion, a request that infuriated Vandegrift, who stormed over to Colonel Hunt's command post demanding action. Hunt promptly relieved Maxwell by radio and put the battalion's exec, Maj. Milton O'Connell, in command. At 1600, Hunt, with part of Company L, departed Kukum by boat and reached Kokumbona at 1750, minutes before sunset. Hunt, who was popular with the men, made the battalion's morale soar with his mere presence. Hunt ordered the battalion to dig in on the high ground 2,000 yards east of Kokumbona and remain there until early morning, when the attack against the Japanese would resume.[25]

In the meantime, Company I was making its move against the Japanese at the Matanikau. The company left its bivouac at 0610 and marched westward along the coastal track, killing two Japanese en route. At about 1600, Company I ran into a wall of Japanese machine gun fire about 2,000 yards west of the river. Ten minutes later, Lieutenant Colonel Whaling, executive officer of the 5th Marines, joined Company I. The company tried to outflank the Japanese with two squads, but the Japanese also stopped this move with machine gun and mortar fire. With the coming of nightfall, Company I dug in.[26]

With hostile forces closing in from the east and west, the situation looked desperate for the Japanese. At 1640 Kadomae urgently radioed Rabaul, requesting two companies of infantry with machine guns and battalion guns, as well as provisions for 1,600 men. Fearing encirclement, Kadomae ordered his shattered command to retreat southwest to the mountains at 2300, bearing forty wounded. Kadomae's timing was fortuitous, because at 0300 on the 28th, Hunt's marines began their march toward Matanikau village. After a grueling trek in the thick underbrush and heat, all they found in the village was abandoned ammunition, material, and twenty dead Japanese—the Kokumbona vagabonds had slipped away during the night. By 1500 all of Hunt's marines had returned to Lunga by Higgins boat. Marine losses totaled three dead and nine wounded, all of them from Company B.[27]

From start to finish, the Kokumbona raid was a complete fiasco. The marines possessed a two-to-one superiority in combat troops against a poorly armed foe and came away empty-handed. Maxwell was rightly blamed for the failure, notwithstanding the unfamiliar terrain and difficult tactical situation. Like the advance after the 7 August landing, Maxwell again proved too cautious and too inept in the handling of his battalion. Even though it was made clear, according to Colonel Thomas, that he was to defeat the enemy and return via land not sea, Maxwell requested evacuation by boat early in the afternoon. Maxwell's ineptness not only cost him his job, but also cost the best opportunity for the marines to eliminate the Japanese naval garrison. Even before the last of Hunt's boats began arriving at Kukum, Vandegrift and Thomas began contemplating solutions to some of the division's leadership problems.[28]

On the 29th, Kadomae and his men arrived at Tassafaronga Point, where they established their front line along the Bonegi River. Kadomae's haggard, debilitated seamen and laborers were hungry, exhausted, and depleted in number. Part of Kadomae's problem was that he had too many mouths to feed. Lieutenant Tanabe's 84th Guard Unit was down to 130 men and armed with just one heavy and two light machine guns. The Takahashi Unit of about 110 men had lost little since landing on 16 August and was still equipped with two heavy and five light machine guns and four 50mm mortars. The 11th and 13th Construction Units totaled 1,350 seamen and laborers, but only 220 carried rifles.[29]

The Last Days of August

Two days after the abortive Kokumbona raid, another convoy—cargo ships *William Ward Burrows* and *Kopara*,

APDs *Little, Gregory,* and *Colhoun,* and escorts *McFarland, Gamble,* and *Tracy*—arrived off Cactus-Ringbolt. There the convoy disgorged air wing ground crews, provisions, and supplies. Before the air raid that day, the *Burrows* fled for the relative safety of Tulagi Harbor, where it was inadvertently grounded before dusk. It took days of unending effort by the ship's crew to unload and finally free the ship on 2 September. Miraculously, the Japanese failed to attack the *Burrows,* let alone find the lame-duck vessel.[30]

The last days of August saw a renewal of the Eleventh Air Fleet's assault against Henderson Field. On the 26th, seventeen Bettys and nine Zeros plastered the airfield at noon, destroying 2,000 gallons of precious aviation gasoline. Heavy weather foiled the airstrike on the 27th, but on the evening of the 28th, three Bettys harassed the marines with a nighttime raid, dropping approximately twelve bombs and killing at least two in the 11th Marines. At noon on 29 August, eighteen bombers and twenty-one Zeros attacked the airfield, inflicting "slight damage" to base ammunition dumps. The next day saw a change in tactics, with the Japanese sending in eighteen Zeros first, followed by a strike by bombers and fighters three hours later. It didn't work. The Japanese lost at least eight fighters, but the Americans lost two P-400 Aircobras in the aerial duel. The Bettys, however, scored big by sinking the APD *Colhoun* off Lunga Point.[31]

About this time, the health of Vandegrift's marines took a turn for the worse. Although battle casualties had not yet reached 300, more than three times that number were suffering from a host of ailments, such as gastroenteritis, dysentery, dengue fever, and the worst ailment of all—malaria. The numerous swamps, streams, lagoons, and rain-filled bomb craters and fox-holes on the island provided an ideal breeding ground for malaria-carrying mosquitoes. Because the troops lacked an adequate supply of mosquito netting and medicines to prevent the spread of this debilitating illness, it is not surprising that in August the division hospitals treated 900 men for malaria alone. The symptoms of malaria—fever, chills, nausea, headaches, and delirium—left men bedridden and cursing the tiny mosquito. "I really thought it was the end of the world," recalled one American on Guadalcanal afflicted with the disease. "It sucks the life blood out of one, and even after one improves you feel listless for days or weeks."[32]

The heat and humidity on Guadalcanal presented the marines with another set of challenges—heat stroke and heat exhaustion. Casualties from the heat were common on work details and on daylight excursions like those to the Matanikau. The climate was obviously the main problem, but a lack of discipline was a contributing factor. "This 1942 model recruit we are getting can drink more water than six old-timers," observed Gunnery Sgt. H. L. Beardsley, Company G, 5th Marines. "We have to stress water discipline all the time." On lengthy excursions where water sources were scarce or nonexistent, however, the marines quickly discovered that one canteen was not enough to sustain a man for a day. Consequently, an extra canteen was issued. This expedient helped greatly, though it resulted in a large turnover of canteens in each regiment.[33]

Jungle rot was another by-product of the climate. Cuts and scratches simply would not heal in the heat and humidity. Sometimes these would become infected, drawing swarms of flies that tried to feed on the pus oozing from the painful red sores. The flies, of course, increased the likelihood of further infection. Painful fungus infections of the foot, resulting from those who wore their shoes and socks both day and night, were also troublesome. Navy doctors and pharmacist mates were usually able to nurse the marines through these and other more acute sicknesses like dengue fever and malaria. However, in severe cases, patients were sometimes flown off the island to rear echelon bases, such as Auckland, New Zealand, and Nouméa, New Caledonia, where better conditions and treatment facilities existed.[34]

Nearly as devastating to the health of the 1st Marine Division was malnutrition. Strict rationing was still being imposed, with two meals per day. Hunger was a constant companion, and the men were always weak. With the regular arrival of Turner's transports, the variety of meals improved a bit but not much. Besides rice, the marines ate Spam, C-rations, K-rations, and corned beef—lots of corned beef. "The cooks did their best to camouflage the corned beef," wrote Pvt. Bob Shedd of the 1st Battalion, 5th Marines. "We had it plain, warmed up, cold, sliced and dipped in batter and fried with pickles. But it was still corned beef!"[35]

In addition to the heat, chow, and bugs, the Americans on Guadalcanal began to develop an intense hatred of two airborne Japanese nocturnal pests, named "Washing Machine Charlie" and "Louie the Louse." In late August these planes began to pay nightly visits to the Americans on the island. Charlie was a twin-engine plane, which usually dropped bombs, while Louie was a single-engine floatplane that provided flare illumination for naval bombardments. Rather than inflict heavy damage, the mission of these planes was one of harassment—to deny rest, fray nerves, and destroy morale—a mission, as the Americans can attest, they accomplished all too well.[36]

Taking to foxholes before Japanese bombings and shellings was a daily ritual for the Americans on Guadalcanal. Although there is little or no humor in enduring the shock and horror of enemy bombings and shellings, it did give cause to one comic incident that caused no injury except in pride and dignity. Private George Haertlein recalled one noontime raid when his unit ran for the nearest foxholes after the air raid alarm sounded. Haertlein caught a glimpse of one panic-stricken, solitary marine diving headfirst into a foxhole everyone else avoided—a latrine trench. After the raid was over, Haertlein saw the soiled marine running for the cleansing waters of the ocean wearing all his clothes and his pack and rifle. Nearly everyone who witnessed the humiliating act, except for the marine involved, thought the incident was hilarious. "Let your imagination run wild on the names he acquired," Haertlein wrote.[37]

Bad weather foiled Japanese attempts to bomb Henderson Field on the last day of August. This was a good thing for the Americans, because they may have noticed a fat target anchored off Tulagi. This was the U.S. transport *Betelgeuse,* which was transplanting a battery of 5-inch coastal and 90mm antiaircraft guns from Tulagi to Guadalcanal. These guns, the property of the 3d Defense Battalion, would be a welcome addition to the island's defenses. The 5-inch coastal guns were emplaced at Lunga Point, where they provided yeoman service, holding units of the Imperial Navy at bay; bombardments by Oscar practically ceased.

On 1 September the marines guarding the beach at Kukum witnessed a curious sight. They saw hundreds of "old men," averaging thirty-one years of age, landing on the beach from the transport *Betelgeuse*. These men, 392 in all, were members of the 6th Naval Construction Battalion (CBs, or Seabees, as they were called). They brought with them two bulldozers and other engineering equipment and immediately took over the maintenance and improvement of Henderson Field. The Seabees also began work on another airfield, a primitive grassy strip one mile east of Henderson Field called Fighter One.[38]

Work on this fighter strip was probably the result of a recent visit to Guadalcanal by RAdm. John S. McCain. During this fact-finding mission, McCain spoke with squadron leaders, pilots, and crew chiefs about the importance of their work and what he expected them to do. More important, the admiral spoke informally with Vandegrift and his staff, "expounding convincingly" on an aspect of the campaign that the marines had not fully appreciated. The admiral told them that Guadalcanal could be a "sinkhole" for the limited Japanese air and naval power. This prophecy was already beginning to come true. Holding Henderson Field was vital. If Guadalcanal was lost, McCain believed that the Allied advances after the Coral Sea and Midway would be squandered. According to Lt. Col. Merrill Twining of division operations, "This good talk made our ears roar." It also enabled the marines to understand better the importance of Guadalcanal, especially that their sacrifices were not in vain.[39]

Giving added impetus to McCain's words, on 3 September one of Vandegrift's old friends flew in to Guadalcanal for assignment. Vandegrift's friend was none other than Brig. Gen. Roy S. Geiger, commander of the 1st Marine Air Wing. Geiger was a legend in Marine Corps aviation. Commissioned the same year as Vandegrift, he served in Panama, Nicaragua, the Philippines, and China. In 1917 he received his "wings"—only the forty-ninth naval aviator and fifth marine to do so. Geiger fought in the skies over France and Belgium during World War I and won the Navy Cross. After that war, Geiger's interest in aviation continued, and he led squadrons in Haiti, Santo Domingo, and Nicaragua. With the appearance and temperament of a Roman emperor, Geiger drove those under him as he drove himself—unmercifully. Although he was there to partially support the foot-slogging marines, Geiger would do everything in his power to ensure that Henderson Field would fulfill McCain's "sinkhole" prophecy.[40]

6 The Cactus Express

"Expect to Annihilate Them"

Rear Admiral Tanaka and the remnants of his battered convoy pulled into Shortland harbor on the evening of 26 August. But before dropping anchor, the commander of the Eleventh Air Fleet, VAdm. Nishizo Tsukahara, directed him to transport 300 troops of Ichiki's Second Echelon to Guadalcanal the following night. Tanaka went a step better, assembling 390 troops, four 37mm antitank guns, and provisions for 1,300 men for immediate embarkation on the destroyers *Umikaze*, *Yamakaze*, and *Isokaze*. These ships weighed anchor the following morning and set sail for Guadalcanal. Tanaka, however, received an order from Admiral Mikawa, stating that the landing was supposed to occur on the 28th not the 27th. Upon receiving Tanaka's reply that the destroyers had already departed, Mikawa ordered Tanaka to recall them immediately. Tanaka was now frustrated and furious. For the third time in a week, he had received contradictory orders from the Eleventh Air Fleet and Eighth Fleet commanders.[1]

At 0330 on 28 August, the transports *Sado Maru* and

Asakayama Maru, carrying the bulk of the Kawaguchi Detachment, pulled into Rabaul harbor. There, 450 soldiers of the 1st Battalion, 124th Infantry, and one regimental and two antitank guns of the 124th Infantry were transferred to three destroyers of Destroyer Division 11 for departure to Guadalcanal. Soon thereafter, Kawaguchi's transports left for Shortland with new cargo, including two 75mm antiaircraft guns and a hospital unit.[2]

As Tanaka struggled with the latest pair of contradictory orders, the four destroyers hauling Major Takamatsu's 2d Battalion, 124th Infantry, were rapidly closing in on Guadalcanal. But because of the length of the journey and a shortage of fuel, the destroyers were unable to synchronize their arrival time with darkness. As a result, Cactus aviators spotted the speedy quartet at 1700 on 28 August, about seventy miles north of Guadalcanal. An air strike of eleven SBDs promptly took off from Henderson Field and located the four Japanese "tin cans" at dusk.

The ensuing air attack was unusually accurate. The *Asagiri* took two bombs, blowing up in a horrible explosion. One hundred thirty-six crewmen of the *Asagiri* and eighty-three soldiers survived the blast. The dive-bombers also shattered *Yugire* with a near miss, killing thirty-two sailors and wounding forty. The *Shirakumo* likewise suffered from two near misses, killing two sailors and flooding its forward boiler room leaving it dead in the water. Sixty-two of Takamatsu's men and his two battalion guns were also lost. Only *Amagiri* was undamaged in the attack. Severely rebuffed, the surviving destroyers limped away for Shortland with the *Shirakumo* under tow.[3]

The effect of this bombing was dramatic and far-reaching. Tanaka signaled Mikawa on the evening of the 28th that the presence of enemy aircraft on Guadalcanal gave destroyer transportation little chance of success. The commander of the 11th Destroyer Division, Capt. Yonosuke Murakami, who was rapidly approaching Guadalcanal with three destroyers, agreed, and on his own initiative turned back for Shortland. Upon arrival, Tanaka severely reprimanded Murakami for canceling the landing. Believing in the efficacy of destroyer transportation, Admiral Mikawa was angry over Tanaka's signal. But General Futami of the Seventeenth Army considered giving up on Guadalcanal. Other staff officers of the Seventeenth Army, however, recommended that a final decision be made after the completion of the next reinforcement.[4]

On the morning of the 29th, General Kawaguchi's transports arrived at Shortland, where he and senior officers of the detachment met with Tanaka aboard the latter's flagship. Tanaka planned on landing the Kawaguchi Detachment according to the Seventeenth Army and Eighth Fleet reinforcement plan. Kawaguchi, however, proposed to take the transports to Gizo Bay, where the detachment would embark in armored barges for the final trip to Guadalcanal. Naturally, Tanaka was shocked by Kawaguchi's proposal to use barges. Kawaguchi and his senior commanders, however, remained adamant. It was barges or nothing. Tanaka suggested they consult their superiors and meet again the following day, to which Kawaguchi agreed. Wasting little time, Kawaguchi radioed the Seventeenth Army at 1100 with his plan to transport

the detachment over 200 miles by barge from Gizo
Island to Guadalcanal. Yet Hyakutake hedged on a
decision until the results of that night's run by the
Cactus Express were known.[5]

At noon on the 29th, Captain Murakami, who was
still smarting after Tanaka's reprimand, set out for the
third time in as many days for Guadalcanal. At Shortland, Tanaka also ordered troops and artillery of
Ichiki's Second Echelon to embark on *Patrol Boats 1, 2,
34,* and *35* for a landing on Guadalcanal the following
night. At 2230 on the 29th, Murakami's destroyers
landed their troops and artillery at Taivu without difficulty. Earlier that day, Captain Kadomae reported that
an enemy convoy of two transports, one cruiser, and
two destroyers was anchored off Lunga Point. Admiral
Mikawa ordered Murakami to attack this force after the
landing at Taivu was completed, but, incredibly, Murakami ignored this order because of the presence of
enemy aircraft on this moonlit night. (Vandegrift had
dispatched fourteen SBDs during the night to protect
the U.S. transport *William Ward Burrows,* which had run
aground off Tulagi.) The failure proved unfortunate
for the Japanese, especially Murakami, who was
relieved of command.[6]

Despite Murakami's successful reinforcement run
the night before, Kawaguchi and Tanaka wrangled
over the use of barges again on the morning of the
30th. Building his case for the use of barges, Kawaguchi recalled his campaign in Borneo where the
detachment successfully navigated 500 miles in barges
(Kawaguchi used them with success in the Philippines,
too). As Kawaguchi explained, barges had another
advantage in that they could lift all of the detach-

ment's weapons, equipment, and supplies, unlike Tanaka's destroyers. Tanaka argued that control of the air was a prerequisite for a barge's safe passage, but the Americans maintained air superiority over the southern Solomons. Later that day, Kawaguchi received a visit from Major Takamatsu, who reported to him in tears over the drubbing his battalion took at the hands of the Cactus Air Force.[7]

Based on their memoirs, there remains a wide difference of opinion between Kawaguchi and Tanaka on who said what and what was agreed on in this meeting. Kawaguchi thought he had Tanaka's blessing on the barge plan. He claims that Tanaka insisted that using "destroyers was a mistake and that army barges should be used with destroyers escorting." Tanaka, however, denies that he ever endorsed Kawaguchi's barge plan. But Mikawa's chief of staff wrote in his diary that both agreed on using barges. This, coupled with Tanaka's signal on the evening of 28 August, seems to substantiate Kawaguchi's claim of Tanaka's compliance. Since they were unable to proceed with the barge plan until they received final approval, Tanaka ordered about 150 men of Ichiki's Second Echelon to embark on the destroyer *Yudachi* for a rendezvous with the four patrol boats that had left Shortland the previous day.[8]

In what was probably meant to placate Kawaguchi, Hyakutake and Mikawa reached a strange compromise regarding the use of barges. They decided that the main force of the Kawaguchi Detachment would go to Guadalcanal by destroyer while the rest went by barge. The order specified that the landing point would be east of Henderson Field at Taivu Point. An alternative site for the landing on the northwest coast of Guadalcanal was also designated in the event that the barges were unable to land at Taivu. Although the Seventeenth Army wanted the barges to transport most of the detachment's heavy equipment and supplies with about one company of troops with machine guns, Kawaguchi decided to let Oka organize a convoy for about 1,100 men. For this journey, Kawaguchi chose the remainder of Takamatsu's 2d Battalion, 124th Infantry, and Oka's headquarters with a small portion of the regimental artillery.[9]

General Hyakutake was less than thrilled when he learned of Kawaguchi's plan to transport more than 1,000 troops by barge. It is evident that Hyakutake had little hope that the barges, which had a top speed of seven and one-half knots, would be able to run the gauntlet past the Cactus Air Force and land at Taivu Point. Indeed, convinced that Kawaguchi's force would be split and further weakened, Hyakutake met with Admiral Mikawa on the 31st to explore the alternative employment of the First Echelon of the Aoba Detachment (the 2d Battalion, 4th Infantry), a part of the newly assigned 2d Division. Apparently, the two agreed that Kawaguchi's force needed more muscle, because Hyakutake decided to give the unit to Kawaguchi rather than employ it in the Rabi operation in New Guinea. Kawaguchi was fortunate to have this crack unit added to his order of battle, and it would prove to be more than an adequate replacement for the 2d Battalion, 28th Regiment, which was lost at the Tenaru River.[10]

Later that evening, in the wardroom of *Sado Maru*, Kawaguchi lectured that "faith is our strength" and exchanged toasts in a previctory celebration. It is certain that Kawaguchi read General Hyakutake's exhortation to the detachment:

> The operation to recapture Guadalcanal Island is a truly important one which will determine supremacy in the entire Pacific. Already, the main force of the Ichiki Detachment and the Naval Guard Units are at Guadalcanal and are stoutly maintaining their positions. Likewise, the Imperial Navy is fiercely engaging the enemy every day. Although I know that your Unit's organization, transportation, essentials, etc. are not always satisfactory, the situation does not permit a moment's delay. Relying upon the skill of command and the power of determination, attack the enemy exploiting your strengths against their weaknesses. Since their infantry is probably not yet toughened to jungle warfare, you should expect to annihilate them. Battles always reach critical turning points. The glory of victory will be given to the side which looks up to it and always believes in it. At present your unit must immediately prepare your equipment and take to the field. I will be praying for a hard fought battle and your speedy success.[11]

In the meantime, the Cactus Express continued to run according to schedule. At 2100 on the 30th, *Yudachi* and the four patrol boats made a bloodless landing at Taivu, putting ashore 500 troops, four 37mm antitank guns of the 8th Independent Antitank

Company, and the four 75mm guns of the 28th Regimental Gun Company. These vessels were spotted and bombed by two U.S. planes at Taivu while they were discharging their cargo. But a combination of poor visibility and heavy antiaircraft fire made it impossible for the planes to score any hits. Later the next night, the destroyers *Umikaze, Kagero, Kawakaze, Suzukaze, Amagiri, Fubuki, Hatsuyuki,* and *Murakumo* completed Tanaka's largest "express" run to Taivu Point, bearing Major General Kawaguchi and 1,200 troops. They disgorged the 35th Brigade Headquarters; the 3d Battalion, 124th Infantry; part of the 67th Line of Communications Hospital Unit; a platoon of engineers; and two small communication units.[12]

Edson's Raiders

The Kokumbona raid made it abundantly clear to General Vandegrift that he had some serious leadership problems in the upper echelons of the 5th Marines. Colonel Gerald Thomas, more than anyone else, probably drove this point home to the commanding general. Both wanted to exterminate those Japanese who remained on the island, but they proved elusive. More disturbing was the increasing presence of the Cactus Express, and that meant one thing—more Japanese. Even though Vandegrift now fielded six rifle battalions, these were needed to protect the airfield from another attack that both he and Thomas were sure would come. Vandegrift not only needed more troops, but those who were well led and offensive-minded. Thus, on 28 August, Vandegrift ordered General Rupertus to ship the 1st Raider and 1st Parachute battalions from Tulagi to Guadalcanal at the earliest opportunity.[13]

Lieutenant Colonel Gerald Thomas, the dark, handsome, bushy-eyed officer in whom Vandegrift placed so much trust, was forty-seven years of age at the time. He joined the marines in 1917 and as a sergeant fought in France in World War I, participating in the grim battles of Belleau Wood and the Meuse-Argonne. His performance impressed his superiors so much that he won a field commission in September 1918. Thomas served overseas during the interwar years, including a tour in Peking, China, where he first met then Lieutenant Colonel Vandegrift. Thomas immersed himself in his work. Along with his intelligence, Thomas possessed a good degree of tact and the gift of persuasion that won him many arguments. Of course, not everyone liked the talented, hard-driving Thomas. He offended some and stepped on a few toes. Among those who disliked the talented upstart were Col. Capers James, Vandegrift's chief of staff, and Col. Leroy Hunt, commander of the 5th Marines. Personality conflicts aside, the commanding general trusted Thomas and that is all that really mattered.[14]

Colonel Merritt A. Edson, the commander of the 1st Raider Battalion, met with Vandegrift and Thomas at the general's headquarters on the 29th. There, Edson digested the details of his command's transfer and was briefed on the division's situation on the island. Because Maj. Robert H. Williams, the commander of the 1st Parachute Battalion, was still recovering from wounds he suffered at Gavutu on 7 August, Edson learned that he would command Williams's outfit as well. Little is known about Edson's reaction to his unit's transfer to Guadalcanal, but he must have been elated. Edson, a fiercely aggressive officer, had spent a boring, relatively uneventful three weeks on Tulagi, organizing patrols in search of Japanese stragglers on Florida Island in the Solomons.[15]

Known as "Red Mike" for his carrot-colored hair, Colonel Edson was one of the Marine Corps's finest leaders and infantry tacticians. Commissioned in 1917 at age twenty, Edson saw no action in France in World War I but saw plenty in the late 1920s in the jungles of Nicaragua. There, Edson mounted several expeditions in search of rebel bandits and won the Navy Cross. Although disqualified from flight service for vision problems in 1927, he was, nevertheless, a deadly shot with a weapon. Soft-spoken, small in stature, and weighing only 140 pounds, Edson did not fit the Hollywood image of a marine. With his helmet on, his men thought he looked like a mole. But Edson had the courage and heart of a lion and knew how to lead men in battle. Respected by all, Edson, however, was not universally loved. Many Raiders said he was cold and overzealous for battle, prompting some to call him "Mad Merritt the Morgue Master."[16]

The Raider battalion that Edson helped create in the summer of 1941 was a special outfit. It was employed in various roles, such as amphibious landings, amphibious raids, and commando operations behind enemy lines. The 1st Raider Battalion had already carved a niche in Marine Corps history, having taken heavily fortified Tulagi in the Watchtower landings. As a marine unit specializing in amphibious operations, a key component of the 1st Raider Battalion was the navy's APD. Indeed, from its genesis the

Raider battalion was known as the "APD Battalion." The APD was a special ship. Its high speed and small size made it ideally suited for hit-and-run raids. The only drawback was its size—each APD could carry only 155 men. Thus, six APDs were needed to haul the entire battalion to its destination.[17]

Sergeant Frank Guidone recalls the training and esprit de corps of the Raiders. "Small unit tactics, individual and crew-served weapons were stressed as well as hand-to-hand combat, movement at night, and special operations, including the use of rubber boats in stealth landings at night from the APDs. But most of all," Guidone emphasized, "we knew each other well and the bond was strong. We were confident and proud of the marine Raider image even though other marine infantry showed us some disdain—or was it jealousy."[18]

As befitting a special unit, the 1st Raider Battalion was organized differently from the standard marine rifle battalion. A light infantry force, it consisted of four rifle companies each numbering 130 marines, one weapons company of 204 men, and one headquarters company of 139 troops. Although the Raiders had nothing heavier than the Browning .30-caliber air-cooled machine gun and 60mm mortar (Edson preferred the 60mm over the 81mm because it was much lighter), the battalion was outfitted with additional demolition, intelligence, and pioneer elements. Gunnery Sergeant Angus Goss's demolition team, in particular, proved its worth on Tulagi by destroying a large number of heavily defended dugouts.[19]

Like the Raiders, the Parachute battalions were employed as light shock troops. When called upon, they could act as a reconnoitering and raiding unit, as a spearhead that seized and held critical terrain features, and as a self-sustaining force placed in an advantageous tactical situation. "This battalion was unique in that it really was 'The Old Breed,'" recalls Major Williams, commanding officer of the 1st Parachute Battalion. "All sergeants, and many corporals, were on their second four-year enlistment. Some staff NCOs had eight or ten years' service. An attitude of professionalism therefore characterized the battalion," wrote Williams. "Add to this the boundless esprit of the early parachute units and the quality of the men—who had to pass something approaching a flight physical to be accepted for parachute training—and you have a truly elite unit."[20]

The Parachutists had already fought with distinction in the Solomons, having taken the twin islets of Gavutu-Tanambogo. But the Parachutists assaulted these islands conventionally rather than from the air. Indeed, the marine paratroopers would never take an enemy objective from the air in the entire war. Compared to the standard marine rifle battalion, the 1st Parachute Battalion was tiny. It was comprised of one headquarters and three rifle companies. Even though the official table of organization listed 583 men, it stormed Gavutu's beaches with only 397, including navy medical personnel. But the main problem in the battalion was not its size, but its weaponry. It was armed with a folding stock variant of the troublesome Reising submachine gun.[21]

With the regular appearance of the navy's APDs, the transfer of the Raiders and Parachutists to Cactus finally became a reality. The Raiders were transferred in two echelons on 30 August and 1 September, while the Parachutists went to Guadalcanal on 3 September by way of the navy's YPs, converted California tuna boats. Colonel Edson arrived on the island aching for a fight. As Lt. Col. Samuel Griffith, executive officer of the 1st Raider Battalion, later wrote, from the moment he set foot on Guadalcanal, Red Mike Edson "began to urge the need for reconnaissance in force toward either Esperance or Taivu." Colonel Thomas agreed with the need to hit the Japanese hard.[22]

The product of Thomas and Edson's first collaboration, and the beginning of a long friendship, was a reconnaissance of Savo Island, where native patrols reported small numbers of "Japan man." Using the APDs *Little* and *Gregory,* Griffith's orders were to take two companies there on the morning of the 4th and return by nightfall. After enjoying an unopposed landing, the Raiders scoured the volcanic island for ten hours, but found no enemy. Thomas and Edson originally planned a similar operation against Cape Esperance the following day, but Hashimoto's Cactus Express played the role of spoiler that night. Both the *Little* and *Gregory* were blasted to the bottom in a onesided action by the destroyers *Yudachi, Hatsuyuki,* and *Murakumo.* With the loss of the *Colhoun* to Japanese bombers on 30 August, the U.S. Navy had lost half of its APDs in just one week.[23]

The Barge Convoy

While the Japanese buildup at Taivu Point proceeded at a rapid pace, Col. Akinosuke Oka's barge convoy was leapfrogging its way down the Solomons chain.

Oka assembled sixty-one large and small Daihatsu motorized barges manned by about 450 men of Lieutenant Colonel Wakiya's 6th Independent Shipping Engineer Regiment. Their cargo included supplies and trucks as well as the 2d Battalion, 124th Infantry (less the 7th Company), and organic units of the 124th Regiment, including one 75mm regimental and two 37mm antitank guns—about 1,100 soldiers in all (see Table 7).[24]

Table 7
Composition of the Oka Barge Convoy

6th Independent Shipping Engineer Regiment

124th Regiment Headquarters

124th Regimental Signal Unit (less one part)

124th Regimental Gun Company (1 platoon)

124th Regimental Antitank Company (less 1 platoon)

124th Motor Transport Company (trucks) (one part)

2d Battalion, 124th Infantry Headquarters

5th Company

6th Company

8th Company

2/124 Machine Gun Company

2/124 Trench Mortar Platoon

Part of the 24th Water Purification Unit

Special Radio Squad

Source: *Diary of First Lieutenant Kashii, 31 August entry, SOPAC-CIC: Item 575: M-2 619483.*

Before recounting the barge expedition, it will help to review the basic geography of the Solomon Islands.

Running on a northwest-southeast axis, the Solomons consist of two groups of islands, which on a map resemble a set of several footprints. Bougainville, Choiseul, Santa Isabel, and Malaita together make up the northern half of imprints; Vella Lavella, New Georgia, Guadalcanal, and San Cristobal make up the southern half. Kawaguchi had ordered Oka to use Gizo Island in the New Georgia group as his staging point and to travel down the southern chain of islands, but for some unknown reason, Oka decided to proceed down the longer northern chain. More important, the landing point was supposed to be Taivu Point, but Oka instead chose to land at Kamimbo Bay on the northwest tip of Guadalcanal.[25]

The first half of the journey was uneventful. The transports *Sado Maru* and *Asakasan Maru* left Shortland at 0800 on 1 September and arrived off the northwestern side of Santa Isabel and Long Island by 0300 on the next day. There, Oka's troops and equipment were transferred to barges. For the journey south, Oka chose to rest by day and travel by night. The convoy left Long Island at 1700 and anchored at Finanana Point on Santa Isabel at 0300 on 3 September.

There, Oka's barges were detected by search planes and promptly strafed by eleven SBDs in the morning and seven SBDs and two F4Fs in the afternoon. Bullets damaged some barges, but Oka kept to his timetable, arriving at a point between Santa Isabel and San Jorge Island at 0500. Although Oka had carefully camouflaged his boats, another wave of thirteen SBDs spotted him again on the morning of 4 September. These SBDs, led by Major Mangrum, subjected Oka's barges to vicious strafings, damaging one-third of them. Two

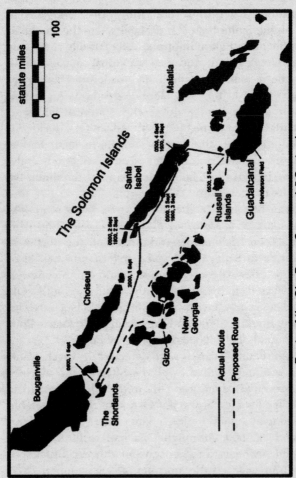

Route of the Oka Barge Convoy, 1-5 September

more attacks occurred later in the afternoon in lesser strength.[26]

After screaming profane oaths at the U.S. planes, the Japanese immediately began the task of repairing their boats before initiating the longest and most dangerous leg of the journey to Kamimbo Bay, a distance of about fifty-seven miles. Oka planned on leaving San Jorge Island at 1900, but because of low tide, he was unable to do so until 2130. When the Japanese finally reached open water, they found that the choppy seas and heavy winds threw spray into the barges and that many repaired holes began to leak. Taking on water, some barges began to falter and fall behind. At 0430 the cruiser *Sendai* and three destroyers arrived to provide escort, but these vessels could do little to help the soaked and shivering infantrymen, who feverishly bailed to keep their craft from sinking.[27]

Oka's barges were scheduled to arrive at Kamimbo Bay by 0500 on 5 September, but that hour passed without Guadalcanal in sight. Finally, at 0620 the Japanese saw the tips of Guadalcanal's mountains peeking over the horizon. Their joy, however, was short-lived as the unmistakable silhouettes of two "long-nosed planes" (P-400s) came into view twenty minutes later. These were followed shortly by six rotund F4Fs. The barges were sitting ducks, and the fighter pilots lined up on the leading fifteen, subjecting them to deadly strafing runs and killing Major Takamatsu and many others. Using small arms and mounted machine guns, the Japanese fired back and shot down one of the Wildcats but that did little to alleviate the punishment they were receiving.[28]

The first hulls scraped bottom on Guadalcanal's

shore at 0740. Oka's badly leaking barge finally grounded at 1120 at Garbanga, about seven miles southeast of Kamimbo. At 1400 he learned that the main group of about 300 troops had landed with Colonel Wakiya at Kamimbo Bay. The remaining 700 were scattered at various locations, from Santa Isabel and San Jorge in the north to Savo Island in the south, where 450 soldiers had landed on the evening of the 5th. One diarist with Oka proudly noted that the sacred color of the 124th Infantry also arrived safely that night.[29]

Over the next seven days, the Imperial Navy corralled these scattered detachments and landed them on Guadalcanal. By the 9th, most of Oka's unit was on the island. Oka's artillery and machine gun company and a portion of the 2d Battalion Headquarters, part of the 5th Company, and a small part of the 8th Company were still stranded on San Jorge Island, but these units made it to Guadalcanal in time to participate in Kawaguchi's attack. Japanese records show that about ninety men died in Oka's barge convoy. In view of the losses in men, equipment, supplies, and, more important, time, the barge convoy cannot be regarded as anything but a complete failure. It was a bad omen for Kawaguchi, Oka, and the Japanese.[30]

Kawaguchi Moves Out

Dawn on the first day of September revealed a pleasant tropical setting for Kawaguchi and his newly landed men as they sat among the thatched huts of the village of Tasimboko. Under tranquil azure skies, palm trees gently stirred in the cool breeze along the beach, where white crested waves pounded rhythmically on the shore. As they sat at breakfast in this beautiful, tropical setting, the serenity of the moment was shattered by U.S. aircraft, which began flailing the Taivu area blindly with machine gun fire and bombs. Screams filled the air as explosions toppled trees and sent clumps of dirt and Japanese bodies into the air. The attacks lasted throughout the day, inflicting casualties on the Japanese, some of whom sought shelter in their newly dug foxholes. Twelve Japanese succumbed to bombs and bullets that day, and one near miss damaged Kawaguchi's hearing, creating what he later described as an "irritating" difficulty in speech.[31]

And these attacks had other "irritating" effects as well. On the evening of 1 September, the destroyers *Urakaze, Uranami, Tanikaze,* and *Shikinami* ferried the 465 troops of the 1st Battalion, 124th Infantry, to Taivu. But because of the dogged attacks of three SBDs and a lack of landing boats, which Kawaguchi's shore party failed to provide, the destroyers were unable to land everyone. During one pass, the SBDs strafed and scored a near miss on one landing craft, killing four and wounding a like number. Five soldiers were killed and five were wounded during the landing. The Cactus fliers also wounded one sailor. Japanese antiaircraft fire relegated one SBD to the scrap heap at Henderson Field.[32]

Despite the morale-suppressing attacks from the Cactus Air Force, Kawaguchi issued his first written order on Guadalcanal on the afternoon of the 1st. It called for a gradual march westward and for a reconnoitering of American positions around the airfield. Ichiki's Second Echelon, now christened the Kuma

("Bear") Battalion, was ordered to guard the beaches between Berande Point and Tasimboko. The 1st Battalion, 124th Infantry, would start out early on the 2nd for the village of Tetere. Following this battalion's departure, the 3d Battalion, 124th Infantry, would advance south along the east bank of the Balesuna River for a distance of about four miles. There the battalion would turn and march west for approximately twelve miles, until it reached the attack position south of the airfield. Kawaguchi would maintain his headquarters in the jungle south of Tasimboko until the detachment moved out.[33]

Much to Kawaguchi's chagrin, the aerial onslaught by the Cactus Air Force continued that night and throughout 2 September. The attacks were so concentrated and persistent that Japanese correspondent Gen Nishino counted seventy aircraft sorties. The area from Taivu Point to Tasimboko was covered with blackened bomb craters and smoldering tree trunks. "I received several near misses from these bombings and strafings," wrote First Lieutenant Matsumoto, a company commander in the 1st Battalion, 124th Infantry. "The enemy continued his bombing attacks almost all day long—four times in the morning and twice in the afternoon. Therefore, I stayed in the trench all day. I haven't any appetite. Although I think that these bombings are a test of intestinal fortitude," Matsumoto lamented, "it is maddening to be the recipient of these daring and insulting attacks by the American forces."[34]

The day after these "maddening" air attacks, a patrol dispatched by Kawaguchi searched the Koli Peninsula, but found no sign of marines. Accordingly,

Kawaguchi ordered the Kuma Battalion to Koli Point, where it could observe the Americans at Lunga Point. On the afternoon of the 4th, Kawaguchi was the recipient of more good news. He learned that the leading elements of Oka's convoy would be landing that night at Kamimbo Bay, some forty miles west. Kawaguchi ordered fencing expert 1st Lt. Hakusuji Nakayama to take three men on a long, hazardous trek west to personally provide Colonel Oka with maps and orders detailing the attack. He told Nakayama of the mission's import, that a coordinated attack was the key to victory. Kawaguchi sent them off with the only personal item of food he had in his possession—a can of sardines.

In the meantime, Admiral Hashimoto's express continued its shuttle runs to Taivu Point. On the night of 2 September, two destroyers, two patrol boats, and the minelayer *Tsugaru* put ashore two regimental guns and a like number of antitank guns. They also landed one 75mm antiaircraft gun of the 45th Antiaircraft Battalion (two guns were brought but one was damaged during unloading and was returned), 150 soldiers, and provisions. No reinforcement run was scheduled for 3 September, but a large "express" run was executed on the 4th. The light cruiser *Sendai* led eleven destroyers, six of which debarked about 770 soldiers of the 2d Battalion, 4th Infantry, and 200 men of the Kuma Battalion at Taivu Point without incident. The following night, the destroyers *Fubuki, Shirayuki, Amagiri, Kagero,* and *Yugure* disgorged another 370 troops and provisions.[35]

At 1630 on the 5th, Kawaguchi issued another order directing a further advance west. One infantry company plus the machine gun platoon of the Kuma Battalion would probe the area around the village of Rengo. The newly landed 2d Battalion, 4th Infantry, dubbed the Aoba Battalion, would march west, occupying Tagoma Point by the 7th. Kawaguchi's order tentatively set the date of the attack for the night of 12 September.[36]

As Kawaguchi's brigade marched west, General Hyakutake radioed Kawaguchi on the evening of the 5th, offering an additional battalion to the five already assigned. This battalion would be available, Hyakutake estimated, on 11 September. But Kawaguchi, confident his 6,200 men were sufficient for the attack, rejected the offer, stating, "It would not be advisable to postpone the day of the attack to wait for reinforcements." Since no moon was expected on 12 September, Kawaguchi maintained that the conditions on the 12th would be perfect for a night attack. While it is true that Kawaguchi had faith in the night attack, his confidence appears to have sprung from faulty intelligence—the latest of which came from Captain Kadomae—that only 2,000 marines were on Guadalcanal.[37]

At Tasimboko on the evening of 5 September, Kawaguchi stepped into a barge and motored west along the coast to the village of Tetere. There, Kawaguchi radioed Seventeenth Army with a message containing several requests. First, he asked for air attacks against the airfield commencing on 9 September until sunset on the 12th. On the date of the attack, he requested that the Imperial Navy stage a diversion off Lunga Point and destroy any Americans who attempted to flee from the island. In what was probably an effort to avoid "friendly fire," Kawaguchi also requested that warships abstain from shelling the airfield on the 12th.[38]

On 6 September Kawaguchi's attention turned from planning to the bad weather. Heavy rains made life miserable for the Japanese, who spent most of their time holed up in their trenches. But the bad weather proved damaging to Kawaguchi's timetable as well. The rains flooded rivers and streams and made trails muddied and difficult to cross. The transport of the detachment's artillery and ammunition was particularly difficult. Nobody could convince the newcomers to Guadalcanal, especially the Japanese, that September was not a part of the rainy season. The lost time forced Kawaguchi to put off the date of the attack to the 13th.[39]

Second Lieutenant Genjirou Inui, a platoon commander in the 8th Independent Antitank Company, took note of the wretched weather in his diary. Inui wrote that it rained practically the entire night of 6 September. Having no shelter, his troops endured a miserable night in the open and were, in his words, "soaked to the bone." Like the Americans on the island, disease and fungus infections were taking their toll on the Japanese. Lieutenant Inui complained that many of his men had dysentery and "crotch rot," yet added that the morale of his company remained high. All expected a quick and easy victory over the Americans.[40]

At the village of Tetere on the afternoon of 7 September, Kawaguchi issued his plan of attack to "rout and annihilate the enemy in the vicinity of the Guadalcanal Island airfield." Unlike Ichiki's attack plan, Kawaguchi's called for an approach inland, culminating in a surprise night attack south of the airfield. His attack scheme also called for a division of forces. At 2200 on the 13th, the Left Wing Unit under Oka, composed of his scattered 2d Battalion, 124th Infantry, and regimental units, now about 900 soldiers in all, would attack from the west. It would seize 35-Meter Height (the hill where Vandegrift's command post was located) northwest of the airfield and destroy any enemy along both banks of the Lunga River. The Kuma Battalion, with the four Model 94 (1934) 37mm guns of the 28th Regiment Antitank Company attached, comprised Kawaguchi's Right Wing Unit. At midnight this battalion, led by Maj. Takeshi Mizuno, would break through and annihilate the enemy along the left bank sector, "thus giving," in the words of Kawaguchi, "repose to the departed souls of the Ichiki Detachment commander and his men."[41]

The Central Body south of the airfield would deliver Kawaguchi's main attack at 2200. This force was composed of three battalions of infantry: the 1st Battalion, 124th Infantry, led by Maj. Yukichi Kokusho; the 2d Battalion, 4th Infantry, commanded by Maj. Masao Tamura; and the 3d Battalion, 124th Infantry, under Lt. Col. Kusukichi Watanabe. Kokusho's 870 men (with one 75mm regimental gun and two 37mm antitank guns of the 124th Infantry attached) were designated the Left Front Line Unit. Kokusho's soldiers would simultaneously destroy enemy positions south of the airfield and "firmly secure" 15-Meter Height (Pagoda Hill) northwest of the airfield, and assist, if necessary, in the capture of 35-Meter Height. The Right Front Line Unit, Watanabe's nearly 800 soldiers, would pierce enemy positions southeast of the airfield, then push north toward the coast and "destroy the enemy in that area." The nearly 800 men of Tamura's 2d Line Attack Unit would advance between the front line units and annihilate any enemy along the way to the coastline. The support forces of the Central Body included the 6th Independent Signal Unit, a special radio squad, the 67th Line of Communications Hospital Unit, and an engineer force. The latter, under 1st Lt. Yoshio Hoshino, was comprised of a platoon of the 7th Engineer Regiment (seventy-seven men) and a platoon of the 15th Independent Engineer Regiment (sixty-four troops). Kawaguchi set X-day, the date of the attack, for 13 September (see Table 8).[42]

Noticeably absent from Kawaguchi's plan of attack was a reserve force. Kawaguchi admitted this was a "drastic decision" contrary to military orthodoxy, but he was convinced that a night attack in unfamiliar jungle would make it difficult, if not impossible, to throw in a reserve at the right moment. Thus, each battalion would be essentially on its own during the battle.[43]

Kawaguchi's orders also called for the artillery unit, led by Capt. Isao Nakaoka, to fire on the eastern side of the American perimeter. The bombardment would commence at 1830 and last until 2000. This diversionary bombardment would also serve to soften up the marines' defenses before the Kuma Battalion's attack. Nakaoka was given nearly all of Kawaguchi's artillery for the mission. His ad hoc unit consisted of the four Model 41 (1908) 75mm regimental guns of the 28th Regiment and two 75mm guns of the 124th Regiment. The Model 41, which weighed about 1,200 pounds, was perhaps the oldest-looking artillery piece in the Japanese arsenal. It fired a fourteen-pound shell up to

7,800 yards. Nakaoka also had the four remaining German 35/36 37mm antitank guns of the 8th Independent Antitank Company (the other two guns having been left at Taivu Point) and two machine gun platoons of the 4th and 124th Infantry Regiments.[44]

Table 8
Kawaguchi Detachment Order of Battle for the September Counteroffensive

Central Body (Major General Kawaguchi)

    Detachment Headquarters

    Detachment Guard Company

    1st Battalion, 124th Infantry

        One 75mm gun of the 124th Regimental Gun Company

        Two 37mm guns of the 124th Regimental Antitank Company

    2d Battalion, 4th Infantry

    3d Battalion, 124th Infantry

    One Platoon, 15th Independent Engineer Regiment

    One Platoon, 7th Engineer Regiment

    67th Line of Communications Hospital Unit

    Part of the 24th Water Purification Unit

    6th Independent Radio Platoon

Left Wing Unit (Colonel Oka)

    124th Infantry Headquarters

    124th Regimental Gun Company (one 75mm gun)

    124th Regimental Antitank Company (two 37mm guns)

    124th Regimental Signal Company

    124th Regimental Machine Gun Company

    Part of the 124th Regimental Transport Company

2d Battalion, 124th Infantry (Maizuru Battalion)
3d Battalion, 4th Infantry
Part of the 24th Water Purification Unit
6th Independent Engineer Regiment
Special Radio Squad
Kadomae Naval Unit

Right Wing Unit (Major Mizuno)
    Kuma Battalion
        28th Regimental Antitank Company (four 37mm guns)
    Nakaoka Artillery Unit
        28th Regimental Gun Company (four 75mm guns)
        8th Independent Antitank Company (four 37mm guns)
        Two 75mm guns of the 124th Regimental Gun Company
        10th Company, 124th Infantry

At Taivu Point
    One Company, 28th Independent Engineer Regiment
    1st Company, 2d Field Artillery Regiment (four 75mm guns)
    One 75mm gun of the 45th Antiaircraft Battalion
    Two 37mm guns of the 8th Independent Antitank Company
    Imaizumi Large Launch Unit

Before the day ended, Kawaguchi was the recipient of intelligence that changed his newly revised plan of attack. A 2300 message from Seventeenth Army relayed a report from Tokyo that "a large enemy convoy with marines aboard arrived at the Fiji Islands on the 5th." The message ended asking Kawaguchi how soon he could begin his attack. Kawaguchi answered that he

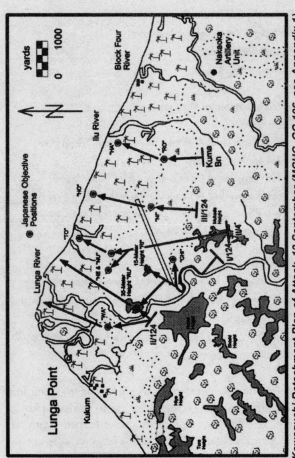

Kawaguchi Detachment Plan of Attack, 12 September (MCHC, GC-106, see Appendix 1)

would attack on 12 September, and, depending on how much progress the detachment made in the jungle that day, he might even be able to launch the attack earlier. Recklessly, Seventeenth Army notified the Imperial Navy that Kawaguchi would commence his attack on 11 September.[45]

In the drizzling rain the following day, Kawaguchi gathered his officers for a final battle briefing. With his handlebar mustache dripping water, Kawaguchi injected caution: "As you know, gentlemen, the Americans have been strongly reinforced with men and supplies. Perhaps they are stronger than we are. Above all, their air force cannot be underestimated. Our troops must also overcome difficult terrain problems before we even reach the enemy lines. We are obviously facing an unprecedented battle. And so, gentlemen, you and I cannot hope to see each other again after the fight." Kawaguchi concluded: "This is the time for us to dedicate our lives to the Emperor." The gathering then toasted to their success with a few drops of *sake*.[46]

7 | The Tasimboko Raid

Hit and Run

In early September, Martin Clemens's native scouts reported that between 200 to 300 poorly equipped, half-starved Japanese occupied Tasimboko with defenses there oriented to the west. Given the Cactus Express's frequent shuttle runs to Taivu Point, confirmed by aircraft sightings and ULTRA intelligence, Lt. Col. Gerald Thomas and his deputy, Lt. Col. Merrill Twining, wanted to verify enemy strength in that area. As they began laying the groundwork for this mission, Colonel Edson came to division headquarters on the morning of 6 September with a similar scheme. The result of their efforts was a plan for a classic hit-and-run raid against the Japanese—exactly the type of mission for which the Raider battalions had been created.

The scheme, as originally conceived, had the Raiders landing at daybreak 3,000 yards east of Tasimboko, in order to take the Japanese from the rear. One company would follow the beach to the west, while two other companies looped inland to envelop the village from the south. Edson's weapons company would support the attack on Tasimboko with mortar fire, while the other rifle company was slated to protect the rear. The APDs and aircraft from Henderson Field would provide ground support. Following the destruction of the enemy supplies and installations, the Raiders were to return by nightfall.

Vandegrift's approval for the raid came easy, but the APDs were scarce of late with the losses of *Colhoun*, *Little*, and *Gregory*. With *Stringham* occupied elsewhere, this left just the *McKean* and *Manley* available for the mission. Hence, two patrol boats from Tulagi, YP-346 and YP-298 (nicknamed "yippies") were added to supplement the lift. But this augmentation still fell short of what Colonel Edson needed. Thus, he was compelled to divide the Raider-Parachute Battalion into two echelons (see Table 9).

Table 9
Composition of U.S. Assault Force
for the Tasimboko Raid

Assault Force		**Reserve Force**	
Raider Battalion		Parachute Battalion	
HQ Company	35	HQ Company	36
Company A	150	Company A	96
Company B	140	Company B	76
Company C	130	Company E (Raiders)	104
Company D	46		
Totals:	501		312*

---

*The official report from which these figures were taken states that the total of the Reserve Force was 348 men. Based on the units listed, however, this writer calculated a figure of 312. Company C, 1st Parachute Battalion, consisting of only about 35 men, is not in this report. It is not known if the total of 348 was a miscalculation or if a typographical error occurred somewhere in the unit totals.

Source: *Report on the Tasimboko Raid.*

As darkness began to fall on Lunga Point on 7 September, the *Manley* and *McKean* arrived off Kukum with a new look, sporting deception schemes of green paint and camouflage netting. In this new battle dress, the two ships looked ready for a raid. The embarkation of Edson's assault force began after nightfall, but before getting under way, Edson was handed a new intelligence report from D-2. It stated that the enemy was now estimated to number as many as 3,000 men, but these troops, the report confidently said, were believed to be half-starved and poorly equipped, and only "two out of ten were armed." The unflappable Edson was not moved by the higher estimate, and soon the four ships were under way, leaving Lunga Point behind them in the darkness. The sight of the YPs as they sailed was almost comical, according to Lt. Col. Samuel B. Griffith. With the YP engines pounding loudly, belching showers of bright red sparks, many marines were amazed they were not spotted by the enemy.[1]

Unbeknownst to the sailors and marines on these four ships, the Cactus Express was making another run to Taivu Point this night. But heavy rains, evidently, prevented the two forces from detecting each other. The Americans on these four vessels were fortunate that they were not detected and blown to bits like the *Little* and *Gregory* three nights earlier. This evening's express was Kawaguchi's final reinforcement, but he did not know it. Without notifying Kawaguchi, Hyakutake and the Eighth Fleet decided to forward supplies and a battery of 75mm field guns to Taivu. These, the property of the 1st Company, 2d Field Artillery Regiment, 2d Infantry Division, were ferried by the minelayer *Tsugaru* and the destroyers *Umikaze, Suzukaze,* and *Kawakaze.* The artillerymen, fifty-three in all, joined the 250 or so garrison troops Kawaguchi left behind to guard the supply base at Tasimboko.[2]

Before first light on 8 September, the ragtag American fleet arrived off Taivu Point. Higgins boats were lowered, and the first wave of Raiders climbed into them. However, just as the boats were about to leave the line of departure, an event occurred that, according to one Raider officer, was "a stroke of genius on the part of nobody except our good Lord." Steaming west toward Lunga Point were the cargo ships *Fuller* and *Bellatrix* and the destroyers *Hull, Hughes, Zane, Hopkins,* and *Southard.* This convoy, in addition to the raiding force, apparently gave the Japanese, who saw this armada gathering in the gloom, the impression that a major invasion was under way. Consequently, most of the Japanese troops in the area panicked and disappeared into the bush. A few signal troops stayed long enough to get off an urgent message to Hyakutake, however, reporting that an American fleet of four transports, one cruiser, and six destroyers were putting troops ashore at Taivu Point.[3]

Following preparatory air strikes against Tasimboko by two Wildcats and four Aircobras, the first wave of Raiders splashed ashore at 0520. No opposition was encountered, a fact the Raiders found a bit puzzling. At 0615 the second wave hit the beach. Forty minutes later, Edson's assault companies moved out, leaving platoon-size Company D behind to secure the landing area. Marching west along the coastline the Raiders found an abandoned 37mm antitank gun 500 yards from the landing point. By Japanese standards, this was a modern-looking piece with rubber tires and a split-trail carriage. Strewn about in disorder about this gun were backpacks, ammunition, life preservers, shoes, and entrenching tools. A short distance west, they found more of the same, including freshly dug slit trenches and foxholes and another 37mm antitank gun identical in appearance to the other. This second piece was unmanned and pointed to the west. These two German-made Pak 35/36 guns, the former property of the 8th Independent Antitank Company, could have wreaked havoc on the Raiders during the landing, but, fortunately, the gunners had disappeared into the jungle.[4]

At 0740, Edson radioed division: "Repeat bombing mission 0745. Ten-minute concentration. Troops apparently well-armed and equipped." On the receiving end of this transmission was Vandegrift, who, along with Colonel Thomas and others, remained huddled around the division's radio dugout throughout the day. As Thomas pointed out, "Edson was always meticulous in planning his communications." This day was no different. The Raider commander practically provided a play-by-play account in Morse code of the entire raid. Edson's communications platoon was equipped with the TBX radio, a 120-pound behemoth requiring a three-man crew to carry and operate. A low-power set, the TBX had a maximum range of just twenty miles, although its range was greater over water. In order to reliably maintain communications, one of Edson's communicators stayed aboard one of the APDs to act as a relay to division headquarters. This arrangement worked well throughout the raid, though the TBX crew ashore had to constantly tear down, march, and set up in order to send messages and keep pace with the advance.[5]

General Geiger's Cactus Air Force promptly responded to Red Mike Edson's radio request for additional air support. At about 0800, aircraft began lashing out against Tasimboko again, as the Raiders waded across the waist-deep Kema River. Soon thereafter, the Raiders of Company B saw and eagerly fired at a small group of Japanese on the beach alongside some collapsible boats. The Japanese answered with cracks of rifle fire and chattering Nambus. As the fusillade swelled in volume, the Raiders heard a loud explosion, which Edson thought at first was mortar fire. But the Japanese were not firing mortars at the Raiders. They were firing a 75mm mountain gun at point-blank range! The Raiders aggressively responded to this fearful sounding piece by unlimbering their .30-caliber machine guns. The Japanese apparently were in no mood to stay and fight, because they abandoned this field piece in a small clearing and began backtracking toward Tasimboko.[6]

Before capturing this artillery piece, Edson's communicators tapped out another message to Vandegrift at 0855. Edson reported that the Raiders had come in the "back door" and had captured two (37mm) field pieces. After stating that the Japanese were withdraw-

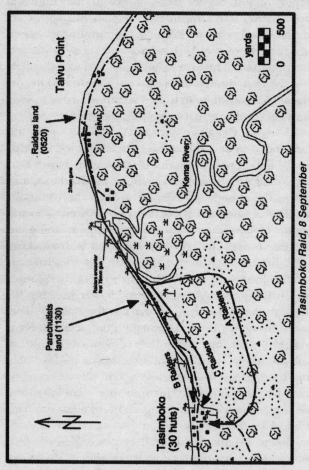

Tasimboko Raid, 8 September

ing to Tasimboko, Edson admitted that the enemy's
strength was unknown but was believed to be as estimated. Red Mike finished the transmission by requesting that the air support be maintained and that boat
crews be sent from Kukum to retrieve the captured
antitank guns.[7]

Edson's original plan called for two companies to
envelop Tasimboko from the south after crossing the
Kema River. The Raiders, however, discovered that the
main tributary of the river that ran parallel with the
shore was too deep and marshy to cross by foot. With
the beach on one side and the tributary on the other,
the Raiders found themselves channeled down a narrow neck of land. As a result, Edson was forced to
advance in echelon with Maj. Lloyd Nickerson's Company B leading the way, followed by Company A, commanded by Capt. John W. Antonelli, and Company C,
temporarily led by Capt. Robert H. Thomas, in that
order.[8]

As the Raiders zigzagged down this narrow corridor
to make themselves less inviting targets, Major Nickerson reported to Edson that small groups of Japanese
were seen filtering east on the other side of the tributary. Edson ordered Captain Antonelli to take a patrol
and outflank the Japanese there. This patrol, however,
found no sign of the enemy, and at about 0900, Company A, led by native scouts, curved inland to outflank
Tasimboko from the south. But the jungle was so thick
and swamp-laden that it took over two and one-half
hours for the company to get into position to support
the attack on the village.[9]

As the Raiders advanced west toward Tasimboko
under light opposition, they came upon more signs

that a large Japanese force was now on the island. As
the Raiders entered one clearing, they gazed upon
large stacks of medical supplies. They also saw foxholes and slit trenches carefully camouflaged with
palm fronds in which Kawaguchi's troops had sought
refuge from American aircraft only a week earlier. Farther along, they surveyed large stockpiles of provisions, such as canned meat and sacks of crackers, and
mounds of backpacks and life preservers. The abandoned equipment and supplies clearly indicated that a
large, newly landed Japanese force was in the area and
possibly setting a trap.[10]

Meanwhile, Japanese opposition steadily increased
as the Raiders moved on Tasimboko. Spearheading
the drive was Capt. John Sweeney's 1st Platoon of
Company B. As Sweeney's platoon exited the clearing
where they found the abandoned 75mm field piece, it
spotted another 75mm field gun a short distance
southwest. Three Japanese gunners quickly manned
the gun, frantically depressed its muzzle, and began
firing at Sweeney's platoon at point-blank range. The
first two or three rounds whistled over their heads but
exploded in treetops to the rear, showering the 2d Platoon of Company B with shrapnel. This platoon, led
by Capt. Rex Crockett, suffered several casualties,
including the death of one Raider and another who
lost an arm. Sweeney's platoon immediately opened
fire and killed two of the Japanese before the third
fled into the jungle.[11]

After silencing this field piece, Sweeney's platoon
covered only a few yards before being stopped by surprise fire from three Japanese firing a Nambu.
Sweeney taunted the Japanese with several shouts of

"Baka" ("you fool"), which immediately provoked a burst of machine gun fire each time he yelled it.

In the midst of this shouting and shooting match, the battalion operations officer, Maj. Robert S. Brown, crawled up to Sweeney to ask why his platoon was not advancing. A few shouts of *"Baka,"* followed by short bursts from the Nambu, gave Brown the answer he was looking for, and he left, apparently satisfied. A short time later, Sweeney's occasional taunts distracted the Japanese gunners sufficiently to allow three of his Raiders to outflank the position and to kill the Japanese manning the machine gun.[12]

In the meantime, another 75mm mountain gun began to harry the Raider advance. Like the other artillery pieces, however, this gun was too close to be effective; most of the shells whistled over their heads and exploded hundreds of yards to the rear. Correspondent Richard Tregaskis, who was taking cover in a lightly wooded jungle break, described the artillery blasts as "scary," as the shells whistled just inches above his head. Tregaskis was so close to the enemy muzzle that he could feel the blast of hot air each time the gun fired. As they had with the other Japanese guns, the Raiders easily outflanked this piece and killed its crew at about 1030.[13]

Before this third 75mm artillery piece was seized, heavy rains began pelting the island, reducing visibility greatly and forcing Edson's air support to return to Henderson Field. At 1038, Vandegrift radioed Edson that ten planes would support him in one hour, but added that the fliers were having problems differentiating between friend and foe. One concentration of Japanese, either Colonel Watanabe's battalion or the

Tasimboko Garrison, was located by pilots two miles southwest of Tasimboko.[14]

It did not take Edson long to respond to Vandegrift. At 1045, Edson asked for a coordinated air and naval bombardment of Tasimboko and announced that he had captured another 75mm gun. He also said that 1,000 life preservers had been overrun. Red Mike also requested that troops be landed west of the village to outflank the Japanese. If this was not possible, he asked that instructions regarding his embarkation be issued. Haunted perhaps by Goettge's memory, Vandegrift replied that another landing was not possible and ordered Edson to re-embark and return to Kukum.[15]

Edson's anxiety continued to increase as he closed in on Tasimboko. Bad weather had forced his air support to return to Henderson Field. But, more important, Edson feared he was either walking into a trap or that the Japanese were circling around his flank to cut him off from the landing point. With these thoughts running through his mind, Edson learned that his men had seized a fourth 75mm gun. Taking these weapons seemed too easy; hence, the fear of a trap prompted another transmission from the Raider commander at 1130. Edson reported that he had captured six field pieces and that he was "advancing slowly against machine gun and rifle fire." He estimated that he had run into "1,000 well-armed, well-equipped troops." Edson explained that his position was untenable after dark without the landing of additional troops west of Tasimboko. After requesting continual air support and stating his intentions to withdraw shortly, he added ominously, "Hostile pressure increasing, request instructions." Vandegrift replied fifteen minutes later: "Instructions to withdraw and re-embark already issued." But Edson ignored this order and kept his Raiders pointed at Tasimboko.[16]

About this time, the situation began to brighten for Edson—both literally and figuratively. At 1130, the *Manley* and *McKean* began landing the reserve force, composed of the Parachutists and the Raiders of Company E, 2,000 yards east of Tasimboko. Edson wanted the force landed there to provide flank and rear protection for the Raiders and to tie in the forty-six men of Company D. According to Edson's request, the two APDs added insult to injury to the Japanese by shelling Tasimboko with their deck guns. Soon thereafter, Captain Antonelli's Company A, which had set out two and one-half hours earlier to envelop the village from the south, appeared on the defenders' flank and rear. Following a brief firefight, the Japanese bolted at about 1230, leaving behind dead in large and small clusters sprawled over six Nambu machine guns. Colonel Griffith noted that Antonelli's men had shot many of the dead in the back. The rains then stopped and the jungle grew quiet. As if reflecting the sudden change of fortune, Tregaskis noted that rays of sunlight began to shine on the Raiders.[17]

As the Raiders entered Tasimboko, they saw a surprising sight. Before them were vast stockpiles of assorted supplies, including cases of food and sacks of rice. Large caches of ammunition for machine guns as well as artillery and mortars were also found, prompting one officer to estimate that the ammunition totaled more than 500,000 rounds. In addition, ten collapsible boats completely equipped with outboard engines were found along the beach. Within one of

the thatched huts was a powerful short-wave radio station, which was strong enough, in one communications officer's estimation, to reach Tokyo.[18]

A brief inspection of the Japanese corpses revealed
that they had recently come from Guam, the Dutch
East Indies, and the Philippines, clear indications
that the garrison was comprised of troops from the
Ichiki Detachment, the 2d Division, and the Kawaguchi Detachment, respectively. This information was
obtained from backpacks, diaries, and pictures of
Javanese women, souvenirs, and money. The Raiders
also discovered that the four captured 75mm guns
had been manufactured in Germany by the Krupp
Works. In contrast with the antitank guns found earlier, these guns were antiquated-looking with large
spoked wheels. A translation of the markings on each
barrel revealed: "Model 41 [1908] mountain gun."
The Raiders also noted that the gun sights were of
English manufacture. American ammunition with
Dutch labels and Allied tommy guns were found as
well. Some marines gathered souvenirs from the
dead. One Raider liberated a corpse of its binoculars
and camera.[19]

With the enemy vanquished, Edson decided to stay
put in order to destroy as much of the captured booty
as possible. Nearly everything the Raiders and Parachutists could get their hands on was systematically
destroyed. Troops demolished a radio generator, bayoneted thousands of cans of beef and crab, ripped open
sacks of rice, and emptied them into the surf. After
removal of the breechblocks, the captured artillery
was towed by boat and pushed over the side into deep
water. Not everything was destroyed, however. The

Raiders kept the transmitter, six Nambus, and a large amount of papers, notebooks, and maps. Food, *sake*, medical supplies, some of Kawaguchi's personal effects, and 81mm-mortar ammunition were also brought back. Many weary marines returned with pockets overflowing with canned food and other goodies. Everything else was burned. At 1430 Red Mike radioed Vandegrift that the Japanese had withdrawn to the southwest and that he was destroying Tasimboko and as much of the abandoned supplies and equipment as possible. Edson also told Vandegrift that he was planning to re-embark at 1530 unless otherwise directed. At 1435, Vandegrift radioed a "well done" and ordered him to return to Kukum. Edson did, and at 1730, all hands were under way, leaving behind them a wrecked shoreline dotted with several fires and plumes of black smoke reaching skyward.[20]

Without a doubt, the Tasimboko raid was a resounding success. Colonel Griffith later recalled it as "one of the really very successful small operations of World War II." He was right. At a cost of just two dead and six wounded, Edson had, in one quick stroke, destroyed Kawaguchi's supply base, which included a two-week supply of provisions for 6,000 men. Japanese losses totaled at least twenty-seven, although as many as fifty were believed to have perished. But the raid's effects transcended mere logistics and casualties. The documents captured by the marines revealed much about the Japanese.[21]

In addition to superb planning, the timing of the Tasimboko raid played a role in its success. As Edson later said, "All of the signs indicated there were five to ten Nips in the area to every one of us and the lack of opposition looked like a trap." This certainly would have been the case had the Raiders landed three days earlier. Indeed, Japanese records show the last remnant of Kawaguchi's main force left Taivu Point just the day before. Had Edson's Raiders landed even one day earlier, it might have been a Goettge patrol revisited, but on a much larger scale. Providence, fate, or luck—whatever you call it—plays a large role in war, too.

Some of the Japanese around Tasimboko apparently believed friendly forces were attacking them. Around the time the Raiders entered the village, they heard a Japanese soldier shouting *"Yama, Yama,"* the password used by Ichiki and Kawaguchi's men at the time. This belief was not too far-fetched, since shots were exchanged between Japanese forces on at least one occasion during a landing at Taivu Point early in the month.[22]

One final, comical event relating to the Tasimboko raid is worth mentioning. In one of his transmissions to division, Edson reported: "1,000 life preservers overrun." At some point during the relay process through the APDs, the message was mistakenly altered by Raider communicators and was received at division headquarters as "1,000 live prisoners taken." As a result, when the ships arrived off Kukum, division was all set to greet the Raiders and Parachutists with guards, interpreters, and a welcoming party for the prisoners.[23]

"That bunch at Tasimboko was no motley of four hundred Japs," Edson told Colonel Thomas after returning from the raid, "but two or three thousand well-organized soldiers." Later that night, after having examined the captured documents, Capt. "Pappy"

Moran, the senior Japanese linguist of the division Intelligence Section, found ample evidence to sustain Edson's conclusion. Native scouts soon brought word that columns of Japanese—as many as 3,000—were snaking their way west from Tetere. At division operations on the morning of 9 September, Thomas knew that the Japanese were preparing for another attack, but the question was where. Edson thought that the narrow, grassy, 1,000-yard-long, coral hogback south of Henderson Field offered a natural avenue of approach. Running parallel to the Lunga River, this unnamed ridge was surrounded by thick jungle except on its northern extremity. Several spurs emanating from the ridge's sides gave it the appearance of a serpent or insect from the air, a resemblance that prompted the Japanese to call it "the Lizard" or "the Centipede."[24]

Since late August, Thomas and Twining were of the opinion that the division's defenses were facing the wrong way. They believed that the exposed southern flank, which could be reached under the cover of the jungle, posed a greater threat than the beaches. The two, however, were unable to convince Vandegrift, who still insisted that the coastal flank was under the greatest threat. On 9 September, Thomas and Edson tried to change Vandegrift's mind again, in light of the new and building threat. Complicating matters was Vandegrift's sudden decision to move his command post from its original location to the ridge south of the airfield. Vandegrift wanted his command post moved to a more protected location to get what he hoped would be "a good night's sleep." But even with this move the commanding general remained uncon-

vinced that a major realignment of the division's
defenses was needed. Thomas then scored a limited
concession. Since the Raiders and Parachutists were in
need of some rest, and since the command post
needed some kind of security force, Thomas recommended that the Raiders and Parachutists be moved
to the ridge. Vandegrift agreed to this proposal.[25]

Japanese Reactions

On the morning of 8 September, as Kawaguchi was
preparing to leave Tetere, he heard the disturbing
sounds of booming and crackling bellowing westward
from Taivu Point. Later, a young lieutenant, who had
been tasked to guard the Japanese supply base at Taivu
Point, ran to Kawaguchi to make a report: "Last night
without any notice one company of the 2d Field
Artillery Regiment of the Sendai Division landed.
Later, warships and transports came to the same spot.
At first," the young officer explained, "we thought they
were our own forces, but instead they were of the
enemy. The sick and wounded as well as the newly
landed artillery unit also joined in the fight. But the
enemy force was several times greater than our own.
Four of our field artillery guns were captured, and we
had to retreat." The panting young officer then asked
for instructions. Kawaguchi resisted the temptation to
turn about and crush the Americans. He did, however,
order 1st Lt. Shingo Shimokawa's 10th Company and
a platoon of machine guns to temporarily protect the
detachment's rear at the Belesuna River.[26]

Word of the Tasimboko raid alarmed many at Seventeenth Army Headquarters. General Futami and vis-

Henderson Field, the object of the six-month-long campaign for Guadalcanal. This photograph was taken about three weeks after the 1st Marine Division captured it on 8 August 1942.

Major General Alexander Archer Vandegrift (first row, fourth from left) and high-ranking officers of the 1st Marine Division took time out of their busy schedule on August 11 to pose for this photograph at the division command post. Lt. Col. Gerald Thomas is seated to Vandegrift's left.

Lieutenant General Harukichi Hyakutake, Commanding General of the 17th Army. Originally responsible for taking Port Moresby, Imperial General Headquarters also gave Hyakutake the unenviable task of recapturing Henderson Field. (Japan War History Office)

Colonel Kiyonao Ichiki, commanding officer of the 28th Infantry Regiment and leader of the Japanese forces at the Battle of the Tenaru. The decoration around Ichiki's neck is the Order of the Sacred Treasure (3rd Class), normally awarded for long and meritorious service. The campaign medal on his left breast (center) is for service in the China Incident, 1937–45.

With few exceptions, the U.S Marines enjoyed a leadership advantage over the Japanese at Bloody Ridge. One of those who played a key role during the fighting was Major Kenneth D. Bailey, who along with Colonel Edson, won the Medal of Honor for his heroic actions. Bailey, however, would not live to see it. The major lost his life to a Japanese bullet at the 2d Battle of the Matanikau. (USMC photo, courtesy John Sweeney)

Soldiers of Ichiki's elite assault group washed up on the beach after the Battle of the Tenaru.

A marine poses with a captured Japanese 70mm Model 92 (1932) battalion gun. This distinctive, lightweight piece could be broken down and man-packed into several loads. It was used in both low and high-angle fire and was an effective weapon. During this and other campaigns, the marines sometimes thought they were being hit with mortar fire when in fact they were being attacked by this artillery piece.

Major General Kiyotake Kawaguchi (center) and officers of the 35th Infantry Brigade staff. This photograph was taken probably in the Palau Islands shortly before the brigade left for Guadalcanal. The Japanese characters on the building read, "Kawaguchi Detachment Headquarters."

An excellent view of the Japanese destroyer *Umikaze*. This vessel transported Major General Kawaguchi to Guadalcanal on the night of 31 August, in one of the many runs made by the Cactus (Tokyo) Express in the campaign. The need to transport troops and supplies to Guadalcanal on high-speed ships made it necessary for the Japanese to impress vessels such as these into this new and unfamiliar role as transport. (Naval Institute Press)

Japanese soldiers of the Kawaguchi Detachment marching in a coconut grove toward battle. (Japan War History Office)

Colonel Merritt "Red Mike" Edson (pictured here as a brigadier general), commanded the 1st Raider and 1st Parachute Battalions at the Battle of Bloody Ridge. Edson is wearing the Medal of Honor, which was awarded for his leadership during the battle.

A fine shot of one of the two high-speed transports (APDs) used by the Raiders in the Tasimboko Raid, *Manley*. During the Guadalcanal campaign, the APDs were used by the U.S. Navy to ferry men and supplies to the marines as well as take part in raids like the one at Tasimboko. Losses due to Japanese air and surface attacks were heavy. "We Marines felt keenly the loss of these brave little ships," Merrill Twining wrote. "To my mind, no group in the Pacific accomplished so much with so little." (Naval Institute Press)

Pictured in the background is Pagoda Hill, or as the Japanese called it, 15-Meter Height, one of the main objectives of Major Kokusho's 1st Battalion, 124th Infantry.

A marine sentry on Hill 80 of Bloody Ridge in search of the Japanese to the south. This photograph gives some idea of the inhospitable terrain that surrounded the ridge. Mount Austen looms in the background.

Marines leaving the northernmost part of Bloody Ridge after a patrol. Henderson Field is located just to the left of this photograph. This remarkable shot, looking generally north, illustrates the importance of Bloody Ridge. Whoever controlled the ridge controlled the airfield.

An excellent shot of Hill 123 on Bloody Ridge, looking north, as the brave and determined Japanese soldiers of Major Tamura and his 2d Battalion, 4th Infantry, saw it.

A shot from Hill 80 on Bloody Ridge looking generally southwest. This picture clearly illustrates the ridge's dominant position in the region. Note the shallow depressions where the marines fought on 12 September.

iting staff officers from Imperial General Headquarters urged that Kawaguchi turn about and crush the new American threat at Taivu. But Colonel Matsumoto successfully argued that the airfield remained the critical objective and that if it could not be retaken Kawaguchi could at least be able to prevent its use. Hyakutake feared that Kawaguchi was "sandwiched" between the marines at Lunga and Taivu. The Seventeenth Army needed access to its troops in the East Indies desperately, but it lacked the shipping to bring them to Rabaul. As a result, the Imperial Navy dispatched two light cruisers to Djakarta to embark 780 troops of the 16th Infantry Regiment, including the regimental headquarters and the 3d Battalion, for immediate lift to Rabaul. In the meantime, Hyakutake ordered the Nankai Detachment to halt on its Port Moresby offensive for several days, until he could reach a decision on whether it would be diverted to Guadalcanal.[27]

On 9 September, Seventeenth Army asked for Kawaguchi's views on where to land the 3d Battalion, 4th Infantry (minus one company), and a platoon of 75mm guns. Kawaguchi had rejected a similar offer four days earlier but now requested that the battalion be landed west of Taivu Point, where he was gathering his forces. However, Hyakutake thought that Taivu remained occupied by the Americans and decided to instead disembark the 3d Battalion, 4th Infantry, at Kamimbo Bay. This landing, Hyakutake hoped, would establish a more direct line of communications to the island in the event that Kawaguchi failed.[28]

General Kawaguchi had no intention of failing, but he was learning that he had underestimated the difficulties he would face in Guadalcanal's thick and tangled jungles. Knobby roots and vines twisted across the ground, creating not only barriers but also trip hazards to the unsuspecting. Sharp thorns and stout vines barred any type of movement, necessitating the use of machetes to clear a path. This was exhausting work. The poor quality of his maps was another problem that vexed the general. The only map he possessed was a worthless hydrographic chart that only provided accurate information about the coastline. Even though Imperial Navy aircraft had provided an accurate aerial mosaic, it covered only the Lunga Point area. No aerial photographs from Taivu to Koli and south of Lunga were available—the area he desperately needed. Consequently, Kawaguchi was forced to navigate on this jungle-covered island by compass alone.[29]

In typical Japanese fashion, General Kawaguchi's scheme of maneuver was complex. It called for four columns advancing independently from Koli Point to their predesignated attack points south and southeast of the airfield. Kawaguchi and his headquarters began the march at Rengo before dawn on 9 September, advancing in a southwest direction with Tamura's 2d Battalion, 4th Infantry, in the lead. This date had special significance for the 4th Infantry Regiment. It marked the anniversary when the regiment received its near-sacred regimental color. Lacking time for the traditional toast with *sake,* the battalion took a few moments to celebrate the occasion to face east and pray.[30]

Of the four columns, Kawaguchi's had the most trouble during the march west. Kawaguchi was using a faulty compass, which resulted at times in a magnetic deviation of between twenty and forty degrees. Thus, when they thought they were advancing west, they were actually marching northwest. This direction took the column surprisingly close to the coast, at which point it turned back. This maddening problem later prompted Kawaguchi to write: "Thus we moved in a tremendous zigzag pattern and wasted a lot of time. An army fighting without a map is just like a merchant doing business without an abacus."[31]

Major Kokusho's 1st Battalion, 124th Infantry, snaked across the Metapona River after dusk on 8 September and bivouacked near Tagoma Point. Kokusho planned on turning south at dawn, but a wide-open plain nearly one-mile wide stood in his way. In order to remain undetected, Kokusho decided to cross the open plain and the Nalimbiu River on the night of 9 September. At 0800 on the 10th, the battalion resumed the march, but it had a difficult time slicing its way through the nearly impenetrable jungle, advancing only one-half mile every two hours. Later that afternoon, the battalion met Kawaguchi's errant column and completed the remainder of the trek with Kawaguchi. The latter part of the march was enlivened a bit when Kokusho's column encountered American patrols and exchanged shots before noon on the 12th.[32]

Colonel Watanabe's 3d Battalion, 124th Infantry, was supposed to march to Koli Point before going south, but for some unknown reason, Watanabe plunged southwest on the afternoon of 8 September at Berande Point. By dawn the following morning, Watanabe had advanced about nine miles southwest of the river's mouth. Making excellent time after snaking

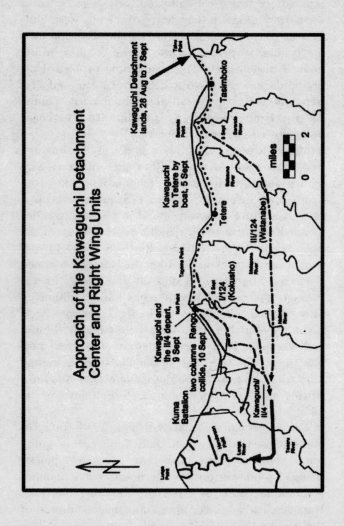

Approach of the Kawaguchi Detachment
Center and Right Wing Units

across grassy plains during the night of the 9th, Watanabe's soldiers were compelled to hack their way through the jungle with machetes on the morning of the 10th. By dusk, Watanabe reached a point he believed was eight miles southeast of the airfield. At dawn the following morning, the battalion started the advance again, and by early morning it had crossed the Tenaru River and had contacted Kawaguchi.[33]

Tasked with protecting the detachment's right flank along the shore, Major Mizuno's Kuma Battalion remained at Koli Point until the evening of 9 September. At 2230, Mizuno struck out southwest along the coastal track to a branch of the Tenaru River, where he dived south into the jungle for a distance of about two miles. Around 1400, Mizuno's battalion ran into Kawaguchi's wayward column, which was heading northwest. At dusk Mizuno trudged west until dawn on the 11th, when it was about two miles from the Tenaru River's mouth. Although his van had encountered a Company G, 1st Marines, patrol on the afternoon of the 11th, Mizuno kept his troops pointed at the airfield but made little progress the rest of the day. When dawn greeted the island on the 12th, Mizuno estimated that he was about five miles from the mouth of the Ilu River.[34]

Compelled to advance along the coast, Capt. Isao Nakaoka's artillery unit encountered less jungle but faced other troublesome obstacles. The artillerymen left Tetere at 1050 on the 8th but were immediately strafed by aircraft supporting Edson's raid on Tasimboko. Since the guns could not be disassembled for movement in the jungle, Nakaoka decided to move at night along the coast. The recent rains vexed the gun-

ners, however, as they exerted all their strength to pull
the artillery (eleven or twelve men towed each gun)
along trails or beaches with the wheels of the guns
being sucked down by mud or sand up to half their
diameter. In addition, the artillery shells had to be carried by hand when the carts used for hauling the
ammunition broke down. The task of towing each gun
by hand, recalled one Japanese officer, "was almost
beyond human strength."[35]

On 10 September, Kawaguchi received word that the
marines were reinforcing their positions along the Ilu
River. His plan previously called for the artillery unit to
shell the Americans as a distraction, but Kawaguchi
believed that the detachment's approach had thus far
been undetected. As a result, Kawaguchi decided on 11
September to make a slight alteration of plans by having the artillery unit begin the bombardment at 2200
on the 12th to coincide with the time of the main
attack. By doing so, he hoped to maintain the element
of surprise. At 1630 on 11 September, Seventeenth
Army notified Kawaguchi that bombers of the Imperial
Navy planned on attacking the north end of the enemy
airfield at noon on 12 September. This message was
the last Kawaguchi had with higher headquarters for
nearly a week.[36]

Meanwhile, Colonel Oka was making good time as
he advanced east toward the airfield. At 0740 on 11
September Oka met Captain Kadomae at the latter's
headquarters near the Matanikau River where they
exchanged information. Kadomae decided to make a
coordinated attack with Oka, using his motley band of
naval troops and laborers. Kadomae handed Oka an
intelligence report on American strength and posi-

tions obtained from a captured P-400 pilot shot down on 30 August. The prisoner revealed that about 5,000 marines, commanded by a major general, defended the airfield with thirteen tanks and fifteen planes. He also disclosed that three lines of barbed wire protected the east and that additional wire lined the airfield mainly to the east and north. The prisoner estimated that the caliber of the marine artillery was about three inches and was located north and south of the airstrip.[37]

With this intelligence in hand and time running short, Oka issued his attack order just before noon on 11 September. His hastily devised plan called for an attack at 2200 in conjunction with Kawaguchi's main assault on the 13th. While Kadomae's seamen attacked the coastal area, the 2d Battalion, 124th Infantry, thereafter called the Maizuru ("Dancing Crane") Battalion, would aim its assault at the Lunga River bridges near 35-Meter Height and the airfield. The 3d Battalion, 4th Infantry, would advance to a forward position using Colonel Wakiya's twenty remaining barges and assume a position behind the Maizuru Battalion as the "2nd Line Force." In a maneuver coinciding with the main assault, Wakiya's barges would arrive off Lunga Point on the night of 12 September in a conspicuous feint to distract the Americans and prevent their escape.[38]

8 The Gathering Storm

Edson's "Rest Area"

As events rapidly escalated toward the largest clash yet on Guadalcanal, debate on the allotment of scarce resources festered at the upper echelons in Hawaii and Washington, D.C. In accordance with an order from the Joint Chiefs of Staff, Adm. Chester W. Nimitz directed Vandegrift's boss, VAdm. Robert L. Ghormley, on 8 September to give General MacArthur one reinforced regiment of "experienced amphibious troops" along with the required shipping. Admiral Turner answered Ghormley the following day by stating, "The only experienced amphibious troops in SOPAC are those in Guadalcanal, and it is impracticable to withdraw them." Under the assumption that they had their eyes on the 7th Marines at Samoa, Turner stretched the truth by pointing out that the regiment was in no condition to execute an assault. (The regiment, however, was very prepared, having engaged in extensive training on the island during the last two months.) Not one to mince words, Turner then laid it on the line: "I respectfully invite attention to the present insecure position of Guadalcanal. . . .

Adequate air and naval strength have not been made available. . . . Vandegrift consistently has urged to be reinforced at once by at least one more regiment. . . . I concur."[1] Turner's message apparently forestalled this transfer to MacArthur, but it is evident that those in the upper echelons in Hawaii and Washington were ignorant of the precarious situation on Guadalcanal. The marines on the island would have only been eager to "respectfully" inform them.

Back on Guadalcanal on the morning of 10 September, Colonel Edson spoke with key officers of the battalion at his command post in a coconut grove near Kukum. He explained that they were moving to a "rest area" south of the airfield in an effort to get away from the bombing and shelling. Edson's Raiders found this explanation a bit odd, since they had found the breezy, sylvan glades along the beach quite restful compared to recent sites, including Tulagi. Following a breakfast of captured rice and dehydrated potatoes, the Raiders and Parachutists packed up their gear and trudged the short distance to the ridge, where Edson predicted the Japanese would attack. The arrival to their new home was delayed by a noontime air raid, but they arrived in time to set up camp before dark. The Raider bivouac was located in the jungle flat between the ridge and the Lunga River. The battalion enjoyed a hot meal and settled in for a relatively peaceful night. The peace would not last.[2]

The dominant terrain feature in Edson's rest area was the ridge. It was slender, winding, and grass-covered, with three distinct hillocks—one on both ends and one in the middle. At 123 feet above sea level, the hill in the middle—appropriately called Hill 123—was the highest. This hill overlooked Henderson Field and dominated the rest of the ridge to the north and south as well as the surrounding jungle. About 600 yards south rose the second highest hillock, Hill 80. There the ridge sloped off sharply into the thick jungle to the west, south, and east. Commanding the approach to and from the airfield was the northernmost hillock. It was approximately sixty feet high and, unlike the other two hills, had no designation.[3]

Aside from the ridge, two other terrain features in the area were important. The first was a narrow dirt trail, which ran along the entire length of the ridge. Easily identifiable, this footpath served as a convenient marker and would serve as a reference point for the marines during battle. The second terrain feature was a deep, impassable lagoon, which stood between the ridge and the Lunga River in the jungle flat. This stagnant body of water, about sixty feet wide and several hundred feet long, was located about 200 yards west of Hill 80. The lagoon would hamper movement and break the continuity of any defensive dispositions in the area.[4]

On the morning of the 11th, the approximately 840 Raider and Parachute effectives[5] received a rude awakening, as Red Mike Edson rapidly deployed them in and around the ridge. Suddenly, their rest area became a front-line battle position. Using the trail on the ridge as a boundary, Edson deployed the Parachutists on the left (east) and the Raiders on the right (west). On the Parachute Battalion's front, Edson placed the approximately ninety men of Capt. William McKennan's Company A. The company's right was anchored on Hill 80 with its front extending down the slope and into the jungle east and northeast about 600 yards. Captain Dick Johnson's Company C—about only thirty Parachutists strong—manned part of Edson's reserve line about 300 yards to the rear of McKennan's company. Backing up Johnson's company a short distance to the rear in a wooded draw were the approximately seventy-five Parachutists of Company B, led by Capt. Justin Duryea. The Parachute Battalion Headquarters Company was located in the draw east of Hill 123 near Company B. Edson screened his open left flank with patrols by dispatching several patrols into the tangled jungle to the south.[6]

The length of the Raider Battalion's front stretched 900 yards from the Lunga River to Hill 80. On the right of this front, Edson placed the Raiders of Company C, reinforced with a machine gun platoon from Company E, a total of about 130 men. Company C's right flank was anchored on the east bank of the Lunga River and extended to the western edge of the lagoon. A swamp, however, isolated a platoon on the left, further weakening the Raider company's position. To the left of Company C, Edson disposed the 130 men of Major Nickerson's Company B, with a machine gun platoon from Company E attached. Company B's left tied in with Company A Parachutists on Hill 80 and extended down into the jungle with its right flank against the lagoon. Edson added the 150 Raiders of Captain Antonelli's Company A to Edson's reserve line on a spur about 300 yards to the rear of Nickerson's company. Company A's left tied in with the Parachutists of Company C and extended a short distance into the jungle. Edson placed his command post, the approximately thirty-five men of Company D (Edson used this company as a replacement pool), and the 60mm mortars of Company E about 100 yards behind Company A.[7]

Given the complexities of the terrain, Edson deployed his companies brilliantly. Placing them on just the ridge would have left his flanks wide open for the Japanese to envelop. On the other hand, placing his companies on the front only would have left his position untenable, with an enemy penetration at any point. Edson's compromise of placing his troops on both the ridge and in the jungle was not foolproof, but, considering the terrain and the strength of his mongrel battalion, it was the best deployment possible under the circumstances.

The rest of the division's defensive scheme suffered obvious weaknesses. With Vandegrift unwilling to reorient the division's defensive scheme, a series of "strong points" using the support battalions of the division were maintained instead. On the right flank of the Raiders' position, the 1st Pioneer Battalion sat on both sides of the Lunga. The 1st Engineer Battalion manned a position to the left rear of the Raider-Parachute Battalion to provide some protection in case of an enemy breakthrough in the thick jungle east of the ridge. Another gap in the defenses existed between the Lunga westward to the sea. To afford some protection there, the 1st Amphibious Tractor Battalion sat perched on a ridge that the Japanese called Kuma ("Bear") Height in the middle of this gap. Vandegrift's official after-action report confessed, "These measures were not altogether promising," and he was right. Vandegrift was really pressing his luck against an enemy known for its ability to infiltrate.[8]

As the Raiders and "Chutes" worked at improving their new positions on and around the ridge, air raid sirens began wailing about noon. Looking up, they saw twenty-seven Bettys and fifteen Zeros approaching in the typical shallow V formation. This sight failed to alarm, since a good mile separated them from the airfield, the usual target. But this time the Japanese dropped some bombs and "daisy cutters" on the ridge and the surrounding area. The marines on the ground, however, took some solace in watching one Betty and one Zero fall during the raid. Lieutenant Colonel Griffith overheard one Raider corporal sarcastically and profanely complaining about the division's so-called rest area.[9]

One unit on the receiving end of this bombing was a Company A detachment of twenty-five Raiders on patrol south of Company C's position. The mission of this detachment, led by Platoon Sgt. Joe Buntin, was to determine the size and location of the Japanese force that Edson expected. The patrol was pushing south in the thick jungle along the east bank of the Lunga River, where it ran into a Japanese patrol about 1130. The firefight was beginning to taper off when the Japanese bombers droned overhead. Buntin's patrol was shocked to hear explosions as sticks of bombs fell downward from the Japanese bombers, peppering the ridge, the jungle flat behind them, and the area where the two patrols were fighting. No one in Buntin's patrol was hurt, though many were shaken by the experience. The bombing also ended the firefight. When Buntin's patrol later returned to their bivouac, they were greeted "by a scene of destruction," as one Raider described it. Japanese bombs demolished the bivouac, killing two Raiders and wounding several others. The returning patrol was also disappointed to find that bombs had destroyed their tents and lean-tos and ruined their galley.[10]

On the afternoon of 10 September, General Vandegrift simultaneously closed down his old command post by the airfield and opened his new one on the ridge. It was nestled on a heavily wooded L-shaped spur on the northeast side of the ridge. With the jungle encroaching on three sides, the staff complained about the cramped working conditions. The engineers made the location somewhat comfortable for the general by erecting a small-screened shack with two small bedrooms and a large working area. Adjacent to the general's quarters was the operations tent, covered with an old Japanese tarpaulin and set up with phones and maps. With the exception of Vandegrift, everyone hated the new spot, including Lieutenant Colonel Twining, who ruefully called the new locale "Robbers' Roost."[11]

During that same afternoon, Gerald Thomas gave Merrill Twining a ride in his jeep to the new command post. Thomas had just returned from a visit to the Pagoda, where he was given an "unofficial" copy of a top-secret letter flown in on the daily flight from Nouméa. Thomas handed Twining the letter. In it, Ghormley provided Nimitz with a bleak estimate of the situation—the Japanese were gathering strong naval, air, and amphibious forces at Rabaul and Truk for a major effort to retake Guadalcanal. The Japanese offensive was expected anywhere between ten days and three weeks. Ghormley said he lacked sufficient forces to stop it, identifying shortages in carriers, cruisers, destroyer transports, and cargo ships. He concluded with a veiled statement questioning whether he could support Vandegrift. Twining was shocked as much as Thomas by Ghormley's letter.[12]

The source of Ghormley's intelligence on the Japanese buildup apparently came from ULTRA. Indeed, American radio intelligence experts in Hawaii and Washington detected clear and unmistakable signs that a major Japanese attempt to retake Henderson Field was in the making. This attempt, however, would come much sooner than Ghormley had anticipated. On 10 September, Admiral Nimitz warned that the Japanese carrier "*Shokaku* may be preparing for operations with part [of] Desron Three and 17th Army against probably Guadalcanal." What made this warning more ominous was the fact that Nimitz had already deduced through ULTRA that the Japanese were sending troop reinforcements from the Philippines to Rabaul. In the CINCPAC ULTRA Bulletin for 12 September, Nimitz said that the Japanese were contemplating an early attack in the Guadalcanal area, and that they may attempt to recapture the airfield using paratroopers. This conclusion was based on two Japanese messages that were deciphered on the 11th. One message instructed Kawaguchi to display two signal flares, fifteen meters apart, to reconnaissance planes overhead. These signals were to be displayed for the first ten minutes of each hour from 2300 to 0400 once the field was recaptured. In the event that the Americans still held the airfield, Kawaguchi was ordered to display flaming torches to indicate that planes could not land on the field. Another message from Eighth Fleet on the 10th instructed Captain

Kadomae to transmit continuous radio signals when the airfield was in friendly hands.[13]

12 September: Frustration and Disappointment

The 12th of September began just like any other day for the Americans on Cactus. "Like a slender white line of cloud across the blue sky," twenty-five Betty bombers and fifteen Zeros appeared over Lunga Point just in time for lunch. Their bombs demolished Vandegrift's main radio station, cooked off some gasoline, and destroyed a trio of SBDs on the ground. A few bombs also landed on the ridge, wounding several Raiders. The good visibility offered the antiaircraft gunners an opportunity to blast two Betty's out of the sky. Ironically, a bomb from one of the disintegrating bombers landed in the midst of the 1st Battalion, 124th Infantry, killing one Japanese soldier and wounding four. In a spectacular aerial display, American fighters retaliated by shooting down an additional four bombers and one Zero, and the marines on the ground took great delight, whooping it up as if they were at a football game.[14]

On the 12th, Admiral Turner and a small entourage flew in to Guadalcanal from Espíritu Santo to get a firsthand look at the situation. Vandegrift whisked Turner away to his new command post, where the admiral broke out a bottle or two of scotch. Informally, they discussed Ghormley's message to Nimitz (a copy of which Turner brought with him) and the deployment of the 7th Marines. The good news was that Vandegrift was finally going to get the services of this regiment; the bad news was that Turner wanted to disperse the regiment in small parcels around the island to prevent the Japanese from landing additional reinforcements. The admiral's strategy was flawed, however, in that powerful Japanese detachments were already on the island and could easily wipe out these isolated pockets. Vandegrift urged Turner to land the regiment in the perimeter, but the matter remained unresolved until the next day.[15]

Meanwhile, the Raiders and Parachutists spent the 11th and 12th digging in, cleaning weapons, and sharpening bayonets and knifes. There was no time for rest. The effort to dig foxholes in the hard, coral ridge was particularly difficult, considering the men's weakened physical state and the direct exposure to the sun. Some succumbed to heat stroke. Lacking picks and shovels, they managed to scratch just shallow depressions in the topsoil and coral. Digging in the soil in the jungle flats was easier, but still difficult in the suffocating heat and humidity. Using bayonets, firing lanes were cleared, and along Company C Raiders' front, they strung double apron wire to form a barrier, albeit a weak one, against enemy attacks.[16]

Supervising the work on Company C Raiders' position was Maj. Kenneth Bailey, who just flew in from Nouméa after recuperating from wounds suffered on Tulagi. Bailey was an aggressive, bright, and enthusiastic officer, adored by nearly all. Edson was elated by the return of this fine officer. The battalion, however, greeted his return with extra enthusiasm when it was learned that he brought along bags of mail that had piled up in Nouméa. This was the battalion's first mail call since they landed in the Solomons. Although the Raiders had little time to read letters and to sample goodies sent from home, the fact they had any mail at all made spirits soar. This boost in morale, however, was dampened by small clashes with enemy patrols to the south. The Raiders were tense as they made last-minute improvements to their positions. They knew the Japanese were coming.[17]

As Edson's men prepared their positions, Kawaguchi and the men of his Central Body, numbering approximately 3,000, were endeavoring to reach their predesignated assembly areas. Kawaguchi wanted all of the battalions at their assembly areas by 1400, but the jungle was not cooperating. Shortly after dawn, Kawaguchi spoke with Major Kokusho. "We are terribly behind schedule," Kawaguchi said after wiping sweat from his brow. "Do you think we can reach our attack positions by [1400]?" Since Kokusho had the farthest to travel, Kawaguchi felt that if Kokusho could make it, so could the other battalions. Kokusho thought about it for a few moments and replied, "We should be able to make it. At least we will try." Kawaguchi was tempted to postpone the attack by one day. But with the difficulties of communicating with his five battalions and artillery in the jungle, Kawaguchi decided to go forward with the attack.[18]

The prospects for Japanese success brightened that morning when a captured American flyer disclosed that the southern flank was the weakest portion of the marine perimeter—precisely where Kawaguchi planned on striking. He also revealed that American aircraft would be unable to detect them underneath the jungle canopy. Kawaguchi distributed this encouraging news to his commanders and told them that he was convinced that the attack would be successful. At

1225, the Kuma Battalion reported it would attack that night. Likewise, the artillery unit reported that, although it had just repulsed about 400 marines on the coastal road, it would be ready for the assault. But not all of the news was encouraging. Colonel Oka revealed that only two companies would participate in that evening's assault and that Colonel Wakiya's barges were incapacitated and would not be able to transport the 3d Battalion, 4th Infantry, in time to join the attack.[19]

As the day progressed, it became apparent to Kawaguchi and his commanders that they were far behind schedule. Indeed, all of the battalions reached their assembly areas late. The 1st Battalion, 124th Infantry, arrived at 1800, four hours before the scheduled attack time of 2200. The other two battalions, the 3d Battalion, 124th Infantry, and the 2d Battalion, 4th Infantry, reached their assembly areas at 2200 and 2300, respectively. Even worse, when the latter two battalions advanced, they lost their sense of direction in the moonless night and drifted off course. Leaving behind its artillery to quicken its pace, the 3d Battalion, 124th Infantry, errantly angled northwest between the ridge and the Lunga River, while the 2d Battalion, 4th Infantry, groping in the darkness, got lost entirely and did not participate in this night's fighting. Major Kokusho, commander of the 1st Battalion, 124th Infantry, found the advance extremely difficult in the rugged jungle. As a result, at dusk he, too, decided to leave his artillery behind and advance north along the Lunga River, wading in rapid, waist-high waters. Kokusho's 2d Company took the lead followed by the 1st, 4th,

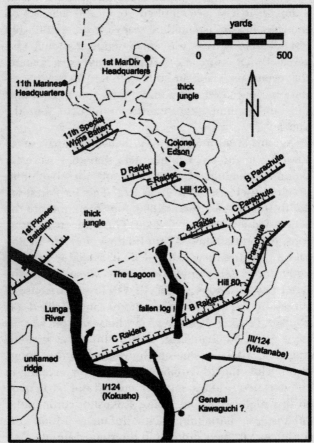

Bloody Ridge, Night of 12-13 September

3d, and Headquarters Companies, in that order.[20]

As darkness fell on the island on 12 September, tension levels rose as exhausted marines standing watch expected the Japanese to strike at any moment. The creatures of the night did little to alleviate the tension as they rustled in the bushes and vegetation. Private John W. Mielke, a Company E machine-gunner attached to Company C Raiders, was in his foxhole near the Lunga River when a large iguana scampered over to inspect his foxhole. Mielke could not bear the thought that the reptile would rustle in the bushes all night, so he scared it off with the tip of his bayonet. Soon, Mielke and other marine sentries along Company C's front heard talking, thrashing, and other strange noises in the distance and they were not iguanas.[21]

Colonel Edson was convinced that a major attack was imminent. Clashes with Japanese patrols and sightings by Clemens's native scouts made it evident that a major Japanese force was coiled to his front. In order to knock this enemy force off balance, Edson decided to conduct a reconnaissance-in-force the next morning with the entire battalion. In preparation for this operation, Edson gathered his commanders at his command post early in the evening. Edson's plan was simple. He would hit Kawaguchi's legions hard, with the Raiders of Company A taking the lead. The operation would never get off the ground, however, because the Japanese had plans of their own this night.[22]

As Edson's meeting broke up at about 2115, the Raiders and Parachutists heard Louie the Louse buzzing overhead and saw a falling flare, casting an eerie glow on the ground. Fifteen minutes later the cruiser *Sendai* and three destroyers unlimbered their guns on the perimeter, but most of the shells soared over the ridge and exploded harmlessly in the distance. Five shells, however, did land in the Raider command post area, but only one exploded. Twenty minutes later, the four warships stopped shelling, but they remained on-station off Lunga Point as part of their mission to prevent the Americans from escaping out to sea.[23]

Thereafter, the sporadic firing grew in intensity, as Japanese soldiers and U.S. marines tossed grenades and exchanged rifle, machine gun, and mortar fire. At 2200, Captain Nakaoka's artillery unit then added their six 75mm guns to the medley of battle. This shelling, which lasted thirty minutes, was largely ineffective, though shrapnel killed three pilots. Nakaoka's bombardment could have been useful, but Kawaguchi chose a bad time to commence it. Indeed, the Americans mistakenly believed that it was a resumption or a continuation of the flailing they had received only minutes before from the *Sendai* and her consorts. For Kawaguchi, this was unfortunate, because Nakaoka's shelling could have been perceived as an attack from that quarter, and, hence, could have worked as an excellent diversion for his main attack.[24]

Coinciding with the Japanese artillery bombardment, scattered pockets of Kawaguchi's legions roamed the jungle like ghosts and began skirmishing with the Americans. From where Edson stood on the ridge facing south, the Japanese were trading blows with the Raiders of Company C on the right flank near the Lunga River. After having successfully cut through the barbed wire in front of Bailey's com-

pany, the Japanese hit the seam between the two platoons on the left. Repeated attacks and the threat of
encirclement forced part of the left platoon, led by
Capt. John Salmon, to withdraw across the lagoon
over a fallen tree in order to join up with Company B
to the east. This attack, the handiwork of Kokusho's
1st Battalion, 124th Infantry, not only succeeded in
puncturing Company C's line, but also forced the
right-flank platoon of Company B to refuse its flank
to the Japanese.[25]

The survivors of Captain Salmon's platoon were rattled by the viciousness of the Japanese attack and
some men were cut down during the withdrawal. Near
midnight, Captain Sweeney, leader of a Company B
platoon on Hill 80, was surprised to see Captain
Salmon leading a handful of survivors through the
wire. Salmon was as gifted as any young officer in the
battalion, but Sweeney this night found him to be "visibly shaken, in bad shape, and deeply concerned about
several of his men who had been cut off during the
withdrawal."[26]

The 2d Platoon, manning the center of Charlie
Company's line, also suffered at the hands of the
Japanese that night. Private First Class Martin Heitz's
machine gun crew emptied hundreds of rounds into
the attackers, leaving several Japanese screaming and
moaning. But the numerous attackers overran the
machine gun position and the rest of the platoon,
leaving the platoon's position problematic. Like
Salmon's platoon, the 2d Platoon was ordered to move
out across the lagoon by crossing the log bridge.
Under normal circumstances, crossing the slippery
tree would be no easy accomplishment in the dark,

but the task was now much harder with the Japanese infiltrating the area.[27]

Platoon Sergeant Joseph Rushton ordered his squad to the ground to avoid the overwhelming numbers of Japanese around the lagoon. Some of the Japanese took ghoulish delight in chopping and hacking Raider survivors with bayonets and swords. "In sheer terror," Rushton remained frozen on the ground. An ememy soldier stepped on Rushton's leg, cautiously stepped back, nudged him with his foot, and called for help. Rushton then heard the unmistakable and terrifying sound of a sword being drawn from its scabbard. Rushton heard enough. While jumping to his knees in an attempt to shoot his BAR, a Japanese soldier riddled Rushton first with his shoulder-slung Nambu. Hit in the arm and leg, Rushton rolled on the ground once and emptied his BAR into the surrounding Japanese. Rushton, in excruciating pain and bleeding badly, dodged clusters of Japanese and somehow later fought off another trio of Japanese before crawling up the ridge after the dawn where he received treatment.[28]

In the meantime, parties of Japanese from Kokusho's battalion swam the Lunga in what the Raiders thought was an effort to envelop Company C's right flank. This startling development, coupled with the earlier withdrawal of the two Company C platoons to the left, made the right flank platoon's position untenable. Consequently the right flank platoon was also forced to fall back. But some Raiders failed either to receive the order or were cut off by the enemy. Platoon Sergeant Lawrence A. Harrison was in one such group. Harrison directed deadly volleys of machine gun fire at the onrushing Japanese, staving off a potential breakthrough. Another unit left behind was a Company E machine gun section near the Lunga. Soon after the beginning of the attack, the leader of this machine gun section, Sgt. Warren Morse, fired his machine gun incessantly into a large group of Japanese that walked right up to the muzzle of his gun. The Japanese had apparently believed that the firing lane Morse had so painstakingly prepared was a trail. Private First Class Mielke contributed to the carnage that Morse had created by throwing all the grenades he had at the Japanese.[29]

Morse's machine gun section was not assailed again this night, but it was still a night filled with terror and uncertainty. Sporadic rifle fire and screams of a Raider or two being tortured heightened tension levels that had already reached the breaking point for some. As dawn approached, Mielke heard some Japanese talking to their rear. The Raiders pulled their guns into a tighter circle in expectation of another attack, but it never came. Taking advantage of a lull in the action, Mielke turned to World War I veteran, Platoon Sgt. "Pappy" Holdren, and asked whether the blood baths of Belleau Wood or the Argonne Forest were as bad as this night. Pappy looked back at Mielke and ruefully answered, "No, this is the worst situation I've been in."[30]

Holdren would have gotten no arguments from other Raiders who fought this night. Corporal Robert Youngdeer, a member of Company E, 1st Raider Battalion, recalls the loneliness and terror that first night:

The night was pitch dark there in the jungle and had it not been for the few marine

buddies there with me I would have felt more
alone than ever. . . . When the naval bombardment ceased, I heard the splashing of many
people wading [in] the river coming toward
our positions. Then the Jap became verbal, as
fast as that. I could hear Japs behind us, they
were a noisy lot. [They probably] had to keep
some sort of contact there in the pitch black
jungle. I heard what must have been firecrackers popping as well as much firing of small
arms.[31]

Casualties suffered during this opening round
between Kawaguchi's legions and Edson's Raiders
were light. The total number of Japanese casualties is
unknown, but appear to have been greater than the
Raiders who reported one killed and eleven missing;
ten from Company C and two from Company E.
Although several American bodies were later recov-
ered, positive identification on the badly decomposed
corpses was impossible.[32]

Information on the Japanese attack is sparse and
sketchy. Although details are lacking, without a doubt
Major Kokusho's 1st Battalion, 124th Infantry,
attacked the Raiders that night. In order to avoid the
tangled jungle, at dusk, the battalion began the march
in the Lunga River and waded north toward the American line. The 2d Company led the march followed by
the 1st, 4th, Headquarters, the 3d Companies, in that
order. After advancing two kilometers, Kokusho's
patrols encountered Company C's front line and
"received heavy hostile gunfire." About this time 1st
Lt. Shoutarou Manuo's 1st Company and 1st Lt. Kazuo

Yamaguchi's 4th entered the jungle, groped their way north toward the sound of battle, and hit Charlie Company's line. Although the battalion reserve, 1st Lt. Matsumoto's 3d Company, did not participate in the fighting that night, 1st Lt. Meitaro Matsuyama's 2d Company attacked the Raiders near the Lunga River. This is the unit that undoubtedly slithered around the right flank platoon of Company C to infiltrate the rear.[33]

The official Japanese history records that later in the battle, presumably after midnight, Kokusho's battalion became entangled with Colonel Watanabe's 3d Battalion, 124 Infantry, in the thick jungle. This effectively shut down Kokusho's attack. In an effort to separate the two battalions, and thus halt any confusion, Kokusho ordered his troops to the opposite bank of the Lunga. But by the time this aggravating task was complete it was nearly dawn—too late to resume the night attack.[34]

Watanabe's battalion reached the wire fronting Company C's line about 0100, but his troops apparently made little headway after mixing with Kokusho's battalion. At first light on the 13th, Watanabe's men came under heavy shellfire, killing First Lieutenants Takahumi Kojima and Kozo Hotta, commanders of the 9th and 11th Companies respectively. The official history also records that Watanabe's battalion continued the attack on the American right flank until 1400.[35]

General Kawaguchi's command group floundered in the darkness and the thick jungle as well. The general aimed his command group at 15-Meter Height north of the airfield. But he found that the terrain was too difficult to advance through and ordered his command group to the Lunga, where they waded north. The darkness seemed to swallow his command group. When he looked around, he saw only seven or eight men, and he began to wonder if he had gone too far ahead of the rest of the detachment. Later, when it became impossible to advance because of the depth and flow rate, Kawaguchi, who was soaked from the chest down, crawled out of the water on the east bank at daybreak. Although Kawaguchi began the night confidently, he was now boiling over with anger and exasperation. He later complained "Due to the devilish jungle, the brigade was scattered all over and was completely beyond control. In my whole life I have never felt so disappointed and helpless."[36]

The fortune of Kawaguchi's two wing units was no better. After using the last of their fuel to cook their dwindling ration of rice, the men of the Kuma Battalion started their advance at 2000. They made little progress in the pitch-black jungle, however, and were unable to contact the marines by 2200. During the night, they heard the sounds of battle to the west, but they were unable to attack any U.S. position. At dawn, the soldiers had discovered that their attack had failed to take place, because their assembly area was much farther east than they believed. At daybreak, they were still about three miles southeast from the mouth of the Ilu River.[37]

Oka's Left Wing Unit, the Maizuru Battalion, now led by 1st Lt. Kuniyoshi Yoshida, floundered as well. Yoshida planned on leaving Kadomae's headquarters on the Matanikau at sunset on the 11th, but for some unknown reason he failed to do so. Oka's command group, composed of his regimental headquarters, the regimental machine gun company, the Maizuru Battalion light mortar unit, signal troops, and a part of Kadomae's Naval Guard Unit, however, had made excellent progress. By dawn on the 13th, Oka had advanced to the jungle on the southwestern side of Shishi ("Lion") Height, a mile west of the Lunga River. Although Oka had reached an advanced position, he was still too far south to stage any type of attack or diversion.[38]

"There Will Be No Surrender of This Place"

At dawn on 13 September, the Japanese south of the ridge were subjected to an unpleasant reveille as American cannon and machine gun fire from strafing P-400s and F4Fs came raining down on them. Marine artillery and mortars added their voices to the chorus as the Japanese scurried to obtain whatever cover was available. Flying bullets and shrapnel inflicted casualties upon the Japanese. This fire also destroyed Kawaguchi's short-wave radio, eliminating his only way of communicating directly with Rabaul. Kawaguchi still had his brigade radio, but to reach Rabaul required radio relay through the Imperial Navy. At 0550, Kawaguchi decided to regroup his forces for another attack the next night.[39]

Later that morning Red Mike called on his company commanders for a meeting during breakfast. "They were testing, just testing," Edson said. "They'll be back. But maybe not as many of them. Or maybe more. I want all positions improved, all wire lines paralleled, a hot meal for the men. Today, dig, wire up tight, get some sleep. We'll all need it." But Edson had three companies do more than just sleep this morning. He ordered the Raiders of Companies A and D forward on the right flank to retake the ground lost during the night. The Japanese, however, repulsed this effort. Another attempt by the Parachutists of Company A to sweep the area south in front of the left flank also failed this day to a platoon of dug-in Japanese armed with three Nambus.[40]

At Rabaul, Seventeenth Army Headquarters waited anxiously for reports from Kawaguchi on the progress of the attack, but none were forthcoming. Even the Imperial Navy units on the island remained silent. One Japanese radio monitoring station intercepted S-O-S signals from two U.S. planes asking for position fixes. Seventeenth Army interpreted the distress signals as a sure sign of Kawaguchi's attack. American code transmissions stopped near dawn but resumed at 0700, prompting headquarters to believe this was a sign of Kawaguchi's failure. On the other hand, confirmation, or what they believed was confirmation for Kawaguchi's success, came early in the morning, when a Japanese pilot reported seeing two fires fifty meters apart—the prearranged signal of success. The Japanese dispatched two reconnaissance planes escorted by nine Zeros to confirm the report. The flight was greeted by an overwhelming number of F4Fs—twenty-eight to be exact. That should have been all the confirmation they needed, but the Japanese persisted throughout the day in reporting that Kawaguchi held the airfield.[41]

At Colonel Cates's command post in the morning, Admiral Turner spoke with Vandegrift and Colonel

Thomas concerning the deployment of the 7th Marines. The admiral asked, "Now, where do you want the 7th Marines to land?" Thomas answered, "Admiral, you see that beach 300 yards away over there? That's where we want them landed, right in this perimeter." Turner responded, "Well, that's settled. I'll be here in the morning of 17 September."[42]

Admiral Turner departed in the afternoon. Shortly after he left, Colonel Thomas entered the operations tent visibly upset. From his shirt pocket he unfolded an "eyes only" handwritten note from Ghormley to Vandegrift and handed it to Twining. It had apparently been given to Vandegrift just before Turner left. Like his official message to Nimitz, Ghormley summarized his heavy losses and stated that he was no longer able to support Guadalcanal—the marines were on their own. Ghormley gave Vandegrift authorization to make whatever arrangements were necessary. For Vandegrift, this meant only one thing—surrender. Vandegrift soon entered the tent in the same state of mind as Thomas. Not noticing Twining in the dim light, he forcefully told Thomas, "As long as I am here there will be no surrender of this place. We will continue as we are. Tell Bill Twining to prepare a plan of withdrawal up the Lunga using our amphibian tractors if it becomes necessary." Twining recalls this as the only occasion during the campaign that Vandegrift used the word "surrender."[43]

Vandegrift also met with General Geiger that afternoon. The two discussed the precarious situation in which they found themselves. At the end of their meeting, Vandegrift said, "Roy, if the time comes when we may lose control of the airfield, I want you to gas

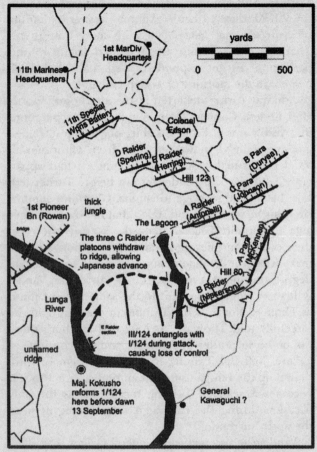

Bloody Ridge, Japanese Advance, Night of 12-13 September

up your planes and fly them out." Gazing at his old friend with seriousness and determination, Geiger replied, "All right, Archer, I'll fly the planes out, but I'm staying here with you."[44]

Meanwhile, back at the ridge, illnesses forced Edson to make some necessary leadership changes in the Raiders. Major Nickerson, the commander of Company B, was suffering from bleeding ulcers, and his executive officer, Capt. Louis Monville, succumbed to a sunstroke. Both required evacuating. As Nickerson's replacement, Edson chose Capt. John Sweeney, an excellent officer and 1941 graduate of Officer Candidate School. But Edson had to make other changes in the company as well. The leader of the 2d Platoon, Capt. Rex Crockett, was in the division hospital with a severe case of dysentery. Crockett's platoon was taken over by Gunnery Sgt. Clinton Haines, while charge of Sweeney's old unit, the 1st Platoon, passed to Platoon Sgt. Robert Aneilski. These changes due to illnesses were indicative of what was taking place in all the marine units on Guadalcanal.[45]

Red Mike also decided to make a major change in the disposition of his battalion after the failed attempt at restoring the right flank. He chose to pull his front back about 400 yards. This new front, which was only some 150 yards south of Hill 123, offered better terrain from which to defend, especially on the ridge. Now, if the Japanese appeared over Hill 80 to attack the marines on the ridge, they would be forced to advance some 400 yards over clear terrain. Bolstered by elements from other commands, Edson's new front stretched a length of about 1,800 yards. From left to right, Company B Parachutists, Company B Raiders,

Company D 1st Engineer Battalion, and Company A Raiders manned the realigned front. To the rear of Company A, on both banks of the Lunga, stood elements of the 1st Pioneer Battalion.[46]

The new position on the ridge was anchored on two small spurs that jutted out from the main axis of the ridge to the east and west. Captain Duryea's Company B Parachutists defended the spur on the east side, and part of Captain Sweeney's Company B Raiders defended the spur on the west. Sweeney's position would prove critical in the next attack. From the ridge trail on the left to the end of the spur was the understrength 3d Platoon (fewer than twenty men) bolstered by a machine gun section. Manning the middle of Sweeney's line was his old unit, the 1st Platoon. That platoon's line stretched from the spur on the left to a point about 200 yards west of the ridge near the northern tip of the lagoon. Sweeney positioned the 2d Platoon on his extreme right between the 1st Platoon and the Engineer Company.[47]

Red Mike's reserve was composed of four companies of varying strength, positioned a short distance to the rear. On the left, in echelon behind Company B Parachutists sat Company C Parachutists in a draw between Hills 80 and 123 about fifty yards east of the road. Behind Company C, Edson disposed Company A Parachutists about 100 yards east of the trail. On the right, Edson placed the Raiders of Company C, and the remaining elements of Company E, on the crest of Hill 123. The Raiders of Company D were planted a short distance northwest of Hill 123. Edson's command post took up position northwest of Hill 123, about forty yards from the trail. Major Charles Miller, temporarily in command of the 1st Parachute Battalion, set up the battalion command post fifty yards southeast of Edson's.[48]

Although the new positions offered better terrain from which to defend, they presented some new problems. Having no time to string telephone wire to the new positions, the only form of communication Edson had with his companies was the walkie-talkie, which was unreliable in the thick jungle. Fortunately, the units on the ridge would be free of this problem because they were on open terrain. But communicating with those units on the right flank in the jungle would be difficult if not impossible. In order to solve this dilemma, a serious command and control problem, Edson placed his executive officer, the redheaded Lt. Col. Samuel B. Griffith, in charge of the right flank. But Edson had other concerns as well. The Raiders and Parachutists lacked sufficient time to prepare adequate fortifications, and there was no barbed wire, the battalion having used it all in the previous positions. Ammunition was also low. Besides his Springfield, BAR, or Reising, each marine had only one or two hand grenades.[49]

As the Raiders and Parachutists realigned their defenses, Colonel Twining took a stroll over to Edson's command post to assess the situation. Edson, he believed, was in fair shape, but the Raiders and Parachutists appeared utterly exhausted, a state made evident by their mumbling, stumbling, glassy-eyed appearance. Alarmed at their condition, Twining returned to the division command post and urgently recommended that the division reserve, the 2d Battalion, 5th Marines, temporarily commanded by Col.

William J. Whaling, be moved up to replace the Raider-Parachute Battalion. Vandegrift gave the order immediately, but the battalion was unable to cross the airstrip until dark because of continuous air operations. Instead, the battalion was placed in a reserve position to the rear of Edson's mongrel battalion south of the airfield.[50]

Meanwhile, a battery of 105mm howitzers of Lt. Col. Eugene Price's 5th Battalion, 11th Marines, moved to a position from which it could render close support to the ridge. An observer was posted about 150 yards south of Hill 123 at a front-line observation post. Telephone communications were established between Price and Edson's switchboards. A few shots were registered by the artillerymen on a hill south of the ridge in the early afternoon, but accurate plotting was impossible, because that particular area on the division's map was blocked by a cloud in the aerial mosaic. Kawaguchi was not the only one bedeviled by poor maps. In view of the mounting evidence of an attack on the 12th, one cannot help but wonder why this action did not take place a day earlier.[51]

Stepping onto an empty grenade box, Edson addressed the Raiders of Company C late in the afternoon: "You men have done a great job, and I have just one more thing to ask of you. Hold out just one more night. I know we've been without sleep a long time. But we expect another attack from them tonight and they may come through here. I have every reason to believe that we will have reliefs here for all of us in the morning." For these men who endured hunger, thirst, exhaustion, and a lack of sleep, Edson's speech raised their spirits and gave them renewed courage. With the exception of their weapons, courage was about all they had.[52]

Although General Kawaguchi possessed little information on the whereabouts of his three battalions and the enemy's defenses, he issued an attack order shortly before noon. The general said that the assault would take place at 2200 in accordance with the 7 September attack order. In addition, he told the 1st Battalion, 124th Infantry, to use its artillery to destroy the American lighting equipment near the airstrip. He also directed the artillery unit to shift its position to the southwest to fire on enemy tanks, in the event they appeared on the morning of the 14th. The unit was also told not to fire during the attack that night. Finally, the hospital unit was ordered south of the airfield to care for the wounded. At 1500, Major Kokusho assembled his company commanders. He aroused his men with an emotional speech, stating this was a difficult battle and that they must sacrifice their lives for the emperor and for their country.[53]

That afternoon at his temporary command post near Shishi Height, Colonel Oka radioed Kawaguchi, requesting that the attack be postponed until the night of the 14th. Oka believed the delay would give the 3d Battalion, 4th Infantry, sufficient time to join the attack. But Kawaguchi disagreed with the colonel, saying the attack had essentially been delayed a day already (the previous night's attack amounted to no more than a probe). Kawaguchi stated that the attack would take place at 2200 that night.[54]

At 1650, Colonel Oka received unexpected guests—Lieutenant Nakayama and his three men, the group that had been dispatched by Kawaguchi to relay important maps and orders for the attack. Nakayama and his men endured a grueling weeklong trek, traversing some of the worst terrain on the island. They fought hunger, thirst, and fatigue and fought off an angry native and his pack of vicious dogs with swords and bayonets. They were a pitiful sight with their deep cuts and torn and filthy uniforms. Nakayama barely had the strength to make his report to Oka before he and the others collapsed before the colonel's feet.[55]

Although Kawaguchi did not know it, the Kuma Battalion was also in position to launch its attack. Based on the results of a patrol, which located a machine gun emplacement in a grassy plain across the Tenaru River, Major Mizuno issued his plan of attack. They would cross the Tenaru River about two miles south of the river's mouth, cross a 500-to-600-yard-wide plain, and attack the machine gun emplacement in a surprise night attack. After smashing this position, they would push westward and seize the enemy airfield.[56]

9 Bloody Ridge

13 September

As the sun began to set on 13 September, Edson would have been alarmed if he knew the size of the Japanese force coiled to his front. Against his approximately 830 effectives stood a Japanese assault force comprised of three infantry battalions and support units, a force totaling about 3,000 troops. Military theorists have long regarded a three-to-one superiority requisite for success in an attack, and Kawaguchi had such a force. Kawaguchi's soldiers also brought with them a small assortment of light artillery and mortars. In addition to the six 70mm battalion guns and the large number of 50mm knee mortars organic to the three battalions, the Japanese had four Model 97 81mm trench mortars (weight 145 pounds, range 3,100 yards), a 75mm regimental gun, and two 37mm regimental antitank guns. More than offsetting this material support, however, were the twelve 105mm howitzers of the 5th Battalion, 11th Marines, to Edson's rear. Although it is true that only one battery was in position to support Edson, the others could be brought into action quickly if the need arose.

Shortly after nightfall on the 13th, the jungle in front of Gunnery Sergeant Haines's 2d Platoon, Company B of the Raiders, "seemed to come alive," as one marine recalled. "We could hear the jabbering of Japs and movements in the brush." Suddenly, hand grenades and rifle fire from the soldiers of Major Kokusho's 1st Battalion, 124th Infantry, pummeled the platoon. The sudden attack, probably from 1st Lt. Kazuo Yamaguchi's 4th Company, forced one Raider squad of the platoon, then the second, and then the third to fall back to Hill 123, where they remained the rest of the night. A simultaneous thrust also forced platoon Sergeant Aneilski's 1st Platoon back to Hill 123, where it also fought the remainder of the night. After these initial successes, Kokusho gathered his entire battalion in the area where the Raider platoons had been. This was a mistake, because the Japanese gathered there were subjected to what one Japanese officer called a "terrific" mortar and artillery barrage, causing the battalion to scatter like a frightened school of fish.[1]

After reorganizing the companies of his battalion, the sword-wielding Kokusho led his men forward, surging through the more than 300-yard gap that yawned before them on Edson's right flank. Kokusho was a bit too eager in the attack, for his headquarters company raced forward and lost contact with the rest of the battalion, which fanned out in the dense, swamp-laden jungle flat. The commander of the 3d Company, First Lieutenant Matsumoto, led a command section of ten men forward and captured a marine machine gun position following a tough fight and secured it with an attached machine gun platoon. Strangely enough, the Japanese did not molest the marines manning the main line of resistance to the right of the gap; Kokusho's soldiers kept their eyes fixated on their main objective, 15-Meter Height, north of the airfield.[2]

For Red Mike the gaping hole in his right flank was bad enough, but reports began filtering in of a squad of Japanese that had infiltrated into the draw between the Parachutists and the ridge between Hills 80 and 123. Edson warned Capt. Harry Torgerson, acting executive officer of the Parachute Battalion, of the infiltration. Major Charles Miller telephoned Torgerson and told him not to worry, as the Japanese would probably not attack this night. But Edson had little doubt in his mind that a major attack was in the making. At 2015, he notified all companies that he was moving his command post forward to Hill 123. Underscoring his concern of an all-out attack, Edson, about an hour later, ordered the Paratroopers of Company A up on Hill 123 to bolster the hill's defense.[3]

At 2045 the Parachutists reported seeing two white parachute flares, one about 1,500 yards south and the other to the east. This was reported to Edson, who immediately called for artillery support. A battery of 105mm howitzers answered the call by firing a barrage south of the ridge. When the artillery observer reported increased Japanese activity in the jungle about 200 yards from the front, the gunners laid a second barrage there about 2130. The artillery observer believed that this fire created some confusion among the Japanese gathering in the area. The enemy activity in the southern sector was all the evidence that Colonel Price, the commander of the 5th Battalion, 11th Marines, needed to shift his two remaining batteries from their firing positions pointed at the west to the ridge in the south. By 2200, the three batteries of 105mm howitzers were thundering in full support of Edson.[4]

The unfortunate unit on the receiving end of this fire was Major Tamura's 2d Battalion, 4th Infantry. The battalion had advanced to a position close to the ridge just before the shelling began. Just as the shells started raining down upon his men at 2200, Tamura ordered 1st Lt. Yoshimi Onodera's 5th Company and 1st Lt. Tetsuji Isibashi's 7th Company (each about 160 strong) to storm up the ridge's slopes to attack the Americans. After lofting red flares, they surged forward in waves, yelling, *"Totsugeki"* ("charge") and *"Banzai"* at the top of their lungs. Some Japanese buffeted the marines with grenades and mortar fire while their countrymen charged with fixed bayonets.[5]

In the path of this onslaught were Captain Duryea's Parachutists of Company B and the 3d Platoon of Company B Raiders. As the attack began, Duryea sent one platoon leader, Marine Gunner Bob Manning, back to near Hill 123 to fire a 60mm mortar barrage into the draw in front of Duryea's company. Manning fired about thirty-five rounds at the onrushing Japanese before the enemy responded with mortar fire of their own against Manning's position. Screened by smoke, the Japanese persistently attacked the Parachutists' front, and after unremitting hammer blows, Duryeas' company vacated its position on the ridge and reformed in the draw in the jungle on the left flank.[6]

The unauthorized withdrawal of the Parachutists left just the Raiders of Captain Sweeney's 3d Platoon of Company B on the ridge. By radio, Edson asked Sweeney the status of his position. A cultured voice

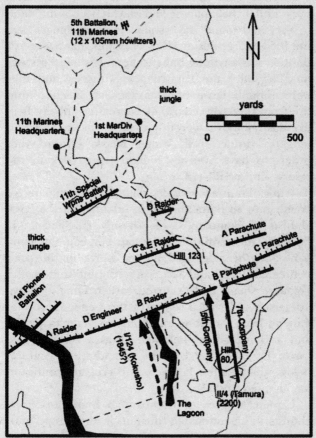

Bloody Ridge, Initial Attacks, Night of 13-14 September

speaking academic English answered, "My position is excellent, thank you." This was no marine. It was a trick. Either the Japanese had captured a marine radio or they had found the frequency or wavelength that the Raiders were using. It was obvious that Sweeney's position was anything but excellent. His left flank was dangling after the Paratroopers withdrew and they were under intense rifle, mortar, and machine gun fire from three directions. Moreover, friendly artillery fire was falling dangerously close. As a result, Edson sent his runner, Cpl. Walter Burak, forward with orders to have Sweeney pull his men back to the reserve line at Hill 123.[7]

While Tamura's soldiers charged, a company of Watanabe's 3d Battalion, 124th Infantry, hit the Parachutists of Company C on Edson's left. The crafty Japanese then infiltrated the gap between this company and the ridge and pushed north in the draw between Hills 80 and 123, where the infiltration of a Japanese squad had occurred earlier. On the ridge, Torgerson received a report of this penetration and, judging from the noise and muttering they made, he and another officer believed it was a company-size force. The two tossed several grenades at the group below, killing a few Japanese and creating confusion among their ranks.[8]

Captain Duryea of Company B found his Parachutists in an untenable situation in the jungle draw and requested instructions from Captain Torgerson. The Japanese had already attacked Duryea's front and left flank and were now enveloping his left rear. He, too, found the friendly artillery barrages falling dangerously near. Realizing that it would be impossible to employ this company and Company C in a counterattack against the Japanese, Captain Torgerson ordered the two companies to regroup behind Hill 123. Accordingly, the two companies scaled the ridge and began pulling back along the single trail atop the ridge with Company B Raiders.[9]

Withdrawing large bodies of troops at night in the confusion of battle is an extremely difficult maneuver. Even with well-rested men, it is no easy task. But Edson's Raider-Parachute Battalion had been on the go for days, with little or no sleep. In the process of pulling back these companies, the Japanese threw some grenades near Hill 123 and yelled "Gas Attack"! During the pandemonium of the moment, the word was passed around to withdraw as they reached the rear of Hill 123. Many marines began withdrawing to the north when Maj. Kenneth Bailey of the Raiders appeared kicking and shouting: "It's a trick! There's no gas." He then gave everyone within earshot a good tongue-lashing. Thus, Bailey's timely and commanding presence averted potential disaster for the marines that night.[10]

During the withdrawal, the forward artillery observer became lost. Naturally, this resulted in the loss of communication between the forward artillery observer and the three batteries of Colonel Price's battalion. Price asked Colonel Del Valle for firing instructions. Wanting to keep the Japanese under fire, Del Valle ordered him to continue to fire on the last concentrations requested until communication could be reestablished. In the meantime, Pfc. Tom Watson, a clerk in the battalion's headquarters battery, and Maj. Charles Nees, the 11th Marines assistant operations officer, volunteered to act as a forward observer and as an artillery liaison officer, respectively. About an hour later, the two were directing pinpoint artillery fire against the onrushing Japanese. Watson would earn a field commission for his actions that night.[11]

As Watson and Nees raced forward, Onodera's 5th Company and Isibashi's 7th Company began another attack, charging in the face of an almost continuous barrage of artillery, mortar shells, and grenades. The din of battle was deafening as they charged up the saddle between Hills 80 and 123. The determined attackers forced the Raiders and Parachutists back to Hill 123, where they formed the last line of resistance. Lieutenant Onodera ordered two platoons of his 5th Company to crawl forward in a lizardlike fashion using the terrain as cover. But the defensive fire from the marines on Hill 123 was too much, killing many, including both platoon leaders. Onodera then gathered his remaining men, including his reserve platoon, and continued the charge. When Lieutenant Onodera fell to enemy bullets, the company's attack slowly fizzled out. Major Tamura found the battle and terrain so confusing, American artillery observers were sometimes behind his attacking companies.[12]

Meanwhile, on Edson's right flank, Major Kokusho continued his headlong charge northward toward 15-Meter Height. The attack was interrupted when Kokusho and his men came upon a pile of American supplies and rations. Kokusho's famished soldiers gorged themselves on C- and K-rations. After taking a puff on an American cigarette, Kokusho ordered the advance to continue. Pointing to a battery of antiaircraft guns (probably of the 11th Marines Special

Weapons Company), he said, "I'm not going to let any of you get in front of me, understand?" Despite a murderous crossfire, the sword-waving Kokusho and a small group of soldiers and artillerymen armed only with bamboo spears seized one of the guns. But as Kokusho leaped onto another gun platform, a grenade exploded in his face and killed him.[13]

The rest of Kokusho's battalion also encountered fierce fire and suffered heavy casualties. First Lieutenant Meitaro Matsuyama's 2d Company broke through two marine lines and made some progress north in the thick jungle. American resistance stiffened, however, and at about 0300 Matsuyama's company came under heavy fire from a marine position. Sergeant Fumio Ota recalls the bloody fight with this unidentified position. "We attacked the American position, but Lieutenant Matsuyama and about 100 men of the company were killed." With the loss of its leader and so many men, the company's participation in the battle ended. Through a combination of casualties and disorientation in the unfamiliar terrain, the rest of the battalion failed to participate in any more meaningful fighting that night.[14]

About midnight, the distinctive hum of Louie the Louse's engine was heard overhead and parachute flares were seen falling at intervals all over the perimeter. Now, with ample illumination, seven Japanese destroyers of Destroyer Division 19 followed up with a bombardment of the Kukum area. The marines believed the bombardment came from a cruiser and two destroyers. At his operations dugout, General Vandegrift heard the guns firing offshore, and, as a precaution, he calmly asked air operations if it was possi-

ble to send a plane aloft to see if any Japanese transports were off Lunga Point.[15]

Back on the ridge, only three understrength companies, Company A Parachutists and Companies B and
C Raiders—perhaps 300 marines in all—defended Hill
123 in a horseshoe-shaped line. The Japanese, supported only by 50mm and 81mm mortars and their
strange, little 70mm battalion guns, stormed the
"horseshoe" with what the marines believed was amazing determination. Private Jim McCarson, a marine
Raider of Company C, thought it was the end. "There
were so many of them that came over the ridge compared to what we had strung out there," McCarson
recalled. "You could shoot two and there would be six
more." Many of the Japanese had to be hit up to eight
times before they were finally stopped. McCarson
believes that some of the Japanese were drugged
(opium was commonly found in Japanese packs) in
order to withstand that kind of fire. One Japanese soldier had been hit at least six times, but he still got up
to continue the attack. He also remembers one Japanese soldier who died within ten feet of him. The
enemy soldier had crawled up the marine position,
dragging his intestines behind him for several yards.[16]

By midnight, the marines had withstood two major
attacks on the ridge, but Edson had no time to rest on
his laurels. He had other problems with which to contend. Edson had no men in position to defend the
now wide-open left flank, and the possibility of being
enveloped there was a major concern. Unfortunately,
Major Miller, the commander of the Parachutists, was
no help. Even though Miller was in a nearby foxhole,
Edson, at this critical point, ordered Captain Torger-

son to launch a counterattack with Companies B and C Parachutists to reclaim the left flank. Forming a skirmish line using two platoons from each company, the Parachutists marched forward, encountering only slight resistance. Soon thereafter, they linked their right flank with the Parachutists of Company A.[17]

Private Irwin Reynolds, a member of the 2d Platoon, Company B Raiders, had taken a position on Hill 123 with the rest of his squad. Reynolds's squad helped stop three banzai attacks with grenades and rifle fire before being ordered to shift to an alternate position. As Private Reynolds was about to make this move, he slipped and fell down a steep incline into the jungle flat below. Unhurt, except in dignity, Reynolds and a few other Raiders were alarmed to discover that they were mingling with a large body of Japanese in the darkness. Although he could make out only their forms, he could smell the distinctive odor of the enemy. "I believe," Reynolds said, "the Japs knew we were among them, but they were as disorganized as we were and didn't want to start anything." He and the other leathernecks were able to climb back up the ridge to safety to rejoin the fight.[18]

Disorientation was common as both sides grappled in close-range combat in the darkness, illuminated sparingly by flares and explosions. Captain Houston "Tex" Stiff, commander of the Company E mortar platoon of the Raiders, discovered this when he headed for the front lines with a half-case of grenades. Unwittingly, Stiff walked through a thinly held section of the Raider line and into enemy territory before realizing his mistake. Stiff did not see any Japanese, but he remembers hearing plenty of them all around him.

Incredibly, Stiff returned safely to the Raider line (avoiding both enemy and friendly fire) to deliver the grenades without receiving a scratch.[19]

Private First Class William Barnes, a 60mm mortar-man in Captain Stiff's platoon, was in the thick of the battle for Hill 123. Having expended all of his mortar shells on the enemy at the peak of the battle, Barnes helped evacuate the wounded. While dropping off some of the wounded at an aid station in the rear, he discovered a small cache of mortar shells and hauled them up to his old position near Hill 123 in order to rejoin the fight. Barnes fired on enemy targets, once again exhausting his supply of shells in defense of the hill. Wanting to help bolster the defense's thinning ranks, he grabbed a rifle and joined in the close-range fight. Even though he suffered serious wounds in the battle, he stayed in the fight until the Japanese were vanquished.[20]

Although the marines on the ridge were outnumbered, the 105mm howitzers of the 5th Battalion, 11th Marines, greatly redressed the odds. The range of most of the firing was an incredible 1,600 to 2,000 yards, well below the previously set minimum of 2,800 yards. The fountains of dirt and flying shrapnel put up in the saddle by the 105s not only covered the marines' earlier withdrawal, but also mowed down many onrushing Japanese intent on taking Hill 123. At about 0200, a Japanese mortar barrage severed the wire providing telephone communications between the artillery observers and the artillery batteries. Needing to relay new firing orders, an artillery observer appeared at the operations dugout at division headquarters. "Drop it five zero and walk it back and forth [left and right] across the ridge," he said. With the batteries only a few hundred yards away, those in the dugout heard a battery officer barking orders "Load. Fire!" A few minutes later, Corporal Burak brought word from Edson that the range was perfect: "It's knocking the hell out of 'em." The 2d Battalion, 4th Infantry, and 1st Battalion, 124th Infantry, lost many men to artillery fire that night. One prisoner said his unit was *"zenmetsu"* ("annihilated") by the fire and estimated that only 10 percent of his company survived.[21]

During the battle the Japanese had nothing to compare with the 105mm howitzer. Their 70mm howitzers, firing at high trajectory angles, were hardly more effective than trench mortars in the dense jungle. But the Japanese did try to sweep the marines off Hill 123 with the only 75mm regimental gun they had at Bloody Ridge. During the night they hefted this field piece up Hill 80 in order to fire it at the marines in a direct-fire mode. Unfortunately for the Japanese, the gun had a short firing pin and was unable to shoot. This was confirmed in the morning, when the marines found thirty to forty unexpended shells lying around the faulty gun. Each 75mm shell had a small dent in the primer. It is quite possible that this gun could have turned the tide in favor of the Japanese. One can easily imagine the frustration and aggravation of the Japanese gunners as they rammed shell after shell home, hoping it would fire.[22]

In the meantime, the Japanese again struck Edson's left flank, where Captain Torgerson had redeployed his Paratroopers. In typical fashion, the Japanese, probably those of First Lieutenant Matsuoka's 3d

Machine Gun Company, used red parachute flares to signal the beginning of the assault. The Japanese surged forward, supported only by grenades and mortar fire. Aided by the illumination of the signal flares, Torgerson's Paratroopers repulsed the attack, combing their ranks with Reising automatics, grenades, and rifles. Although it appeared that this attack was stopped, Torgerson ordered Captain Duryea to move his company in order to furnish flank and rear protection on the east side of Hill 123.[23]

By 0200 Japanese snipers had infested the jungle on both sides of the ridge. Vandegrift's headquarters was the target of frequent sniping, forcing staff and correspondent alike to seek shelter. At about this time Corporal Burak repaired the wire linking Edson's headquarters with division. Red Mike spoke with Colonel Thomas, reporting that he was getting low on grenades and belted rounds of machine gun bullets. Thomas told him that the ammunition would be sent over soon, but at 0300 Edson called again, saying that he was "almost out." Finally, a truckload of grenades and belted ammunition arrived, courtesy of Cates's 1st Marines. The driver of this truck, Lloyd Wiggins of the 1st Marines Headquarters and Service Company, endured heavy sniper fire and other hazards on the ridge to get his precious cargo to Hill 123. A dozen marines, including Major Bailey, Corporal Burak, Sgt. Francis Pettus, and several other volunteers, quickly unloaded the ammunition and hefted the heavy crates to the front line battle positions on hands and knees. In his last contribution to the battle, Wiggins returned to the division hospital with a truckload of wounded.[24]

Those who received these patients were the dedicated navy doctors and enlisted corpsmen who treated more than 200 wounded. Eight corpsmen and one doctor, Lt. Edward P. McLarney, were awarded Navy Crosses for their work that night. Typical of these was Robert L. Smith, a hospital apprentice. Throughout the night, Smith treated and evacuated wounded on the bullet-swept ridge. At dawn, he and a marine corporal spotted an untreated Raider lying near the crest of Hill 123. The corporal urged him to take a break and let someone else tend to the wounded man, but Smith ignored him and headed up the hill to begin treatment. In the act of saving this marine, Smith lost his life to enemy sniper fire.[25]

So far in this bitter fight each side had its heroes, but none were bigger than Red Mike Edson. Fearlessly standing erect in his command post with two fresh bullet holes in his shirt, Edson coolly and calmly directed the battle, a mere twenty yards behind the front line. His presence was needed, because Edson knew how high the stakes were in this deadly game. Behind him, only a mile from where he stood, was Henderson Field. Hill 123 had to be held at all costs. He stood there encouraging, cajoling, and correcting his men. At a desperate point during the night, he was heard rallying, "Raiders, parachuters, engineers, artillerymen, I don't give a damn who you are. You're all marines. Come up on this hill and fight!"[26]

Captain "Tex" Stiff recalls Edson's commanding presence that night:

> When the Japs began attacking . . . the word was soon passed to move up onto the ridge, so we did. This put me in a position to

observe Col. Edson during most of the night. I can say that if there is such a thing as one man holding a battalion (plus the paratroopers) together, Edson did it that night. He stood just behind the front lines—stood, when most of us hugged the ground. Once when I was near him there was a louder crack than usual of a bullet, this one coming from the rear. The Division CP was two or three hundred yards to our rear and their security was getting nervous. Anyway, Edson flinches a bit, then said, "I don't mind the Jap 25s, but those 30 calibers pack a wallop."[27]

Marine casualties in defense of Hill 123 mounted steadily. At about 0400, Edson picked up a phone and told Colonel Thomas: "My losses have been heavy, I need more men." Thomas responded by feeding the companies of the 2d Battalion, 5th Marines, piecemeal into Edson's position. Company G arrived first, bolstering the line on the eastern slope of Hill 123. There the company was buffeted with machine gun fire and suffered many casualties. The two remaining companies, following at intervals, helped fill in the gaps in Edson's defenses around Hill 123. There they helped stave off two more attacks before daybreak.[28]

Edson needed every man he could get, because the Japanese had no intention of quitting. Isibashi's 7th Company knifed through a weakly defended area on the east side of Hill 123 and reached the northeast side of the ridge, where they stood at first light. After the decimation of the 5th Company, 1st Lt. Jin'ichiro Kuroki's 6th Company took up the torch and pressed

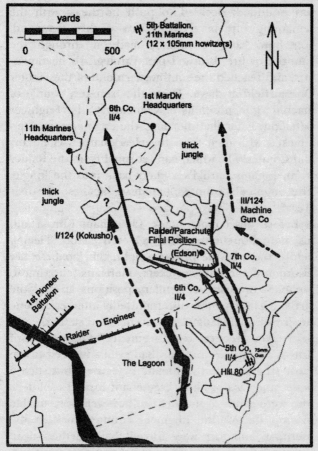

Bloody Ridge, Final Phase, Night of 13-14 September

on, hitting the front right flank of Hill 123. Although half of the company fell to marine fire, Kuroki, who was wounded, decided to push northeast with the remaining fifty or sixty soldiers of his command. Somehow, Kuroki's soldiers made it through the gauntlet of fire, brushed past Vandegrift's headquarters, and reached the southwestern end of the Fighter One airfield at dawn. There they seized a couple of machine gun positions of Company C, 1st Engineer Battalion. Later that morning, the engineers counterattacked with men from the Headquarters Company and Company D, which had returned from the Raider front, forcing Kuroki's soldiers back into the jungle. The engineers counted ten dead Japanese in their area.[29]

Before this counterattack, Lieutenant Kuroki and his men thought they had achieved victory. Fleeing before them in the predawn light, the Japanese saw disordered and panic-stricken Americans scurrying to foxholes, bivouacs, or artillery positions around the airfield. The Japanese also reportedly intercepted one American plain-language transmission stating, "Airfield taken, request reinforcements." One group of Kuroki's men said that they had even advanced to the coast (the battalion's ultimate objective), but such a penetration is not likely. Lieutenant Kuroki's soldiers, who were south of the airfield, however, were unable to stop the Marine Engineer counterattack in the morning, and they were forced to leave their dead countrymen behind amid the American positions. Kuroki's men withdrew to the jungle's edge to wait for reinforcements, but none ever came. "Gulping down their tears," they withdrew to the battalion's preattack assembly point. The first to arrive were ten men, all wounded. The 2d Battalion, 4th Infantry, had lost nearly three-quarters of its officers and men in the fight. Sergeant Shohei Haga of the battalion's headquarters company recalls Tamura being "without speech, dazed, and like a man walking in his sleep," when he realized the enormity of the battalion's loss.[30]

Corporal Carlo Fulgenzi of Headquarters Company, 1st Engineer Battalion, may have encountered part of Kuroki's company just before dawn while he was defending a position on the ridge near the division command post. The eighteen-year-old corporal, fighting off the debilitating effects of malaria, expended all of his rifle ammunition during the night, firing at Japanese infiltrators who had killed or wounded most of his comrades. The young corporal decided to check on a buddy's position, which had gone silent during the night, when he noticed a group of about thirty Japanese walking toward him, laughing and joking. Alarmed, Fulgenzi hid in a roofed dugout, armed with only a .32-caliber Colt pistol. After miraculously surviving a grenade blast thrown into the dugout by the Japanese, the wounded corporal dispatched four Japanese who had jumped into the dugout and killed a fifth topside as he made his way out of the pit. Fulgenzi then helped eliminate a dozen more Japanese and later helped lead a mission to rescue a marine trapped behind enemy lines.[31]

In addition to Kuroki's 6th Company, Lieutenant Matsuoka's 3d Machine Gun Company had also fought its way deep behind American lines. One of Matsuoka's men, Sgt. Sei'ichi Aoyagi, remembers the fighting that terrible night. The company had reached "the edge of the airfield," he recalls, "but the company was pinned down by heavy enemy fire from positions to the west." Aoyagi watched as half of his company fell dead or wounded to enemy bullets. Unable to make any headway, Aoyagi and his comrades crawled back into the jungle and dug in, where they continued to be subjected to heavy fire. Seeing the hopelessness of the situation, the company's attack was called off.[32]

Meanwhile, most of the Japanese withdrew off the ridge at first light, but a group of nearly 100 clung to the southern edge of Hill 80, where they were in defilade and out of reach of marine weapons. Thomas met with Major Bailey and Capt. Dale Brannon, commander of the 67th Pursuit Squadron, to devise a plan to eliminate these Japanese. Using an aerial mosaic, Bailey pointed out the location of the Japanese, and after Thomas's blessing, three of Brannon's U.S. Army Aircobras were in the air by 0600. Using their vast array of 20mm cannons and .30- and .50-caliber machine guns, the trio massacred the Japanese below in only a few passes. Return fire, however, riddled two of the planes, forcing them to make emergency landings at Henderson Field.[33]

During the night at his temporary command post nestled on the west side of a ridge he called "bald mountain," General Kawaguchi watched the battle and waited for reports from his battalion commanders. To Kawaguchi, the arching flares and colorful explosions reminded him of fireworks. Later in the night the reports finally began to filter in, but they were far from encouraging: "Battalion commander killed; battalion completely annihilated; whereabouts of the battalion commander not known." With the coming of dawn, Kawaguchi's attack on the ridge for all intents and purposes had ended.[34]

Dawn revealed a horrific sight around Hill 123. Amid the blackened, smoking patches of grass were grenade cartons, empty shell casings, and ammo boxes strewn about in disorder. Here and there were the tangled and twisted bodies of marines and Japanese soldiers, some of whom appeared to have fallen together, as if they had died in a fierce hand-to-hand struggle. One unlucky marine had his head blown off. On the steep, blood-stained slope of Hill 123 lay about 200 Japanese, some just a few feet from the top of the hill. Many of these were ripped open, exposing their insides. In some places at the bottom of the slope, the Japanese corpses were stacked like poker chips twelve feet high. A similar macabre scene presented itself on the saddle and on Hill 80.[35]

Although the main fury of Kawaguchi's attack dissipated at dawn, large and small pockets of Japanese remained scattered throughout the jungle ravines on each side of the ridge. These scattered pockets and snipers made any type of movement on the ridge hazardous. Occasionally, a Nambu could be heard chattering in the valley below, answered by the deeper sound of American machine guns. Soon teams of marines were dispatched to ferret out these Japanese stragglers. At 0800, a hidden machine-gunner riddled an American jeep bearing five wounded on the ridge. Among those killed was Edson's operations officer, Maj. Robert Brown, who had part of a hand blown off earlier by a grenade. The situation at the division command post was just as hazardous. Early in the morning a Japanese officer and two others suddenly dashed out of the bush shouting *"banzai."* The Japanese officer killed one marine with his sword, before he and another were gunned down near Vandegrift's quarters. The third Japanese soldier managed to escape into the bush.[36]

Radio operator Edward Fee of the 1st Pioneer Battalion, temporarily attached to division headquarters, witnessed this attack by the Japanese trio:

> I was on the far side, looking straight up at them. One marine had his rifle laying across his lap cross legged. He threw his rifle in an arc and caught the first Japanese across his forehead. Down he went. A second marine tackled the second Japanese, and two other marines jumped on his back. This second Japanese had fallen on his own sword and cut his right hand off above the knuckles, back to front. A division chief warrant officer came from 40 feet away downhill, drawing his .45 from his holster. He threw one in the chamber and lifted the flailing Japanese's helmet and blew his brains into the earth below. Stepping over him, he lifted the helmet of the second thrashing, screaming Jap and dispatched him to heaven, too. We never saw the third Japanese again, but heard firing from the right.[37]

At 0830 Colonel Whaling's 2d Battalion, 5th Marines, relieved Colonel Edson's exhausted men on the ridge. Having returned to the Kukum area, the true rest area, the Raiders and Parachutists collapsed in foxholes and spent the rest of the 14th sleeping. It was a well-deserved rest. The unnamed ridge for which they had fought so hard to defend would thereafter be known as Bloody Ridge, Raider's Ridge, and Edson's Ridge. All of them were appropriate titles for this epic battle.[38]

The Wing Units Attack

On the evening of the 13th, Maj. Takeshi Mizuno completed the final preparations for the Kuma Battalion's attack. This was Kawaguchi's Right Wing Unit. Mizuno and his headquarters would lead the assault, followed by 2d Lt. Kiyoshi Sato's 1st Company of about 180 men, and 2d Lt. Toshio Hahara's 2d Company of about 170 men, in that order. Both company commanders had battle experience as survivors of Ichiki's fruitless assault (Hahara as Major Kuramoto's second adjutant and Sato as a platoon commander in the 4th Company). The machine gun platoon under WO1 Kosaku Nakao (about seventy troops) and the 28th Antitank Company (about 140 gunners) led by 1st Lt. Yoshio Okubo would stay behind in reserve near the west bank of the Tenaru River. Reflecting the ad hoc nature of the battalion, both rifle companies consisted of just two, albeit large, platoons rather than the regular three.[39]

Mizuno's plan of attack was aimed at the southeastern sector of the marine perimeter, manned by Lt. Col. William McKelvey's 3d Battalion, 1st Marines. McKelvey's front of nearly 3,500 yards began about 1,500 yards south of the mouth of the Ilu River and ended at a point along the edge of the jungle due east

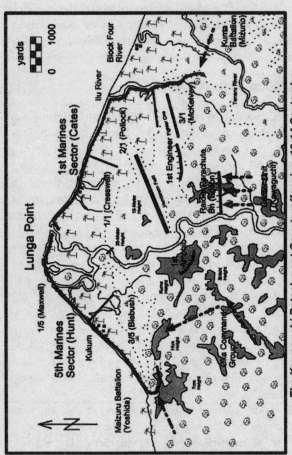

The Kawaguchi Detachment Counteroffensive, 13-14 September

of Hill 80. From left to right his front was defended by Companies L, I, and K, with a machine gun platoon from Company M attached to each company. Barbed wire had been put up about fifty yards in front of the battalion. Unfortunately, McKelvey did not have the manpower to tie in his right flank with Edson's left in the jungle. Thus, a gaping hole of some 2,000 yards existed where the Japanese could simply waltz through and seize the airfield.[40]

At 1900, Mizuno led his battalion forward in column from a point about five miles southeast of the mouth of the Ilu River. Following a two-and-one-half-hour march, he reached the grassy plain with his headquarters and a platoon of the 1st Company after crossing the steep banks of the Tenaru River. But the rest of the battalion was nowhere to be seen. Impatiently, Mizuno threw out his plan of attack and marched toward the American line with the force he had on hand. Almost immediately, American rifle and machine gun fire from a listening post manned by five marines pierced the night, dropping several Japanese in the lead. After throwing several grenades at the marines, Mizuno ordered the rifle platoon to charge the listening post with fixed bayonets. In the face of this overwhelming attack, the five marines bolted.[41]

The marines of Company K, led by Capt. Robert Putnam, manned the threatened sector. When a bloodied survivor of the listening post returned to Company K's line, Putnam ordered an artillery barrage from the 11th Marines concentrated on the now-vacant listening post. This barrage provoked no response, nor did Company K's machine gun fire at a squad of engineers attempting to cut their way through the barbed wire shortly after midnight. Putnam then ordered parachute flares lofted for illumination. In the dim and flickering light, the marines saw the Japanese in the field moving toward them. The machine guns and rifles of Company K's entire line lit up as they fired at the approaching Japanese. Fire from 60mm and 81mm mortars and 75mm howitzers from the 11th Marines also plastered the area, cutting down several Japanese. Among those killed was Major Mizuno, who took a bullet in the head.[42]

Now leaderless, Lieutenant Sato reorganized his platoon for another attack. Following a period of deathly silence, a rifleman in Company K yelled "Japs!" initiating the last and most severe exchange of the night. Covered by grenade and mortar fire, a large group of Japanese managed to penetrate the wire. A deadly hand-to-hand battle ensued, as the Japanese charged with their bayonets. During the fierce struggle, Captain Putnam nearly lost his head to Lieutenant Sato's sword before Sato was shot and killed by Pvt. Marion Pegegrine and his Browning automatic rifle. Just before dawn, Lieutenant Hahara's company finally joined the attack, but return fire from a platoon led by Lt. Bill Sager stopped Hahara's attack dead in its tracks. At dawn, Company K counted some thirty Japanese around their position and an additional twenty-seven ensnared on the wire. One man on the wire was still alive and taken prisoner.[43]

As the sun peeked over the horizon on the morning of 14 September, all was quiet in the 1st Marines's sector. Colonel McKelvey, however, believed the Japanese were hiding in the tall grass in his front. His request for tank support was answered, and at 0945, a platoon of six Stuart tanks of Company B, 1st Tank Battalion, arrived on the scene. The tanks searched the grassy plain thoroughly, but they found no Japanese.[44]

Later that morning, two survivors of the Company K listening post that was overrun the previous night returned to report that a Japanese machine gun was emplaced in a native hut on the opposite end of the field. At 1100 the six tanks left again to destroy this menace. But as the tanks approached the eastern edge of the grassy field, they were also approaching Lieutenant Okubo's four well-concealed 37mm antitank guns. These guns, Model 94s, had a muzzle velocity of 2,300 feet per second and the armor-piercing characteristics sufficient to penetrate the Stuart's armor. Okubo patiently measured the range to the approaching tanks, "1,500," "1,000," and at 500 meters, he yelled "Fire!"[45]

One shell perforated the turret of Tank number 1, killing the platoon commander and the radioman and setting the tank on fire. Tank number 5, immobilized by an exploding grenade, which broke its track, was hit in quick succession by two shells. Filling from the exploding shells began to burn the inside of the tank with a yellow flame and bluish smoke. Efforts to extinguish the fire failed and most of the crew escaped. The tank's commander, however, was not so lucky. As he opened the hatch, a Japanese soldier armed with a flamethrower torched him. Tank number 4, after destroying the emplaced machine gun, toppled down a steep embankment of the Tenaru and turned turtle. Entombed inside, the tank's crew drowned. The headquarters tank was disabled by a hit on the right sprocket wheel about forty feet into the jungle. Retaliatory artillery and mortar fire, called for by Colonel McKelvey, succeeded in destroying one of Okubo's guns.[46]

Surprisingly enough, two small groups of Japanese managed to penetrate Colonel McKelvey's well-defended line during the night of the 13th. One group of about eleven men sliced through Company I's position to the left of Company K. This group of infiltrators spent most of the night hidden near a communications dugout before withdrawing across the field in the morning. The other group, armed with a machine gun, created some excitement later that afternoon when it began firing on some marines from the rear. Tanks, however, rapidly exterminated these pests.[47]

At 2300 on the 14th, the remnants of the Kuma Battalion conducted an ineffective attack against Company K's line, leaving five Japanese dead at the wire. At dawn, nearly 300 Japanese were spotted to the right of Company K's front before a barrage fired by 75mm howitzers scattered them. The Kuma Battalion followed up with another attack on the evening of the 15th, but, like the previous night, the attack was weak and ineffective.[48]

Now we turn our attention to the attack of Col. Akinosuke Oka's Left Wing Unit, composed of three units: the Maizuru Battalion, Oka's command group, and the 3d Battalion, 4th Infantry.

Following losses at sea (a combination of those killed and small pockets still stranded on various islands) the Maizuru Battalion mustered about 650 men out of the original 840. Despite the loss of most of the 7th Company and the battalion artillery, the battalion was still a potent force. For the attack, it mustered the headquarters company, the battalion machine gun company, and the 5th, 6th, and 8th Companies.[49]

At 1815 on 13 September, Lieutenant Yoshida tardily led the Maizuru Battalion on its march from the Matanikau to the American positions southeast of Kukum. At 2240, Oka ordered Yoshida to attack the American antiaircraft positions near the main bridge on the Lunga River. He also ordered Maj. Morie Sasaki, commander of the 3d Battalion, 4th Infantry, to join in the attack along the coastal road. The Maizuru Battalion's path generally followed the coastal trail, though portions of it pushed inland a short distance. With the sounds of battle at Bloody Ridge spurring them on, the battalion came upon the south side of a ridge formation at 2215.[50]

The Maizuru Battalion's assault would ultimately hit a position defended by the unit that fought so well at the first Battle of the Matanikau, Capt. Lyman D. Spurlock's Company L of the 3d Battalion, 5th Marines. Company L defended both the coconut grove along the shore and the main trail to the Matanikau River, as well as a small, steep ridge that was part of a group of ridges the Japanese called Tora Heights. A platoon defended the grove, which was bisected by the trail. On the side of the trail closest to shore, a 37mm antitank gun from the Regimental Weapons Company stood ready. On the other side sat a water-cooled machine gun from Company M. Stretching left (east) of the position ending on a small ridge were the remaining two platoons of Company L. All positions were fronted with barbed wire and were dug in and well camouflaged, with the exception of those on the ridge, where the rocklike coral made digging impossible with the tools on hand.[51]

About 0400 on 14 September, Company L detected the Japanese in the dim moonlight as three columns of infantry—each about a company strong—approached the marines' positions. Marshaling each column was a sword-waving officer cajoling his men. Taking no precautions to conceal their march, the Japanese talked and joked freely as their bayonets glistened and their mess gear and equipment rattled and clanked. One column of Japanese, probably 1st Lt. Masayuki Kamei's 8th Company, approached the marines on the coastal trail. The second, probably the 6th Company, commanded by a First Lieutenant Tauruta, marched about twenty-five yards inland in the coconut grove. The third, 1st Lt. Makoto Hirota's 5th Company, approached another twenty-five yards inland at the ridge. Up and down Company L's line the word was passed to hold fire until the 37mm gun opened up.[52]

When the Japanese on the trail reached a point about twenty-five yards from the line (about 0430), the 37mm fired the first of a dozen or so canister rounds with devastating effect. The entire American line followed the cue, and machine guns, BARs, and rifles swept the three attacking companies. For the Japanese on the trail and in the grove, the attack was over in less than ten minutes. Reeling from the surprisingly powerful enemy fire, Lieutenants Kamei and Tauruta withdrew their men, leaving behind large clusters of their dead countrymen. Marine losses in the brief exchange were extremely light.[53]

Although the two inland attacks were soundly

defeated, Lieutenant Hirota's 5th Company succeeded in driving the marines off of the ridge. Before the attack, Cpl. Zenjiro Tohno's 3d Squad was ordered to destroy the wire entanglements protecting the ridge. After First Class Private Yamagata destroyed a section of the wire, Tohno's squad charged up the ridge at the V point in the American line, followed by the rest of the company. Japanese fire badly wounded 2d Lt. Edward Farmer and wounded six other marines. The Japanese forced Farmer's group back about ten or so yards on the reverse slope, where they held firm for the remainder of the battle. Second Lieutenant John "Flash" Flaherty, Sgt. Ore Marion, and eight other men from the platoon in the grove helped Farmer hold his ground.[54]

Hirota's company made a few half-hearted attempts to attack over the crest of the ridge but was beaten back with machine gun fire and a few well-placed rounds of 60mm mortars and rifle grenades. The marines soon brought in a few reinforcing platoons to stop the Japanese attacks and subjected Hirota's soldiers to heavy fire in the open terrain fronting the ridge. The Japanese dropped to the ground to avoid the heavy fire. Corporal Tohno watched many men of his company die as they attempted to avoid the fierce fire, but there was no place to hide. Tohno recalls lying flat on his face, unable to move even one inch. Only after the firing slackened after dark were Hirota's men able to retreat.[55]

Unable to crack the tough American defenses, Lieutenant Yoshida called off the attack about 1800. Japanese losses on the ridge cannot be stated with complete assurance but were probably more than those suffered in the grove and on the trail. Of the small number of dead Japanese on the ridge was an officer still clutching two leather cases full of Japanese currency. The next day a Company L patrol found a mass grave dug by the Japanese, a short distance south of the ridge.[56]

While the Maizuru Battalion assaulted Spurlock's ridge, the rest of Oka's Left Wing Unit floundered. Colonel Oka's command group commenced its march north toward Hiyo Height at dusk on the 13th. Apparently, Oka had intended on attacking with the Maizuru Battalion, but for some unknown reason, he did not. Sasaki's 3d Battalion, 4th Infantry, located somewhere between the Matanikau and Oka's headquarters, also failed to participate in any meaningful fighting.[57]

An Analysis of the September Counteroffensive

General Kawaguchi's big September counteroffensive, on which the Japanese pinned such high hopes, had been a costly failure. Japanese losses were more than 800 killed or missing, with the 2d Battalion, 4th Infantry, suffering the lion's share, with about 350 killed. The 1st Battalion, 124th Infantry, also suffered heavily, with about 200 fatalities and a like number wounded. The Kuma Battalion lost about 100 dead, while the Maizuru Battalion suffered 120 killed and about sixty wounded. Fatalities in Watanabe's 3d Battalion, 124th Infantry, were comparatively light, with about sixty dead and a similar number wounded.[58]

There was a good reason why Watanabe's casualties were so light. Apparently, only one or two of his companies entered the fight on the night of the 13th. This enraged Kawaguchi. Colonel Watanabe, accompanied by his adjutant and two orderlies, set out during the afternoon of the 13th in an effort to talk to Kawaguchi. But Watanabe and his small entourage lost their way and were pinned down by heavy artillery fire while attempting to return to the battalion. Compounding matters, Watanabe's old battle wound in his left leg acted up, making travel in the thick jungle painful and slow. Watanabe spent the rest of the night trying unsuccessfully to regain contact with his command. Kawaguchi was furious when he learned of the battalion's weak attack and Watanabe's inaction. "This powerful battalion," he later recalled, "which I had counted on most, was thus completely mismanaged. When I heard of this, I could not help shedding tears of disappointment, anger, and regret."[59]

Like the Japanese, American casualty figures are a bit elusive. The 1st Marine Division's historian listed total American losses in all units at 111 killed or missing and 283 wounded, but this writer compiled a total of 104 and 278, respectively. The 1st Raider Battalion reported 37 killed or missing and 103 wounded, while the casualties of the 1st Parachute Battalion came to about 21 dead and 101 wounded. Losses had trimmed the ranks of the Raiders down to about 500 men. Fighting had likewise taken its toll on the tiny Parachute Battalion, which had stormed Gavutu Island on 7 August with 397 men. After Bloody Ridge, Captain Torgerson withdrew with just 86. Because it was no longer an effective fighting force, the 1st Parachute Battalion was withdrawn from the island on 18 September (see Table 10).[60]

Table 10
American Casualties During the
Mid-September Fighting

Unit	Dead	Wounded
1st Raider Battalion	37	103
1st Parachute Battalion	21	101
1st Battalion, 1st Marines*	24	0
3d Battalion, 1st Marines	3	4
1st Tank Battalion	8	0
1st Engineer Battalion	5	15
1st Marine Division HQ	1	0
2d Battalion, 5th Marines	5	39
3d Battalion, 5th Marines	0	16
Totals:	104	278

*1st Battalion, 1st Marines, losses were suffered on 17 September in a patrol action.

Most of the credit for defeating Kawaguchi must go to Edson and his Raider-Parachute Battalion. Although it is true the artillerymen of Colonel Price's 5th Battalion, 11th Marines, played an important role in stopping the Japanese—1,992 rounds of 105mm were expended on the night of 13 September—in ground combat it is the riflemen who ultimately win or lose battles.

Someone was needed to confront the numerically superior Japanese face-to-face and that is what Edson's men did. Indeed, no amount of indirect artillery fire could have stopped the Japanese at Edson's Ridge, or any other battle for that matter. In recognition of his leadership and personal courage, Colonel Edson was awarded the Navy Cross and the Medal of Honor. Major Kenneth Bailey also received the Medal of Honor for his bravery and leadership, but he would receive it posthumously. As for Maj. Charles Miller of the Parachutists, he was ignominiously discharged and sent home.[61]

Captain Harry Torgerson, who replaced Major Miller as the commanding officer of the 1st Parachute Battalion, attributed victory not only to the artillery support but also the "liberal use of grenades." He later reported that his paratroopers had used an extra ten cases of grenades during the night, well over each man's normal allotment. Torgerson believed that these extra grenades "were of inestimable value" to the defenders of Bloody Ridge.[62]

General Vandegrift's tactical leadership during this period faltered. Foremost was his failure to act on the mounting evidence that the Japanese were amassing a large force capable of retaking the airfield. Frequent reinforcement runs by the Cactus Express, the intelligence gathered by Edson during the Tasimboko raid, radio intelligence, and native patrol reports made this clear. An impending overland assault by the Japanese was obvious to the division operations section, but not to Vandegrift. Indeed, both Colonels Thomas and Twining tried to persuade Vandegrift to reorient the division's defenses to face inland rather than toward the sea, but with no success. Almost as damning was Vandegrift's decision to move his command post to the ridge in the face of an imminent attack. Edson's battalion was moved to the ridge only through Thomas's tactful urgings and under the pretext of command post "security" and "rest" for Edson's men. Thomas did this as a last resort to bolster the division's defenses along the southern flank of the perimeter. Without the Raiders and Parachutists on the ridge, the division would have lost Henderson Field. This cannot be denied. Thus, Lt. Col. Gerald Thomas must be regarded as one of the unheralded heroes for the Americans.

At the flag officer level on the Japanese side, Major General Kawaguchi's performance was good, though not without faults. Some historians have characterized Kawaguchi as an obstinate buffoon. This characterization is neither fair nor accurate, especially when one considers that his attack came the closest to retaking the airfield. Only hastiness above and incompetence below prevented Kawaguchi from achieving victory. Considering the circumstances in which he led his force into battle, a force that was short on everything from food and ammunition to vehicles and artillery, his detachment's performance was better than what any reasonable person would expect. In fact, his detachment accomplished more than the Sendai Division's attack in late October, but that is another story.

Kawaguchi's most glaring mistake was his decision to disperse his brigade. Centuries ago, Chinese philosopher and military theorist Sun-tzu wrote about this important principle: "By discovering the enemy's dispositions and remaining invisible ourselves, we can keep our forces concentrated, while the enemy's must be divided." Vandegrift's "division" was indeed divided, with most of it protecting the coast, but Kawaguchi threw away this opportunity by dividing his own brigade into three. Considering how close the

Japanese came to victory and how little the wing units accomplished, the addition of even one battalion in the main assault at Bloody Ridge could have moved the pendulum in favor of the Japanese.[63]

Of Kawaguchi's five rifle battalions only two fought with distinction. Kawaguchi characterized the performance of Major Tamura and his battalion as "brilliant." Indeed it was. Without the initiative of Tamura and his battalion's fearless assault, the Battle of Bloody Ridge would have probably amounted to no more than a minor skirmish. The ferocity and determination of their assault is reflected by its staggering casualty rate. The fact that elements of the battalion managed to punch through Edson's firewall to reach one of the airfields is an accomplishment not to be taken lightly.

Major Kokusho's battalion also fought well. Its inaction after slicing through the marine right, however, is puzzling. There are two possible explanations for the battalion's paralysis. It is possible that no officer was willing or able to take command after Major Kokusho's death. A more probable explanation is that the battalion believed they had captured their primary objective, 15-Meter Height. Indeed, the battalion gleefully reported the hill's capture to Kawaguchi by radio. Thus, disorientation in the "devilish" jungle appears to have once again hurt the Japanese. Despite these difficulties, Kawaguchi came within a hair's width of defeating Edson.[64]

After the war Kawaguchi provided U.S. officers with several reasons why he believed his attack had failed. According to him, the failure to postpone the detachment's initial attack to the 13th was the main reason.

Kawaguchi strongly believed that if his request to post-pone the assault had been approved by Hyakutake, or if he acted on his own initiative to change the date, the attack would have definitely been successful. As contributing factors, Kawaguchi also mentioned the lack of sufficient time to complete preparations for the attack, the lack of adequate maps, and the failure of Watanabe's 3d Battalion "to show the proper fight-ing spirit."[65]

Kawaguchi is probably correct in surmising success if his initial attack had taken place on the 13th. With his weak and ineffective attack on the 12th, Kawaguchi had announced his intention to attack south of the airfield. Thus, his assault the following night had com-pletely lost the element of surprise so essential for suc-cess in a night attack. Moreover, Kawaguchi's men were neither rested nor did they have sufficient time to prepare for the battle. On the American side, Kawaguchi's attack on the 12th enabled Edson to reform his line the following day and permitted the 5th Battalion, 11th Marines, to register its howitzers to the south. The latter is especially important in light of the artillery's important contribution during the bat-tle. Without artillery support, Edson would have prob-ably lost the battle.

Kawaguchi's wing units accomplished nothing in support of the main assault. Major Mizuno displayed an amazing lack of patience in his attack on the east-ern flank. Not only did Mizuno fail to locate the large gap in the marines' line, which would have been located with efficient patrolling, but he also launched his attack with only 100 men, a small fraction of his force. First Lieutenant Yoshida's assault in the west showed poor leadership as well, but in his defense, command of a battalion is normally given to a seasoned major or a lieutenant colonel, two to three pay grades higher than his own. Unfortunately for Yoshida, he was unable to wield much influence with his company commanders, all of whom noisily approached the American line in defiance of Japanese night attack doctrine. Moreover, it appears that Yoshida also failed to patrol effectively—another element stressed in night attack doctrine—to pinpoint American positions. A summary comparison of the Japanese and American officers who fought on Guadalcanal is provided by one enlisted marine who said, "Sure we had inept leaders in our ranks, but fortunately for us, the Japs had many more."[66]

Although some historians criticize the Japanese for employing the night attack, its use on Guadalcanal had merit. During the night, the marines could not use aircraft and tanks in general combat support, weapons in which the Americans enjoyed a decided advantage. Moreover, the Japanese could infiltrate marine positions much more easily. What the Japanese failed to do was adhere to the time-tested tenets of their night attack doctrine. Their doctrine stressed the importance of reconnaissance and familiarity with the terrain before the attack. But because of an unrealistic timeline and promises to Tokyo, neither of these important preliminaries was accomplished. The result was confusion and frustration in a hastily prepared attack.

Of these failings, the lack of proper reconnaissance had serious repercussions for the Japanese. Given sufficient time, Japanese patrols would have discovered

gaping holes in Vandegrift's southern flank. As we
have already seen, between Bloody Ridge and positions manned by the 3d Battalion, 1st Marines, was an
open avenue 2,000 yards wide, providing direct access
to the airfield. Exploitation of this opening would
have given the Japanese easy access to the aircraft,
supply dumps, and all of the command and control
facilities on the island. Already underequipped and
undersupplied, the loss or destruction of these assets
would have been disastrous for the Americans. So
often in war, luck or a lack of it plays an important
role.

Contemporary analysis of Kawaguchi's defeat by the
Japanese is interesting. Seventeenth Army listed several reasons, including inadequate preparation time,
superiority of American firepower, difficulty in communicating and coordinating the complex attack plan
in the jungle, dispersal and separation of one-third of
the 124th Infantry due to the ill-considered barge
expedition, and inferior maps. In addition, the Army
Section of Imperial General Headquarters added inaccurate intelligence on American strength, insufficient
equipment, American air superiority that forced
Kawaguchi to employ the night attack, the unexpected
strength and resilience of the Americans, and the folly
of matching cold steel against a well-prepared defense.
One naval officer provided a succinct analysis of
Kawaguchi's failure: "The army had been used to
fighting the Chinese."[67]

We come to the final question and the one that
really matters: Could the Japanese have retaken and
held Henderson Field with a victory at Bloody Ridge?
The answer to this important question is yes. Merrill

Twining argues that the division possessed sufficient reserves in other sectors to launch an effective counterattack. Although this is true, such a counterattack, launched in sufficient strength, would have been imprudent with Oka and Mizuno's forces attacking on the flanks, especially when one considers that the exact strength of Oka and Mizuno's forces was unknown at that time. On the flip side, the Japanese possessed sufficient reserves (the 3d Battalion, 4th Infantry, and the 3d Battalion, 124th Infantry) in the vicinity, which were at or near full strength, to hold the airfield.

Another point is worthy of consideration. Could the Americans have held had they lost both the 1st Marine Division Headquarters and the airfield? The death or capture of Vandegrift and his staff would have been disastrous to the marines on the island and may have prompted an American surrender. No consideration of this chilling possibility seems to have been given by historians and makes Vandegrift's decision to relocate his command post to the ridge even more foolhardy. Yet, loss of the airfield could have been equally catastrophic. Destruction of the aircraft at Henderson Field would have left the Americans defenseless in the air for a period of time—time enough perhaps for the Japanese to land additional reinforcements from Rabaul en masse and unimpeded.

A Japanese victory at Bloody Ridge would have been disastrous for the American sailors, soldiers, and marines on Guadalcanal. Vandegrift admitted that much by stating that Kawaguchi's September counteroffensive was the only time during the entire campaign he had doubts over the outcome. "Had it been a successful assault," Vandegrift acknowledged, "we would have been in a pretty bad condition." Indeed they would.[68]

The Battle of Bloody Ridge was a relatively small affair compared to the campaigns and battles being fought in Russia and North Africa, but the positive effects on American morale were enormous. It was at Bloody Ridge, against a numerically superior foe, that the Americans proved they could beat the Japanese "superman." The marines would experience many more triumphs on Guadalcanal and during the rest of the war—at Tarawa, Okinawa, and Iwo Jima—but the Battle of Bloody Ridge during the Guadalcanal campaign will live on as one of the Marine Corps's finest hours.

10 The Matanikau

Death March to the Matanikau

Defeat at Bloody Ridge was a horrific and shattering blow for the previously unbeaten Kawaguchi Detachment, but their ordeal was far from over. At 1305 on 14 September, Kawaguchi led his battle weary men away from the blood-soaked ridge that they had tried so hard to take. In order to recuperate after three days of marching and bitter fighting, his hungry, tired, and exhausted soldiers spent the 15th at rest. At 2100 on 15 September, Kawaguchi ordered the detachment to withdraw to the Matanikau Valley, a six-mile journey over some of the worst terrain on the island. Fortunately, the Maizuru Battalion had recently hacked out a trail over the torturous route, appropriately named the Maizuru Road. Kawaguchi's warriors set out on the morning of the 16th with the Brigade Guard Company taking the lead.[1]

On the evening of the 16th, General Vandegrift ordered two companies of the 1st Marines to mount a reconnaissance-in-force south of the ridge the following morning to ascertain the approximate size and location of the Japanese force in the area. Companies

A and B drew the task and commenced their march before dawn on the 17th. The two companies cautiously advanced southwest without opposition until they came under fierce rifle and machine gun fire at the Lunga River. This force was Kawaguchi's rearguard, composed of the 3d Machine Gun Company and a rifle platoon of Capt. Gensuke Bito's 12th Company. Both marine companies fell back, but one platoon from Company B was pinned down. Captain Brush, the commander of Company B, requested permission to mount a rescue effort, but Vandegrift denied Brush's request. Predictably, the abandoned Company B platoon was nearly annihilated by the Japanese in a firefight that ended later that night. The platoon's casualties included twenty-four killed and several wounded. Japanese losses are not known.[2]

On 20 September, Edson's Raiders mounted a similar, grueling, thirteen-hour patrol to determine how far the Japanese had fallen back. Traversing jagged terrain entangled with brambly vines, prickly leaves, and thorn-covered tree branches, the Raiders soon encountered stragglers of Kawaguchi's retreating column. Colonel Edson called in artillery on suspected enemy locations, and he brought machine guns and mortars to prepare the way for the battalion advance. After a firefight, which saw nineteen Japanese fall to flying steel, at a cost of only three Raiders wounded, Edson ordered the battalion back to the perimeter. Edson saw all he needed to see. He confirmed that the Japanese were on the move westward and no longer posed a serious threat to the southern flank of the perimeter. Prizes of the patrol included Japanese flags, rifles, ammunition, and a dismantled pack howitzer.[3]

This booty provided stark evidence of the troubled state of the debilitated Japanese. The last meal Kawaguchi's men had eaten before the Battle of Bloody Ridge was on the morning of the 12th, because they had planned to eat "Roosevelt Meals" after retaking the airfield. The loss of all provisions during the Tasimboko raid no doubt figured in this planning. Thus, the Japanese were forced to supplement their tiny supply of rice with betel nuts, weeds, and small amounts of fruit, hardly the diet needed to sustain one's strength in the debilitating climate on Guadalcanal.[4]

Those Japanese who drew the task of carrying the wounded had it especially difficult. In the 1st and 3d Battalions of the 124th Infantry alone, there were 162 wounded who were so badly hurt that they needed to be carried on litters. Four able-bodied men hefted four patients on each litter, while a fifth soldier handled weapons. Standing by to relieve them as litter carriers were four more men. Only the countless walking wounded were exempt from carrying the litters. But being carried by fatigued stretcher-bearers over the mountainous trail was no joyride for the wounded either. Lacking medicines, Japanese doctors were unable to treat the wounded adequately, resulting in the deaths and suffering of many. Swarms of flies buzzed over stretchers and squirming maggots infested wounds. Many bled to death as the swaying and jolting stretchers forced wounds to split open. Some litter bearers died from hunger and fatigue.[5]

First Lieutenant Matsumoto, commander of the 3d Company, 124th Infantry, aptly described the trying ordeal of this march:

We had never experienced a retreat like this in the China Incident and it is a very distressing event. When I read this diary in the future I believe I'll be carried away with deep emotions. The faithful heroes in battle are not always found in a victorious attack, but also in defeat. The sight of these men who are enduring hardships and hunger, and the afflictions of transporting the wounded is even more beautiful than the picture of them in victory. These are the qualities of only the faithful and well-trained armies. I cannot help but cry when I see the sight of these men marching with no food for four or five days and carrying the wounded through the curving and sloping mountain trail. Hiding my tears I encouraged the weak-willed to march on.[6]

And march they did. On the morning of the 18th, the leading elements of Kawaguchi's snaking column reached Oka's temporary headquarters east of the Matanikau. There, each soldier received a ration of six or seven handfuls of rice, which each man ravenously consumed. On the 21st, the Japanese reached the bivouac of the 2d Battalion, 124th Infantry, where they rested and were given more food.[7]

Of all of Kawaguchi's units, the Kuma Battalion and artillery unit suffered the worst. Through radio contact on the morning of the 22nd, Kawaguchi learned that the two units had become lost in the trackless jungle and were hungry and exhausted. Kawaguchi immediately dispatched a rifle company and a platoon of engineers to guide them to safety. Although small groups of these lost units began to reach the Matanikau on the 26th, some took an additional two weeks to arrive there. When these warriors did arrive, Kawaguchi discovered that their combat value was greatly diminished. Having little strength, half of the soldiers arrived empty handed, while others brought only their rifles. All of their heavy weapons and artillery had either been buried or abandoned in the jungle.[8]

"Despite Serious Fighting, We Have Failed"

At Rabaul, hunger for word on Kawaguchi's offensive remained acute on the 14th. The only scrap of information to fall on Rabaul's table came from Destroyer Division 19, which had bombarded the Lunga perimeter on the night of 13–14 September. The ships reported seeing flares and other signs of battle about two miles east of the airfield, leading some members of the Seventeenth Army staff to surmise that the firing was from Kawaguchi's artillery unit. General Futami, however, was not convinced. Futami believed that Kawaguchi had either become lost or that he was still making preparations for the attack. Support for the latter view came from Colonel Matsumoto on the afternoon of the 14th. Matsumoto admitted that difficulties in jungle movement made it necessary for Kawaguchi to put off the attack from the 12th to the 13th and that it was now scheduled for 2200 on the 14th. The source of Matsumoto's faulty information is not known.[9]

On the morning of 15 September, the Seventeenth Army finally received General Kawaguchi's long-awaited report of the battle. Two staff officers rushed the report to Futami, who saw from their expressions that the attack had failed. Kawaguchi's report provided a brief and stunning synopsis of his defeat at the hands of a surprisingly resilient American foe. The detachment commander ruefully admitted that he had suffered serious casualties and that he was withdrawing his forces west across the Lunga River. "Despite serious fighting we have failed," Kawaguchi proclaimed. "I am sorry." Hyakutake was shocked when he read the report, but he believed that Kawaguchi had done all he could to win the battle.[10]

With the disturbing news of Kawaguchi's defeat foremost in his mind, General Hyakutake radioed Kawaguchi new orders on the afternoon of the 15th. Kawaguchi was directed to occupy a point west of the Matanikau as close as possible to the enemy airfield, where he could both gather intelligence and obstruct U.S. air operations. Hyakutake also ordered Kawaguchi to occupy Kamimbo and to secure the lines of communication from Kamimbo to the Matanikau. In light of Kawaguchi's predicament, Hyakutake's signal was a tall order, but Hyakutake rushed reinforcements to the island to help Kawaguchi complete the task. On the night of 15 September seven destroyers disgorged about 1,100 men of the 4th Infantry Regiment at Kamimbo Bay, including the entire 1st Battalion. Also stepping ashore this night was the commander of the 4th Infantry, Col. Naomasa Nakaguma, a bright and aggressive officer. The following night the destroyers *Suzunami* and *Amagiri* reached Kamimbo with badly needed provisions and medical supplies. A replay occurred on the evening of the 18th, when the destroyers *Arashi, Umikaze,* and *Kawakaze* deposited provisions, 170 troops, and four 75mm guns of Nakaguma's 4th Regimental Gun Company.[11]

Word of Kawaguchi's defeat, the Imperial Army's first major defeat of the war, was met with stunned silence at Imperial General Headquarters. The shock of the defeat, however, energized Tokyo into action like never before. In an emergency session called to discuss the Guadalcanal matter, both the army and navy sections now saw Guadalcanal as the site of the anticipated U.S. counterattack. They also agreed that Guadalcanal might develop into the decisive battle of the war. In the same meeting, naval planners asked the Imperial Army if additional ground forces could be rushed to the Southeast Pacific, to which the Imperial Army replied in the affirmative. With the Russians preoccupied with the German front, Imperial Army planners believed that enough units were available in Manchuria to support a major operation in the Pacific like Guadalcanal.[12]

Meanwhile, back on Guadalcanal, at 1400 on the 19th, General Kawaguchi reached the village of Kokumbona, where he temporarily established his headquarters and oversaw the recovery and reorganization of the detachment. The task suddenly took on new urgency with the receipt of a Seventeenth Army message the day before, announcing that reinforcements would soon be brought to the island for another more massive attempt to recapture the Solomons. The promised reinforcements included the 1st Independent Tank Company (the first Japanese armor to arrive on Guadalcanal); the 2d Battalion, 21st Field Artillery Regiment; and the 3d Mortar Bat-

talion. The importance of this message was underscored two days later, when two officers of the Seventeenth Army staff, Majors Kazuo Etsugu and Haruji
Yamauchi, met with General Kawaguchi to gather
intelligence for the offensive.[13]

The coming offensive, requiring even more Seventeenth Army resources, placed General Hyakutake in
an unenviable position. He was in charge of two major
operations but lacked the troops, shipping, and supplies to sustain them both simultaneously. After much
thought, Hyakutake recommended to Imperial General Headquarters the suspension of the Port Moresby
offensive until the Guadalcanal matter was resolved.
This was a bitter pill for the Japanese to swallow. From
his perch on the Owen Stanley Range on New Guinea,
Maj. Gen. Tomitaro Horii, commander of the Nankai
Detachment, reported on the night of 14 September
that the lights of Port Moresby were in plain view,
some thirty miles distant. Although his force was
undersupplied, Horii was willing to proceed with the
operation, subsisting on the spiritual strength of his
men. But Hyakutake would hear none of it and immediately ordered the headstrong general to fall back to
Kokoda. Not only was Guadalcanal becoming a source
of embarrassment for the Imperial Army, it was having
a direct impact on another important front some 800
miles away.[14]

The Arrival of the 7th Marines

While Kawaguchi withdrew his battered and beaten
command westward, General Vandegrift moved his
command post back to its original position northwest

of the airfield. The fury and proximity of Kawaguchi's attack had at last opened Vandegrift's eyes to the dangers of the ridge location. But that's not all. The attack also prompted an urgent call for reinforcements even in the midst of battle. At about 0100 on the 14th, Vandegrift ordered General Rupertus to ship one rifle battalion from Tulagi to Guadalcanal after daybreak. At 0850 Vandegrift reiterated his order, stressing the need for additional riflemen. "Explain to [the] escort commander [the] urgency of getting [a] battalion here," Vandegrift said. "Reply in clear yes or no if he will bring them." Later that day a YP and the transport *Bellatrix* deposited the 3d Battalion, 2d Marines, at Kukum.[15]

This infusion of additional riflemen was welcome, but the best was yet to come. One day late but true to his word, six of Admiral Turner's transports dropped anchor off Lunga Point at first light on 18 September. These vessels deposited 4,157 men of the 3d Provisional Marine Brigade (7th Marines Reinforced), which included the 1st Battalion, 11th Marines, and Company C, 1st Tank Battalion. Support units included Company B, 1st Engineer Battalion; Company B, 1st Service Battalion; and Company B, 1st Medical Battalion. Turner's transports also put ashore 137 vehicles, 60 percent of the tentage, 4,323 barrels of fuel, ammunition, rations, and 90 percent of the engineering equipment by nightfall. The ammunition landed included 10,000 rounds of 37mm canister and 10,000 hand grenades, items that Vandegrift requested on 22 August. Colonel Merrill Twining called the arrival of supplies and the 7th Marines "undreamed-of wealth." But the arrival of this wealth did not occur without cost. While escorting Turner's transports to Guadalcanal, the aircraft carrier *Wasp* was torpedoed and sunk and the battleship *North Carolina* badly damaged by torpedoes from a Japanese submarine.[16]

According to Lt. Col. Gerald Thomas, the 7th Marines were "loaded with talent." But among the many outstanding officers in the regiment one stood out from the rest—Lt. Col. Lewis B. "Chesty" Puller, the charismatic, forty-four-year-old commander of the 1st Battalion, 7th Marines. With his bellowing voice, barrel chest, and jutting chin, Puller's presence was commanding. In contrast with Edson, Puller was an extrovert. "Chesty" was the quintessential no-nonsense field officer. He hated staff work, command post exercises, and superfluous regulations. Puller came to Guadalcanal with two Navy Crosses, which he won in the banana wars, and would eventually become the most decorated man in the Marine Corps. One of those who saw Puller stepping ashore was Edson, who said, "There comes the greatest fighting man in the Marine Corps. We'll have some competition now."[17]

Kawaguchi's recent three-pronged attack prompted General Vandegrift and Colonel Thomas to reappraise the division's scheme of defense. The result of their efforts was the 19 September operations order directing the establishment of a *complete* perimeter defense. The recent addition of four rifle battalions made fulfillment of this order possible. The new scheme called for ten sectors. The 1st Engineer, 1st Pioneer, and 1st Amphibious Tractor Battalions manned the three facing the beach around Lunga Point. The inland portion of the perimeter was divided into six rifle battalion sectors with two assigned to each of the three infantry regiments (the 1st, 5th, and 7th Marines). The remaining sector was assigned to the 3d Battalion, 2d Marines, which along with the 1st Raider Battalion, remained under division control.[18]

The main line of resistance capitalized on the terrain as much as possible. The perimeter followed the grassy ridges west of the Lunga and included all ground, which offered clear fields of fire to defenders. East of the Lunga, the line dipped south then rose crossing over Hill 80 on Bloody Ridge, followed a bearing nearly due east, then followed the edge of the jungle bordering on the large grassy plain where the Kuma Battalion had recently attacked. Defense in depth was utilized on the ridges as much as possible. Defense in depth, however, was impossible to employ in the dense tropical vegetation. Fields of fire were scratched out of the jungle but were limited in range to between fifty and 100 yards. Emplacements consisted of foxholes and splinterproof fortifications, where automatic weapons were erected. The entire front was protected by two bands of double apron barbed wire supplemented by trip wires between the bands. Measures were also taken to stockpile food and ammunition along the entire front. This was done to make positions self-sufficient, in the event that supply lines were severed by an enemy breakthrough.[19]

The deputy D-3, Col. Merrill Twining, admitted the new scheme "was a cordon defense of the worst type," but the dense maze of jungle vegetation imposed its employment and offered the marines several advantages. Not only did it give the marines the ability to man unusually long frontages, but it also denied the

Japanese the ability to infiltrate gaps in the dense jungle. It also gave the marines the ability to amass tremendous firepower. The great disadvantage of the cordon defense, namely its vulnerability to devastating barrages of artillery prior to an attack and breakthrough, did not apply against the Imperial Army. The Japanese were notoriously weak in the use of artillery. Only at Bataan and later at Okinawa did they demonstrate any proficiency in its use. This fact, however, did not totally eliminate all dangers. A surprise night attack on a concentrated front could easily achieve a breakthrough. But the Japanese had thus far displayed the suicidal preference to attack with cold steel instead of heavy weapons.[20]

While the division toiled to erect the new perimeter defense, Vandegrift made some important leadership changes. The catalyst for change was an 8 September letter from the Marine Corps commandant, Lt. Gen. Thomas Holcomb. Vandegrift was asked to ship his surplus colonels and lieutenant colonels home for employment elsewhere in the rapidly growing Marine Corps. To Vandegrift, the timing of this request could not have been better. The challenges of combat had exposed the inadequate performances of a number of key officers. Conspicuous among these were Colonels Capers James, Vandegrift's chief of staff, and Leroy Hunt, commander of the 5th Marines. As one of Vandegrift's closest personal friends, the removal of Hunt was particularly difficult. In his memoirs, Vandegrift explained that he sent back the most senior colonels with the longest amount of time in the division, but this is not true, because he retained the services of Colonels Cates and Del Valle. This explanation was simply Vandegrift's way of making the transfers more palatable for those affected.[21]

Vandegrift had little difficulty filling the 5th Marines commander and chief of staff positions. Lieutenant Colonel Thomas, who had by now become Vandegrift's most trusted confidant, was a no-brainer choice for chief of staff. With this elevation came a temporary promotion to full colonel. One suspects that Vandegrift had his eye on Thomas all along. Replacing Thomas as operations officer was his outspoken and brainy assistant, Lt. Col. Merrill Twining. At the urging of Thomas, Vandegrift chose Col. Red Mike Edson as the new commander of the 5th Marines. Edson's elevation to the top post of the 5th Marines was ironic. The regiment's lackluster performance on Guadalcanal was in part attributable to the fact that Edson had siphoned off some of the unit's best and brightest the previous year, when he formed the 1st Raider Battalion. Now, as commander of the 5th Marines, Edson returned the favor by robbing a handful of officers from the ranks of the Raiders, including Majors Lew Walt and Hank Adams. Lieutenant Colonel Samuel B. Griffith, the newly appointed commander of the Raiders, protested Edson's raid on his battalion, but the division staff gave Griffith an unsympathetic ear. Vandegrift also replaced several older lieutenant colonels with younger, more aggressive lieutenant colonels and majors. After the changes, Vandegrift felt that his division was "much stronger" than it was before.[22]

Disasters such as the Goettge patrol and the 17 September patrol of the 1st Marines prompted a special innovation in the division. Lieutenant Colonel William

J. Whaling, a skilled marksman and hunter, proposed the formation of a special scout troop for patrolling and intelligence collection. Following Vandegrift's eager approval, the unit, known officially as the Scout-Sniper Detachment, eventually consisted of about 100 men. All of these men were avid woodsmen who before the war possessed a special aptitude in navigation and sniping. They also had an uncanny ability to avoid detection and getting shot by the enemy. Colonel Thomas recalled the interview of one red-bearded giant, nicknamed "Daniel Boone," who, when asked why he wanted to join the outfit, replied, "If I lay behind that wire another day I will go crazy. I must find out what is on the other side of it."[23]

The Second Battle of the Matanikau, 23–27 September

As the campaign entered the fourth week of September, General Kawaguchi was suddenly faced with the dual task of fending off an American attack and preparing a lunge of his own. On 24 September, the Seventeenth Army told Kawaguchi that Japanese radio intelligence analysts suspected that the Americans might launch a new amphibious assault in the Solomons. These analysts believed that the possibility of a landing between the Matanikau River and Kamimbo was so strong that precautionary measures were needed. Thus, Kawaguchi ordered Yoshida's Maizuru Battalion and Watanabe's 3d Battalion, 124th Infantry—with the assistance of Kadomae's naval infantry—to occupy the hills along the coast, where they could repel an enemy landing. If a landing occurred, Colonel Nakaguma's 4th Infantry would fall under the detachment's control and cooperate with Colonel Oka to stop the landing.[24]

Colonel Oka, meanwhile, witnessed alarming enemy air activity over Guadalcanal. Realizing that an enemy landing was a strong possibility, Oka scuttled the idea of leading the Kuma Battalion and artillery unit back to the Matanikau. Instead, Oka chose to pull back the Maizuru Battalion, which was east of the Matanikau, to the relative safety west of the river. Lieutenant Hirota's 5th Company was commanded to occupy a position at the foot of Mount Austen. Lieutenant Kamei's 8th Company, which was on the Maizuru Road near the Lunga, was ordered to fall back to the west bank of the Matanikau. Oka also ordered Captain Bito's 12th Company to seize a position on the east bank of the Matanikau at the one-log bridge, called *Ipponbashi* by the Japanese. From that point, Bito would cover the withdrawal of both the Maizuru and Kuma Battalions.[25]

Late on the 24th, Majors Etsugu and Yamauchi completed their three-day inspection trip and radioed their findings to Seventeenth Army headquarters. They reported that the enemy's main line of resistance west of the Lunga extended from Kuma Height to Hiyo Height, and that the fortifications in the west consisted of dug-in positions and trenches fronted with barbed wire. Similar fortifications east of the Lunga were observed extending south of the airfield to the Tenaru River. In addition to the static defenses, they saw approximately thirty aircraft roosting near the airfield. Kawaguchi's officers told them that the barbed wire was not electrified, but they did state that the Americans were using microphones to aid in detection.[26]

Following the appraisal of the enemy's defenses, Etsugu and Yamauchi assessed the terrain of the island, particularly the rugged, mountainous territory around the Matanikau River. They reported that the width of the river averaged forty to fifty meters near the coast, and that the ground between the river's mouth and the northeastern slope of Mount Austen was rugged and took up to four hours to traverse. Not only did the terrain make it difficult to move carts along the river, the two explained, but artillery pieces needed to be disassembled. More important, because of the Matanikau's steep slopes, they stressed that the only place where 15cm howitzers could cross the river was the sand spit at the river's mouth.[27]

General Vandegrift and his staff were aware that the main body of Kawaguchi's force occupied the area around the Matanikau, and that small and large bodies of Japanese survivors and stragglers remained scattered between the Lunga and Matanikau Rivers. Since the time-consuming, labor-intensive construction of the perimeter defenses remained Vandegrift's top priority, large forces could not be spared for extensive forays against the Japanese. Consequently, Vandegrift decided to mount a series of small operations in the area designed not only to eradicate patrols and stragglers, but also to prevent larger forces from consolidating within easy striking distance of the airfield.[28]

The first excursion into this region was assigned to "Chesty" Puller's 1st Battalion, 7th Marines. His orders were clear and simple: March west, scale Mount Austen, ford the Matanikau, and reconnoiter the area

between the Matanikau and Kokumbona village.
Based on Puller's preliminary reconnaissance, Colonel
Griffith's 1st Raider Battalion would march west and
establish a temporary patrol base at Kokumbona.
From there, the Raiders would explore the area west
toward Tassafaronga and patrol south along the native
trail leading to Beaufort Bay and east toward the
Matanikau. Of particular concern to Vandegrift was
the area from Kokumbona to the Matanikau. Vandegrift wanted to rid the area of the enemy. The major
flaw of this plan, however, was that Vandegrift and
Twining expected to encounter no more than 400
Japanese. The marines, however, would encounter
Oka's bloodied yet resolute 124th Infantry, which now
numbered about 1,900 men.[29]

One of Vandegrift's objectives was clearing out
Mount Austen, which peaked at 1,514 feet. In a letter
to Admiral Turner on the 24th, Vandegrift wrote that
he was sure a Japanese observation post was perched
atop the mountain. Vandegrift was right. Coincidentally, the Japanese had established a post there just two
days prior. Taking advantage of its commanding view,
Japanese observers watched every move the Americans
made. Of particular interest were the arrival and
departure of aircraft and ships, troop activity, and the
construction of the perimeter defenses near Kuma
and Hiyo Heights. The Japanese observers kept
detailed logs of U.S. activities.[30]

Numbering about 600 men, Puller's battalion ven-
tured out from the perimeter early on the morning of
23 September along the Maizuru Road. At 0915,
Puller's battalion engaged a small Japanese force after
crossing the Lunga River. This force, consisting of two

patrols and led by First Lieutenants Kojima and
Nakayama, had coincidentally drawn similar assignments to that of Puller. Kojima's patrol was on its way
to reconnoiter the area south of Henderson Field;
Nakayama's was in search of Captain Bito's 12th Company. In a quick and deadly firefight, Puller's men
routed the Japanese, prompting Puller to issue his
humorous, well-known transmission to headquarters:
"Killed Japanese patrol under cloud 6,000 yards south
of Lunga Point." The "cloud" that Puller was referring
to was not in the sky; it was on the division's map. The
aerial photographs taken for this map were snapped
on a cloudy day. Consequently, several cloud-covered
areas were outlined and blanked out with the word
"cloud" to indicate the reason why no detail was
shown.[31]

At 1700 the following afternoon, Puller's point surprised and engaged a Japanese bivouac of sixteen men
relaxing and cooking rice on the northwest slope of
Mount Austen. These men were quickly exterminated,
but the sound of battle alerted the Maizuru Battalion,
which was nearby. As "Chesty" was sampling some of
the cooked rice, enemy machine gun bullets pierced
the hot and humid air, knocking the bowl out of his
hands. Everyone hit the dirt in the knee-high kunai
grass except for Puller, who stood there bellowing
orders to his men. The two sides then locked horns in
a vicious fight. Company B took the brunt of the fire
on the American side, suffering heavy casualties,
including the company commander, Capt. Chester
Cockrell, who was killed. The Japanese slowly pulled
back during the fight, leaving twenty men of Lieutenant Tauruta's 6th Company behind to act as a rear-

guard, while the main body of the battalion withdrew. The battalion did this to comply with Kawaguchi and Oka's earlier order to pull back to the Matanikau.[32]

Sergeant Joseph Gobel of the 3d Platoon, Company B, recalls some of the fighting:

> The 3d Platoon of Company B had taken up defense in the stream and the banks were about four feet high. I heard Colonel Puller call Captain Cox to bring the 3d Platoon of Company B up on the double. I gave orders for the 3d Platoon to move out of the stream and up the bank. Just as we cleared the stream, two machine guns opened up on us. Some of us rolled back into the water, others lay flat, or got behind anything they could find. I rolled over behind a tree. The firing had pinned us down. Bullets were spraying past me within inches. Afterwards, Tommy Thompson said it looked to him like every one of the bullets was hitting me. He told Corporal Toth that he would have to take command, since Sergeant Gobel had been killed. I was not touched except by flying dirt and gravel. In fact, no one in my squad had been hit.[33]

The fighting ended at dusk. But the fighting had cost Puller seven marines killed and twenty-five wounded. After securing the area, Puller ordered his men to dig in for the night on a nearby ridge and radioed headquarters, requesting help with the wounded. Vandegrift told him that he would reinforce

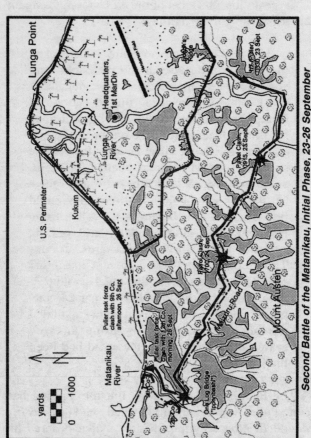

Second Battle of the Matanikau, Initial Phase, 23-26 September

him with a full battalion, the 2d Battalion, 5th
Marines.[34] The next morning, Chesty's men entered
the main Japanese camp. The marines found at least
thirty dead Japanese. "Chesty" estimated that 500
Japanese had recently bivouacked there. The marines
feasted on captured goodies, including tinned crab
and tangerines. Puller liberated a map case, diary, and
sword from a Japanese officer.

The 2d Battalion, 5th Marines, under Lt. Col. David
McDougal, rendezvoused with Puller early on 25 September. Inexplicably, Puller sent the casualties back to
the perimeter with most of his battalion. This group,
led by Puller's executive officer, Maj. Otho Rogers, was
comprised of Companies A and B. Why he chose two
companies when one was sufficient for the task is difficult to fathom. Nevertheless, Puller pressed on with a
task force composed of Company C, part of his headquarters company, and the 2d Battalion, 5th Marines.
The odd organization of this task force would charac-
terize the rest of the battle.[35]

The progress of Puller's task force in the stifling
heat and rugged terrain on the 25th was slow. Following an uneventful evening bivouacked that night, the
task force set out early the next morning. Soon, it
encountered opposition from Captain Bito's 12th
Company at the one-log bridge, where the task force
was apparently supposed to cross. Puller continued
the mission, however, advancing north along the east
bank of the Matanikau toward the sand spit. There, at
1150, machine gun and mortar fire from the 9th Company, now led by Lieutenant Nakayama, lashed out at
the marines as they began to cross. Despite artillery
support from the 11th Marines, two efforts to force a

crossing by Capt. H. T. Richmond's Company G, 5th
Marines, failed miserably, suffering twenty-five casualties in the process. An effort to outflank the resistance
south at the one-log bridge was stopped by Bito's
determined defenders. In the meantime, Colonel
Edson and Griffith's 1st Raider Battalion linked up
with Puller and McDougal near the sand spit.[36]

Edson brought with him a hastily devised plan, presumably from Colonel Twining, which closely resembled the failed Kokumbona operation. Under Edson's
overall command, Griffith's Raiders (with Company
C, 7th Marines) would advance upstream, cross the
river at the one-log bridge, and outflank the Japanese
from the south. While this flanking maneuver was in
progress, McDougal would hold the line and launch
an attack across the sand spit. If the Raiders were successful, the 1st Battalion, 7th Marines (less Company
C), under Major Rogers would land west of Point
Cruz at 1300 in order to take the Japanese by surprise from the rear. Aircraft and 75mm and 105mm
howitzers would provide support for the operation.
The offensive would begin on the morning of 27
September.[37]

From the beginning, the operation did not go well.
As the Raiders approached the one-log bridge, they
came under heavy mortar and machine gun fire from
Bito's 12th Company. Machine gun bullets killed
Major Bailey, one of the heroes of Edson's Ridge, and
wounded several others. An attempt to outflank the
obstinate Japanese defenders with two companies
accomplished nothing besides adding to the growing
Raider casualty list, including the commander, Samuel
B. Griffith. At the mouth of the Matanikau, Naka-

yama's 9th Company, reinforced the night before by the remnants of the 7th Company, the 10th Company, and the remnants of the 124th Regimental Gun Company, also staved off McDougal's effort to cross the sand spit. For the marines, it was a miserable replay of the previous day.[38]

There then occurred a communications muddle, which threw the entire operation into confusion. A series of garbled or ambiguous messages from Griffith led Vandegrift and Edson to conclude that the Raiders had successfully outflanked the Japanese on the west side of the river. As a result, Edson ordered McDougal to renew the attack at the sand spit and ordered the 1st Battalion, 7th Marines, to proceed with the planned landing.[39]

At 1300, Japanese lookouts perched atop Mount Austen saw an American destroyer and nine landing craft discharging hundreds of marines west of Point Cruz. This was the destroyer *Monssen* (DD-436), covering the landing of Major Rogers's 1st Battalion, 7th Marines (less Company C). Rogers, a reservist and post office employee who had never been in battle, ordered Companies A, B, and D to push inland about 600 yards to seize the first ridge, later called Hill 84. Instantly recognizing the seriousness of this landing, Colonel Oka ordered Lieutenant Kamei's 8th Company, reinforced with one 70mm platoon and two machine gun platoons, to attack the invaders from the west. Oka also directed the main body of Captain Bito's 12th Company to fall back and attack the Americans from the southeast. This meant that the Japanese were closing in on the invaders from two separate points.[40]

Almost immediately, Rogers's three companies came under heavy fire. At the top of the ridge a mortar shell blew Major Rogers into two and shattered the arms and legs of Captain Cox. Captain Charles W. Kelly then took command of the isolated and endangered companies, ordering them to establish a perimeter defense around the ridge. Enduring a hornet's nest of flying steel, the marines fought back the best they could. The mortar platoon of Company D had only one 81mm mortar and about fifty rounds to keep the enemy at bay. Master Gunnery Sergeant Roy Fowel directed the mortar fire at the approaching enemy at an incredibly low range of just 200 yards. The tube was so vertical that one marine had to lie on his back with his feet braced against it to prevent it from toppling over.[41]

Despite their best efforts, the Japanese continued to tighten the noose around Kelly's three companies. Unfortunately, nobody bothered to bring a radio on the mission to call for help. Consequently, Kelly's marines improvised by using white undershirts to spell out the word "H-E-L-P" on the ridge. An SBD Dauntless dive-bomber supporting the operation, piloted by 2d Lt. Dale H. Leslie, spotted the signal and relayed the message to Colonel Edson by radio.[42]

Meanwhile, sixteen Bettys and thirty-eight Zeros had made an appearance over Henderson Field at 1330, damaging or destroying several U.S. aircraft on the ground. The bombs also snuffed out all of Vandegrift's communications. The loss of communications in the midst of an offensive was potentially devastating, so Colonel Twining urgently hopped into a jeep and drove to Kukum, where a battalion of the 11th

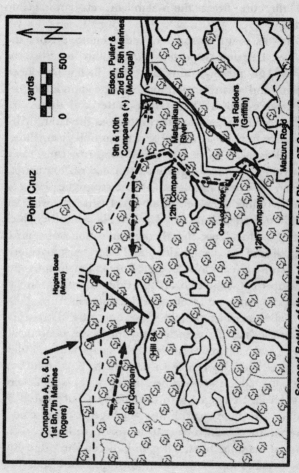

Point Cruz

Companies A, B, & D,
1st Bn, 7th Marines
(Rogers)

Higgins Boats
(Munro)

Hill 84

8th Company

9th & 10th
Companies (+)

Edson, Puller &
2nd Bn, 5th Marines
(McDougal)

Matanikau River

12th Company

One-log bridge

12th Company

1st Raiders
(Griffith)

Matzunu Road

yards

0   500

Second Battle of the Matanikau, Final Phase, 27 September

Marines was supporting the operation. There, Twining arranged to have the battalion's forward observer, who was directing fire at the Matanikau, relay messages to Edson.[43]

At this point, Edson received a message from the Raider Battalion reporting their failure to cross the river. The message also said that Bailey had been killed and Griffith wounded. Edson pondered the message's import. "I guess we better call them off," Edson said. "They can't seem to cross the river." With his battalion isolated and facing annihilation, Puller told Edson, "You're not going to throw these men away!" Puller and a signalman stormed off toward the beach, where they hailed a boat from the *Monssen*. Puller immediately set out toward Point Cruz with ten landing craft trailing the *Monssen* like a mother duck with her ducklings. Visual communication was quickly established between Kelly and Puller by semaphore. This was no easy task for Sgt. Robert Raysbrook, who had to expose himself on the ridge to enemy fire in order to send and receive the visual signals.[44]

Kelly's marines on Hill 84 were in a tight spot. The Japanese had slithered around the ridge and cut off their only escape route to the sea. When Puller ordered Kelly to return to the beach, Kelly told him he was unable to return because he and his men were cut off and engaged with the enemy. Coordinated by Puller, the *Monssen,* with her 5-inch guns, conducted a preparatory bombardment to assist with the withdrawal. Its guns blasted a path between the ridge and the beach, toppling trees and throwing chunks of dirt, foliage, and Japanese into the air. Sergeant Goble of Company B vividly recalls the bombardment:

I looked out on the bay and saw [a destroyer], belching smoke, heading toward us. Then I saw fire from the five-inchers, so I hit the ground. The destroyer fired salvo after salvo, hitting the coconut grove below us. We all let out a cheer. Trees were falling, Japs were screaming, and we were yelling. Between the salvos, many of us stood up to see better. After about 30 minutes, the firing stopped and I was ordered to bring down the rear guard of my platoon.[45]

Company A was ordered to evacuate first, followed by Company B, each with attached machine gun units from Company D. The desperate situation required heroic efforts. Platoon Sergeant Anthony Malanowski of Company A covered the withdrawal with his BAR, dropping large numbers of Japanese until he himself was killed. Things appeared to be going well for the battalion until friendly fire from the 11th Marines began to register on the battalion, inflicting several casualties. Despite this gaffe, the marines managed to fight their way to the shore, where they established a hasty defense.[46]

Herded by Lieutenant Leslie in the air, the first landing craft grounded to a halt just west of Point Cruz at about 1630. But the Japanese were not about to sit idly by while the Americans escaped out to sea. Lieutenant Kamei's 8th Company subjected the marines and the boat crews to a terrific volume of fire from Point Cruz and the shore to the west. Oka also dispatched First Lieutenant Manuo's 1st Company, in order to assist in the annihilation of the Yankee invaders. Marine Johnny Giles, covering the withdrawal on the right, killed several Japanese with his machine gun before he died with only four rounds of ammunition. Signalman Douglas Munro of the U.S. Coast Guard, who led the landing craft to the shore, died while placing himself between the attacking Japanese and the embarking marines. Munro was posthumously awarded the Medal of Honor for his bravery.[47]

The heavy Japanese fire delayed the arrival of some boats in this "Little Dunkirk." Japanese machine guns sprayed the boats and the withdrawing marines, but nearly all of Kelly's marines were evacuated safely. Some did not make it. Looking back at Hill 84, Sergeant Gobel recalls seeing three tracers being fired into the air. Successfully withdrawing these men under heavy fire was nothing short of a miracle.[48]

According to one report, this fiasco cost the 1st Battalion, 7th Marines, eighteen killed and twenty-five wounded. But these figures are subject to considerable challenge. Around Hill 84 alone, the Japanese counted thirty-two American bodies. Other losses were sixteen killed and sixty-eight wounded in the 2d Battalion, 5th Marines, and thirty-six killed and seven wounded among the 1st Raider Battalion. These figures, plus the Japanese count, leave a total of ninety-one killed and 100 wounded. Also, contrary to the claims found in the 1st Marine Division's final report, which stated no weapons were left behind, the Japanese found a host of U.S. weapons around Hill 84. The captured booty included fifteen Springfield rifles, one .30-caliber machine gun, four "automatic guns," one Browning automatic rifle, fifteen boxes of belted machine gun ammunition, and an unidentified weapon the Japanese called a "Czech." According to a Seventeenth Army intelligence report, Japanese losses were thirty killed. Among those killed were the commander of the 8th Company, Lieutenant Kamei, and one of his platoon commanders, a First Lieutenant Shishida.[49]

Back at Rabaul, General Futami was ecstatic when he learned of the battle, labeling it as the first good news to come from Guadalcanal. Vandegrift admitted that the Japanese handled their forces well, "This occasion being the only one in which [they] ever demonstrated a capacity for maneuver," but Oka's forces fought aggressively as well. Indeed, Oka displayed uncharacteristic aggressiveness and aplomb in responding to each American threat. As for the Japanese units themselves, Nakayama's 9th Company, as well as Bito's 12th Company, tenaciously defended their territory without giving up an inch. Having failed miserably at Bloody Ridge, these two companies of Colonel Watanabe's battalion redeemed themselves somewhat in this battle after the fiasco at Bloody Ridge. Likewise, part of the Maizuru Battalion fought well, especially Kamei's 8th Company around Hill 84. For the first time in the campaign, Oka's regiment finally lived up to its reputation.

Although the U.S. Marine Corps official account fails to admit it, the battle was an embarrassing defeat for the marines. Edson correctly referred to it as the "abortive Second Matanikau." American intelligence was again faulty, greatly underestimating the size, strength, and determination of the enemy force. In one of the few times during the campaign, artillery support was not only ineffective, it also inflicted casualties on the marines. Air support was effective only in that Lieutenant Leslie and his SBD came through with some badly needed communications and coordination support for the stranded 1st Battalion, 7th Marines. Naval support, however, came through big, this being one of the few times during the campaign when the navy was called on for tactical gunfire support. Indeed, *Monssen*'s 5-inch guns probably saved Puller's battalion from annihilation.[50]

Not surprising, a lot of finger-pointing took place on the American side after the defeat. Some even blamed the hero of the ridge, Colonel Edson. Puller was disgusted with the botched operation, disparaging the Raiders and their former commander. Griffith echoed Puller's sentiments, accusing Edson of needlessly dispersing the forces at his disposal. Not everyone, however, blamed Edson. Twining blamed Puller for failing to cross the Matanikau at the one-log bridge, as the original plan stated, and also blamed Puller and Edson for hatching the failed scheme, although there is no evidence to support Twining's claim. At the very least, Twining and Vandegrift would have had to authorize the ill-conceived plan. Colonel Thomas later claimed that he was against the operation in the first place and that it was Twining who wanted to expand the perimeter and persuaded Vandegrift to launch the operation.[51]

In defense of both Edson and Puller, both of whom had their reputations marred by this fiasco, division (Vandegrift, Thomas, and Twining) must shoulder most of the blame. The chain of command for the operation and the composition of the force chosen for the job were odd, to say the least. Instead of sending a regiment with a clearly defined chain of command, not to mention battalions that were familiar with each other, Vandegrift sent three unrelated battalions for the task. Moreover, although Edson was clearly placed in charge of the operation, Puller's staff was somehow merged with the 5th Marines staff. In addition, Edson, who was placed in command of the operation late, had no opportunity to brief Puller's executive officer, Major Rogers, before the amphibious assault of the 1st Battalion, 7th Marines. All of these staff failures, coupled with the eagerness of Colonel Oka's 124th Infantry to get back at the marines, doomed the operation before it even got off the ground.[52]

Although the Second Battle of the Matanikau was a defeat, the 1st Marine Division culled a valuable lesson from the loss. In the final report, Vandegrift admitted that a great lesson on this defeat was found in the Field Service Regulations, which warns against "drifting aimlessly into action." Vandegrift wrote, "For in last analysis, this battle was unpremeditated and was fought without definite purpose other than the natural one of closing with the enemy at once and upon every occasion." As painful as this defeat was, however, the marines culled much from the Second Battle of the Matanikau and would aptly demonstrate this in the near future.[53]

On 30 September a lone American B-17 Flying Fortress bomber landed on muddy Henderson Field and laboriously taxied toward a group of officers on the west side of the runway. One of the first to step out of the green, twin-engine bomber was Admiral Chester W. Nimitz. Greeting the thin, gray-haired admiral first was

General Vandegrift, who was pleased to receive a visit from the ranking officer in the Pacific, something Nimitz's subordinate, Adm. Ghormley, failed to do. Nimitz had flown to Guadalcanal to catch a firsthand glimpse of the situation on Cactus. Vandegrift had plenty to show him, including a tour of the perimeter and Bloody Ridge, the division hospital, and the Pagoda, where he spoke with General Geiger. Later that night, Vandegrift discussed logistical problems, reinforcements, and the Japanese with Admiral Nimitz.[54]

The next morning, Nimitz decorated several officers and enlisted men with the Navy Cross, the highest medal he could award on his own authority. The awardees included a few of the most successful pilots, a sprinkling of enlisted men, and some of the commanders who took part in the Battles of the Tenaru and Bloody Ridge, including Colonel Edson. Before climbing aboard his aircraft, Admiral Nimitz promised to give Vandegrift his maximum support. Vandegrift's sailors and marines would need it, because the Japanese were preparing to mount another, more massive effort to eject the Americans from Guadalcanal.[55]

Appendix 1: Kawaguchi Detachment Combat Order A21, 1300, 7 September, Tetere

Author's Note: All times are Tokyo time (Guadalcanal time minus two)

1. Refer to sketch No. 1 on separate sheet for the situation of enemy positions according to the naval report.

2. In accordance with the appended plan of attack on enemy positions in the vicinity of the Guadalcanal Island Airfield, the main body of the detachment will attack the enemy from the rear, routing and annihilating them.

3. The various units will assume their positions to prepare for the coming attack, in accordance with the appended plan of attack on enemy positions in the vicinity of the Guadalcanal Island Airfield. A separate order will be issued in regard to the day after the attack (expected to be the night of the 13th).

4. I will be at Nalimbiu till dawn of X-3. Thereafter, I will proceed with the AOBA Battalion to the site of preparation for attack.

Major General Kawaguchi,
Detachment Commander

Method of Issue

Assemble all unit commanders of the front line and distribute printed copies.

Note: X indicates the opening day of the general attack.

Preparation for Attack

1. The Kuma Battalion will be in charge of the artillery, and on X-4 will advance to the right bank sector of the Higashi [Tenaru] River to protect the change of direction by the main body of the detachment; and, at the same time, it will prepare for a subsequent change of direction. On X-2 at 0100, after having transferred the foregoing responsibility to the Artillery, it will start advancing southward from the vicinity of Lengo. It will pass through the right bank sector of the Higashi [Tenaru] River, and by noon of X it will assume its position according to sketch No. 1 of separate sheet to prepare for the attack.

2. The various central units will prepare for attack in the following manner:

(a) The units of the right front line of attack will concentrate in the vicinity of Nalimbiu on the night of X-4. At dawn of X-3 they will start advancing southward, in general pass through the left bank sector of the Nalimbiu River, and by noon of X they will assume their positions according to sketch No. 1 to prepare for the attack.

(b) On the night of X-4 the units of the left front line of attack will concentrate in the vicinity about 1 kilometer to the southwest of Nalimbiu, and at dawn of X-3 will start to advance southward, generally advancing through the sector along the left bank of the Nalimbiu River; and by noon of X they will assume their positions according to sketch No. 1 to prepare for the attack.

(c) It is essential that units on both sides of the front line of attack keep in close contact with each other as to the selection of the route of advance.

(d) The units of the second line of attack will start their movement on X-3 immediately after the left and right units of the front line of attack, utilize the established routes, and by noon of X will assume their positions according to sketch No. 1 to prepare for the attack.

3. The left wing troops will assume their positions according to sketch No. 1 by noon of X to prepare for the attack.

4. The artillery will be under the command of the right wing commander until 0100 of X-3; thereafter, it will stand alone in the right bank sector of the Higashi [Tenaru] River to protect the changing of direction by the main body of the detachment; and at the same time it will prepare for the attack. During attack preparations, avoid action as far as possible but repulse the enemy if they venture to attack with sea units or tanks from the shore region.

5. Each unit will undertake the establishment of the route of advance as quickly as possible, and at the same time will exercise extreme caution to keep our plans concealed. Do not return fire against air attacks, and keep a good watch toward the shore during the concentration period.

6. Passage through the jungles will be executed chiefly in the daytime, but be sure to make a complete detour around grass fields by day. If passage through a grass field is unavoidable at night, try not to leave any footprints.

7. In case enemy antiaircraft positions exist in the vicinity of our areas for attack preparations, a part of the unit will execute a surprise attack on the night of X-1 and seize those positions.

8. When the enemy attacks during our change of direction, the artillery troops and the various units staying by the shore will do their utmost to check the enemy, while the main body will follow its fixed policy.

Execution of Attack

1. Refer to sketch No. 1 of separate sheet as to the essentials of disposition for attack and the conduct of the attack.

2. On X the artillery will fire on enemy positions in the left bank sector of the Nakagawa [Ilu] River from 1630 for about 1½ hours, and hold the enemy in said area. When the enemy attacks, concentrate the same withering firepower on them, thus safeguarding the right flank of the detachment.

3. On X at 2200 the right wing troops will break through the RO position, then successively the HA position, and will annihilate the enemy in the left bank sector of the Nakagawa [Ilu] River, thus giving repose to the departed souls of the Ichiki Detachment commander and his men.

4. The various units of the central body will attack as follows:

(a) The units of the right front line of attack will

wait till 2000 and will break through the NI position, and subsequently they will charge along the shore in the direction of HO position and destroy the enemy in that area.

(b) The units of the left front line of attack will wait till 2000 and will simultaneously launch attacks on both CHI and RI positions. Following this, a part of the units will firmly secure the RI position, while the main body will concentrate in the sector to the south of RI position and will make appropriate preparations for its use in an ensuing attack. If the right wing troops cannot participate in that action, it will seize RU position in addition and a part of the troops will secure the position.

(c) The units of the second line of attack will advance between the two wings of the front line of attack; and at the same time that the units of the right front line of attack and the units of the left front line of attack at NI position commence their seizure of RI position, they will break through HE and NU positions, which rise up from the area between NI and RI positions; then they will charge along the shore line in the vicinity of TO position and destroy the enemy in that area.

5. The left wing troops will wait till 2000, and its main body will seize RU position and a part will seize WA position; then they will drive on Lunga Point along both bank sectors of Ogawa [Lunga] River and destroy the enemy in that area.

6. Armed boats of the boat unit will cooperate with the navy and will be active on the sea in the vicinity of Lunga Point. They will lead the enemy to believe that this is a landing operation, and will prevent the enemy from escaping.

7. The reinforcements will move along with the detachment headquarters and will be prepared for any exigency.

8. During the preparation for attack the detachment headquarters will move with the AOBA battalion, and during the execution of attack, will advance behind the central body and reach RI position by dawn.

9. The main body of the 28th Independent Engineer Regiment will be responsible for defending the vicinity of Tasimboko.

10. The 1st Company (one gun) of 45th Antiaircraft Battalion will be situated at its present location, and will shoot down enemy planes.

11. During the execution of attack each unit will be on the watch for enemy tank attacks, and at the same time will be prepared to destroy the searchlight facilities and the electrically charged wire entanglements that are expected to be found on the four sides of the airfield.

Appendix 2: Personal Observations of American Forces on Guadacanal by Lieutenant Colonel Matsumoto

Author's Note: Observations made in late September or early October 1942. Translation as rendered by author.

1. The enemy's defensive fires are so well thought out they shoot as though they were expecting our attack.

2. The enemy's gunfire is violent regardless of the time of day or location, including in the middle of the jungle.

3. The bombing made by the enemy's airplanes is the same as the above mentioned items.

4. Due to the rapidity and accuracy of the enemy's artillery fire by means of sound detectors and telephone communication, our movements must be made secretly and quietly.

5. Use tracer bullets to indicate where enemy positions are located.

6. Barbed wire entanglements are established in critical positions in the forest. It is not yet clear whether or not they are electrically charged, since the Ichiki Detachment says they are and Kawaguchi Detachment says they are not.

7. It seems as though they fear the strength of our hand-to-hand combat.

8. The enemy's security at night seems to offer positive opportunity for infiltration due to the possibility of them being off guard on certain occasions.

9. Just before we rush to attack the enemy position, they will withdraw and vigorously concentrate their fire at that position after we occupy it.

10. They do not seem to have any self-confidence in the offensive and night combat.

11. Great consideration is required for receiving commands and liaison among our units in the jungle.

12. Items which require special care:

(a) During bombing and gun attacks, be calm as though dumbfounded.

(b) Thoroughness in discovering the enemy's camouflaged emplacements; approach them quietly and secretly with perseverance.

(c) Firmly and quietly give orders to subordinate officers and NCOs.

(d) Do not let your men talk loud or give out any light during the night or cook with fire during the day.

Appendix 3: Notes on Japanese Tactics and Technique by Col. Merritt A. Edson, USMC

1. The Japanese guns captured and destroyed at Taivu Point GUADALCANAL were Krupp guns and were 77mm instead of 75mm as previously reported [Edson's incorrect here, they were 75mm]. Ammunition for these guns was of Japanese manufacture.

2. The Japanese use snipers during both offensive and defensive action. Their function of harassing our forces and distracting their attention from the main effort is always the same

3. In dealing with enemy snipers it was found most undesirable to allow the assault echelon to become involved with snipers on flanks and rear. In a number of instances, it was found practicable to bypass the snipers with the assault echelon and leave to small follow-up patrols the task of cleaning out snipers.

4. Camouflage is an art with the Japanese. Their camouflage equipment shows careful planning in advance. It blends with the vegetation and terrain of the theater of operations.

5. The troops recently (Sept. 15) encountered on GUADALCANAL are probably fresh from fighting in the Philippines or Malaya. Their equipment corresponds to that used by our raider battalion.

6. Japanese tactics in night actions on GUADALCANAL:

(a) Japanese troops are particularly well trained in night operations and prefer night attacks to those in the daytime.

(b) In making night attacks, the successive objectives are clearly defined terrain features, such as a ridge or stream.

(c) After one attack, it generally requires two to three hours for the Japanese to reorganize themselves and get oriented for the next attack.

(d) In moving troops at night, platoon leaders fire a series of red flares in the direction of advance. The direction of movement could be followed by the defense by the simple expedient of watching the movement of the red flares. (It may be that the color red is used because it least affects night vision.)

(e) The signal for the assault was a flare fired to hang over the objective.

(f) By night, as well as by day, the Japanese invariably try to work small groups into flanks and rear of the defensive position in an attempt to cause panic and to destroy automatic weapons. The best counter for this was the "all around" defense. Those defenders facing the front must continue to do so and let the men on flanks and rear deal with the Japanese that have infiltrated. When this procedure was followed the Japanese were checked.

Appendix 4: U.S. Marine Corps Infantry Regiment Table of Organization (D Series)

Regimental Headquarters and Service Company (173)

Regimental Weapons Company (196)
   Company Headquarters (48)
   75mm Self-propelled Platoon (34)
   3 Antiaircraft and Antitank Platoons (38)

3 Rifle Battalions (933 ea. 2,799)
   Headquarters Company (111)
   Battalion Weapons Company (273)
     Company Headquarters (29)
     81mm Mortar Platoon (76)
     20mm Antiaircraft and Antitank Platoon (24)
     3 Machine Gun Platoons (48)
   3 Rifle Companies (183)
     Company Headquarters (29)
     Weapons Platoon (28)
       Platoon Section (4)

60mm Mortar Platoon (11)
Light Machine Gun Platoon (13)
3 Rifle Platoons (42)
Platoon Headquarters (7)
Browning Automatic Rifle Squad (8)
3 Rifle Squads (9)

Infantry Regiment Total Strength: 3,168

Notes

Introduction

1. Jon T. Hoffman, *Once a Legend: "Red Mike" Edson of the Marine Raiders* (Novato, Calif.: Presidio Press, 1994), 3.

2. George McMillan, *The Old Breed: A History of the First Marine Division in World War II* (Washington, D.C.: Infantry Journal Press, 1949), 1.

Chapter 1

1. Alexander A. Vandegrift and Robert B. Asprey, *Once a Marine: The Memoirs of General A. A. Vandegrift, U.S. Marine Corps* (New York: Norton, 1964), 132–3; Merrill B. Twining, *No Bended Knee: The Battle for Guadalcanal* (Novato, Calif.: Presidio Press, 1996), 66. The basic source for the 1st Marine Division's operations on Guadalcanal from August to December 1942 is Headquarters, 1st Marine Division, *Final Report on the Guadalcanal Operation*, divided into five phases, July 1943 (hereafter cited as *Final Report*), File A-7, Box 7, RG-127, National Archives and Records Administration (NARA).

2. Alexander A. Vandegrift Biographical File, Refer-

ence Section, Marine Corps Historical Center (MCHC); Merrill B. Twining, "Head for the Hills!," *Marine Corps Gazette* (August 1987), 46; Samuel B. Griffith, *The Battle for Guadalcanal* (Philadelphia: J. B. Lippincott, 1963), 22. See also Vandegrift's memoirs, *Once a Marine*. Vandegrift was born on 13 March 1887 and died on 8 May 1973.

3. Vandegrift and Asprey, *Once a Marine*, 132–3; Twining, *No Bended Knee*, 66–7.

4. *Final Report*, III (20 August–18 September), 1–2; Gerald C. Thomas, "Of Coconuts and Their Prelude," unpublished memoir (1976), Thomas Personal Papers, MCHC, 25; Twining, *No Bended Knee*, 66–7.

5. *Final Report*, III, 1–2; Thomas, "Of Coconuts," 25. Quote is from Twining, *No Bended Knee*, 73.

6. Ibid.

7. Eric Hammel, *Guadalcanal: Starvation Island* (New York: Crown, 1987), 126.

8. Artillery data comes from George Forty, *U.S. Army Handbook, 1939–1945* (New York: Scribner's, 1979), and Jack Coggins, *The Campaign for Guadalcanal: A Battle That Made History* (Garden City, N.Y.: Doubleday, 1972).

9. Thomas, "Of Coconuts," 25.

10. Only a small fraction of the Imperial Japanese Army had experience in jungle warfare.

11. Twining, *No Bended Knee*, 69. The 1st Marine Division's total strength is based on COMAMPHIBFORSOPAC letter, serial 0041, 15 August 1942, Operational Archives, Navy Historical Center (NHC).

12. Thomas, "Of Coconuts," 24; Twining, *No Bended Knee*, 73.

13. *Final Report*, III, Annex B (Details of the Estab-

lishment of the Airfield), 1–2, and Annex C (Logistics), 1; Thomas, "Of Coconuts," 26.

14. *Final Report,* III, Annex B, 2; Twining, *No Bended Knee,* 75; quote comes from George C. Dyer, *The Amphibians Came to Conquer: The Story of Admiral Richard Kelly Turner* (Washington, D.C.: Department of the Navy, 1972), 410.

15. *Final Report,* III, 3–4.

16. Herbert C. Merillat, *The Island: A History of the First Marine Division on Guadalcanal, August 7–December 9, 1942* (Boston: Houghton Mifflin, 1944), 54–5; Thomas, "Of Coconuts," 26. COMSOPAC to CINCPAC 131400 Aug 42, Greybook, 650, states that only three days of food were landed.

17. *Final Report,* III, Annex E (Operations Journal), 6; Herbert C. Merillat, *Guadalcanal Remembered* (New York: Dodd, Mead, 1982), 77. This author was unable to fix the exact date on which Vandegrift named the airstrip "Henderson Field." The first mention of Henderson Field in the Daily Operations Journal (Annex E) appears on 17 August 1942.

18. *Final Report,* III, Annex E, 1; COMGEN GUADALCANAL to COMAMPHIBFOR 131015 Aug 42, COMSOPAC War Diary 14 Aug 42, Operational Archives, NHC; Thomas, "Of Coconuts," 26–7. The abandonment of the marines by the navy on 9 August is a controversial topic even to this day. Marine suffering could have been great had the Japanese food supply not been so plentiful. Some sources, such as the *Final Report* (July 1943) and the Marine Corps official history (1958), state that the navy had put ashore thirty and thirty-seven days of food, respectively. Documentary evidence contemporaneous with

the event, however, paints a much different picture.

19. Martin Clemens, *Alone on Guadalcanal: A Coast-watcher's Story* (Annapolis, Md.: Naval Institute Press, 1998), 36–9.

20. Edward Fee, "Beach Party," *Guadalcanal Echoes* (July 1992), 16.

21. Robert Amery to author, letter of 21 July 1999 in author's possession.

22. Ibid.

23. Department of the Army, *Fighting on Guadalcanal* (Washington, D.C.: Department of the Army, 1943), 8.

24. Hammel, *Guadalcanal*, 128; quote is from Clifton Cates, "My First on Guadalcanal 7 August–22 December 1942," unpublished memoir, Clifton Cates Personal Papers, MCHC, 17; J. R. Garrett, "A Marine Diary: My Experiences on Guadalcanal," http://gnt.com/~/jrube@guadaug.html.

25. George Haertlein, "Some Things Were Funny," *Guadalcanal Echoes* (August–September 1996), 5.

26. *Final Report,* III, Annex F, 2–4; Hammel, *Guadalcanal,* 128–9.

27. James A. Donahue, "Guadalcanal Journal," http://users.erols.com/jud55/guadalcanal2.html, 2; Griffith, *The Battle for Guadalcanal,* 74–5.

28. Fee, "Beach Party," 18; John Joseph, "G-2-1 Memories," *Guadalcanal Echoes* (February–March 1999), 26.

29. Joseph, "G-2-1 Memories," 26.

30. *Final Report,* III, Annex F (Intelligence), 1–7; Griffith, *The Battle for Guadalcanal,* 70–1; Richard Tregaskis, *Guadalcanal Diary* (New York: Random House, 1943), 74–7; Merillat, *Guadalcanal Remembered,* 80–4.

31. Griffith, *The Battle for Guadalcanal,* 71–2; Tre-

gaskis, *Guadalcanal Diary*, 72; Donahue, "Guadalcanal Journal," 1.

32. *Final Report*, I, Annex F (Op Plan 7-42); *Final Report*, III, 5–6: Twining, *No Bended Knee*, 68.

33. *Final Report*, III, Annex F, 3–4. The circumstances about the raising of the "white flag" are found in Tregaskis, *Guadalcanal Diary*, 63–4.

34. *Final Report*, III, Annex F, 3–4; Annex J, 2–3. Those killed during the Goettge patrol were officially listed as missing in action. In a report to Rabaul the Japanese garrison on Guadalcanal confirmed that twenty-two Americans were buried after the ambush.

35. *Final Report*, III, Annex F, 5.

36. *Final Report*, III, Annex F, 5–6; Clemens, *Alone on Guadalcanal*, 22, 198–9; Hammel, *Guadalcanal*, 159.

37. The APDs were converted Caldwell and Wickes class destroyers, World War I–era vessels with four stacks. The conversion process into high-speed transports involved the removal of two boilers and their associated stacks, leaving a small hold amidships for cargo and men. Outfitted with davits, this enabled them to hoist and lower four Higgins boats. Ship specifications: displacement, 1,315 tons; length, 314 feet; maximum speed, 24 knots; main armament, 4-inch guns. Each vessel could carry a maximum of about 155 men. An extremely successful innovation, twenty-six APDs, derived mainly from Clemson class destroyers, later joined the six prewar units.

38. *Final Report*, III, Annex J, 3–4; Annex E, 6; Dyer, *The Amphibians Came to Conquer*, 419, 423; John Miller, *Guadalcanal: The First Offensive, The United States Army in World War II* (Washington, D.C.: Historical Division, Department of the Army, 1949), 104; *Dictionary of*

American Fighting Ships, vol. IV (Washington, D.C.: Department of the Navy, 1976), 218; John S. McCain to Vandegrift, letter of 16 August 1942, Vandegrift Personal Papers, MCHC. Some accounts have McCain's letter arriving with the APDs on the 15th, but this would have been impossible, because the letter was dated the 16th. Hence, the letter could have only arrived on the APDs' second run on the 17th.

Chapter 2

1. Saburo Hyashi and Alvin D. Coox, *Kogun: The Japanese Army in the Pacific War* (Quantico, Va.: Marine Corps Association, 1959), 225; Imoto to Griffith, letter of 14 February 1962, Samuel B. Griffith Personal Papers, Folder 9, Box 2, MCHC. Hyakutake was born on 25 May 1888 and died on 10 March 1947.

2. John B. Lundstrom, *The First South Pacific Campaign: Pacific Fleet Strategy, December 1941–June 1942* (Annapolis, Md.: Naval Institute Press, 1976), 24–5, 38–47, 65; H. P. Willmott, *The Barrier and the Javelin: Japanese and Allied Pacific Strategies, February to June 1942* (Annapolis, Md.: Naval Institute Press, 1983), 104–8.

3. Shuichi Miyazaki to Griffith, letter of 1962, Samuel B. Griffith Personal Papers, Folder 18, Box 2, MCHC; Samuel Milner, *Victory in Papua, The United States Army in World War II* (Washington, D.C.: Historical Division, Department of the Army, 1957), 60–7.

4. *Senshi Sosho, Minami Taiheiyo rikugan sakusen, 1, Pooruto Moresubi-Gashima shoki sakusen, Boeicho Boei kenshuji,* Senshishitsu, Asagumo Shinbun Sha, 25 March 1986, War History Series, *South Pacific Army Operations, Part I, Army Operations, Port Moresby–Guadalcanal, Early Operations,* vol. 14 (Tokyo: Defense Agency, Defense

Research Institute, Office of War History, 1986), 250–1; Miyazaki to Griffith letter of 1962.

5. *Senshi Sosho, Nanto Homen kaigun sakusen, 1, Gato Dakkai Sakusen Kaishimade, Boeicho Boei kenshojo,* Senshishitsu, Asagumo Shinbun Sha, 28 September 1971, War History Series, *Southeast Area Naval Operations, Part I,* vol. 49 (Tokyo: Defense Agency, Defense Research Institute, Office of War History, 1971), 442; Richard B. Frank, *Guadalcanal* (New York: Random House, 1990), 87.

6. *Senshi Sosho,* 14:269–71.

7. *Senshi Sosho,* 14:279–80; Griffith, *The Battle for Guadalcanal,* 78.

8. *Senshi Sosho,* 14:280–4, 297; Griffith, *The Battle for Guadalcanal,* 78.

9. *Senshi Sosho,* 14:289–91; translation as rendered in Griffith, *The Battle for Guadalcanal,* 78–9.

10. Quote is from Griffith, *The Battle for Guadalcanal,* 79.

11. USAFISPA, Acofs, G-2, "Japanese Campaign—Guadalcanal Area," 7 August 1943, 4; Masanobu Okada, "Remembrance: Ichiki on Guadalcanal," *Guadalcanal Echoes* (July 1986), 2; Intelligence Center, Pacific Oceans Areas, Bulletin #12-43, *Japanese Land Forces #6,* C15-5, Box 8, RG-127, NARA.

12. *Senshi Sosho,* 14:289–91; Southwest Pacific Area, Allied Translator and Interpreter Section (ATIS), Publication #28, *Enemy Publications* (hereafter cited as ATIS #28), 21 July 1943, Folder 4, Box 124, RG-3, MMBA, 53. In a Seventeenth Army intelligence report published on 16 August, Futami reported that the marines on Guadalcanal "are estimated to number four or five thousand, or at the most ten thousand."

13. "17th Army to Ichiki Detachment, 1500 hours, 13 Aug 42," 20–21, *17th Army Operations,* Part I; "Order for Landing on Guadalcanal Island by the Ichiki Detachment," Part II, William Whyte Personal Papers, Folder 10, Box 1, MCHC.

14. *Senshi Sosho,* 14:297.

15. Okada, "Remembrance," 2; Hayashi and Coox, *Kogun,* 225; Imoto to Griffith letter of 14 February 1962.

16. *Senshi Sosho,* 14:292; *Final Report,* III, Annex G (History of the 1st Marines), 2–4; Okada, "Remembrance," 2.

17. During the campaign, the Americans on Guadalcanal called these runs the "Cactus Express," based on the official Allied code word "Cactus" for Guadalcanal. During the war, correspondents and writers, when referring to these runs, were ordered to omit the code word in order to keep it secret. The person who coined the much more familiar "Tokyo Express" is not known.

18. "Orders for Landing on Guadalcanal Island by the Ichiki Detachment"; *Senshi Sosho,* 14:292; Raizo Tanaka, "The Struggle for Guadalcanal," in *The Japanese Navy in World War II* (Annapolis, Md.: Naval Institute Press, 1986), 160–1; "17th Army to Ichiki Detachment, 1500 hours, 13 Aug 42," 20. According to Ichiki Detachment Order No. 4 of 15 Aug 42, the disposition of Ichiki's First Echelon was as follows:

Arashi	Detachment Headquarters	119
	Part of the I/7 Engineer Regt.	31
Hagikaze	3d Company	125
	Part of the I/7 Engineer Regt.	25

Kagero	1st Company	125
	Part of the I/7 Engineer Regt.	25
Tanikaze	II/28 Headquarters	23
	4th Company	90
	Part of the Detachment Hqs.	12
	Part of the I/7 Engineer Regt.	25
Hamakaze	Part of the II/28 Machine Gun Co.	50
	Part of the 4th Company	15
	Part of the Detachment Hqs.	15
	II/28 Gun Platoon	48
	Part of the I/7 Engineer Regt.	22
Urakaze	2d Company	125
	Part of the Detachment Hqs.	3
	Part of the I/7 Engineer Regt.	22

This plan differs slightly from what was actually landed. For instance, 110 men (two platoons) of the Machine Gun Company were actually put ashore.

19. Ibid. The Imperial Navy's patrol boats were destroyer conversions similar to but less extensive than the U.S. Navy's APDs. *Patrol Boats 1* and *2* were conversions of the old Minekaze class. They displaced 1,390 tons, had a maximum speed of twenty knots, and had a main armament of two 4.7-inch guns. They were fitted with two 46-foot Diahatsu landing craft and could carry up to 250 troops. *Patrol Boats 34* and *35*, conversions of the old Momi class, displaced 935 tons, and had a maximum speed of eighteen knots. The main armament was the same as *Patrol Boats 1* and *2*, but they each were equipped to carry just one 46-foot Diahatsu landing boat and 150 men.

20. Hiroshi Kamei, "Island of Homesickness," *Guadalcanal Echoes* (April 1991 and June–July 1992), 17;

Stanley Jersey, "Observations," *Guadalcanal Echoes* (May–June 1998), 14. Sometimes erroneously called "marines," the Imperial Navy's Special Naval Landing Forces (SNLF) bore little resemblance to units of the U.S. Marine Corps. Even though they took part in early conquests in the Pacific, these lightly trained units were considered garrison troops rather than elite assault troops like U.S. marines. The SNLF were formed at and named after the four major naval bases in Japan—Kure, Maizuru, Sasebo, and Yokosuka—and were given numerical designations as formed. Unlike U.S. marines, they were manned entirely by naval personnel including the officers. However, like U.S. marines, the basic infantry weapons of the SNLF were nearly identical to those used by the Imperial Japanese Army.

21. Kamei, "Island of Homesickness," 17.

22. Ibid.

23. Kamei, "Island of Homesickness," 17; Griffith, *The Battle for Guadalcanal,* 74.

24. Kamei, "Island of Homesickness," 17; *Senshi Sosho,* 49:300, 302; Paul S. Dull, *A Battle History of the Imperial Japanese Navy: 1941–1945* (Annapolis, Md.: Naval Institute Press, 1978), 195.

25. *Final Report,* III, 7.

26. Ibid.

27. Forty, *U.S. Army Handbook, 1939–1945; The World Almanac of World War II* (New York: Pharos Books, 1986).

28. Ibid.

29. *Final Report,* III, 7; William Hawkins to Eric Hammel, letter of 22 May 1963, Eric Hammel Personal Papers, Box 6, MCHC.

30. *Final Report,* III, 7; Hawkins to Hammel letter of

22 May 1963; Merillat, *The Island*, 61; Tregaskis, *Guadalcanal Diary*, 117–20.

31. *Final Report*, III, 8; Annex J (History of the 5th Marines), 4; *Senshi Sosho*, 49:303.

32. *Final Report*, III, 8; Tregaskis, *Guadalcanal Diary*, 124; Ore Marion, "More on the Goettge Patrol," *Guadalcanal Echoes* (April 1989), 6.

33. Tregaskis, *Guadalcanal Diary*, 124–5.

34. *Final Report*, III, 8; Ben Selvitelle, "First Offensive Action on Guadalcanal," *Guadalcanal Echoes* (November–December 1995), 15; Kamei, "Island of Homesickness," 17; Marion, "More on the Goettge Patrol," 6. Quote is from *Final Report*, III, 14.

35. Ore Marion, "The New Reising Gun," *Guadalcanal Echoes* (January 1991), 22.

36. Selvitelle, "First Offensive Action on Guadalcanal," 15; Tregaskis, *Guadalcanal Diary*, 125.

37. *Final Report*, III, 8; Hawkins to Hammel letter of 22 May 1963; Merillat, *The Island*, 63.

38. Marion, "More on the Goettge Patrol," 6, 18. Colonel Hunt wanted his companies back at the perimeter in order to prepare for Ichiki's expected attack.

Chapter 3

1. *Senshi Sosho*, 14:306; Kamei, "Island of Homesickness," 24.

2. Okada, "Remembrance," 2, 13.

3. Ibid., 11.

4. Edward J. Drea, *MacArthur's ULTRA: Codebreaking and the War Against Japan, 1942–1945* (Lawrence: University Press of Kansas, 1992), 12–13; W. J. Holmes, *Double-Edged Secrets: U.S. Naval Intelligence Operations in the*

Pacific During World War II (Annapolis, Md.: Naval Institute Press, 1979), 67–76; Edwin T. Layton, *"And I Was There": Pearl Harbor and Midway–Breaking the Secrets* (New York: Morrow, 1985), 457–63; Willmott, *The Barrier and the Javelin*, 291–343; Merillat, *Guadalcanal Remembered*, 95–97.

5. CINCPAC Bulletin for 26 May 1942, Greybook, Operational Archives, NHC.

6. Drea, *MacArthur's ULTRA*, 58–9, 242.

7. Drea, *MacArthur's ULTRA*, 7. Quote is from Southwest Pacific Area, Allied Translator and Interpreter Section (ATIS), *Exploitation of Japanese Documents*, Publication #6, 14 December 1944, Folder 10, Box 72, RG-3, 1.

8. Ibid.

9. *The Role of Radio Intelligence in the American Japanese Naval War*, vol. IV (Part II), SRH-012, RG-457, NARA, 533–6.

10. L. R. Schultz, "The Ichiki Detachment and COMINT and the Battle of the Tenaru River, Guadalcanal—August 1942," *Spectrum* (Fall 1977), 10–11; CINCPAC to COMSOPAC 172047 Aug 42, Greybook, 654.

11. *Final Report*, III, Annex E, 7; Merillat, *Guadalcanal Remembered*, 99; Frank, *Guadalcanal*, 148.

12. *Final Report*, III, 9; Thomas, "Of Coconuts," 32; Griffith, *The Battle for Guadalcanal*, 81; Hammel, *Guadalcanal*, 156, 162. The *Final Report* mentions that the target of the Brush Patrol was a Japanese radio station at Gurabasu, thirty-five miles east of Lunga Point. However, this station was not operable in August. Taivu Point was the only operable station on the eastern side of the island at that time. But there is another aspect about this mission that bears consideration. With the

receipt of ULTRA intelligence on Ichiki, it is possible that Vandegrift dispatched this patrol to recon the area east, but this is only speculation.

13. *Final Report*, III, 9; Griffith, *The Battle for Guadalcanal*, 82; Okada, "Remembrance," 11; Tregaskis, *Guadalcanal Diary*, 126.

14. *Final Report*, III, 10; Griffith, *The Battle for Guadalcanal*, 82; Okada, "Remembrance" 11; Twining, *No Bended Knee*, 82.

15. *Senshi Sosho*, 14:307–8; Okada, "Remembrance," 11.

16. Vandegrift and Asprey, *Once a Marine*, 138; Thomas, "Of Coconuts," 32–3; Twining, *No Bended Knee*, 83; Griffith, *The Battle for Guadalcanal*, 82–3; Clemens, *Alone on Guadalcanal*, 202. Samuel B. Griffith assumed that the source of this intelligence was an observation post located on Mount Austen. But this post was not established until 22 September. This information only could have come from the Imperial Navy patrols on the island, in this case, the Japanese radio and observation post at Taivu Point.

17. *Final Report*, III, 10–1; Vandegrift and Asprey, *Once a Marine*, 138–9; Thomas, "Of Coconuts," 33.

18. *Final Report*, III, Annex E (Operations Journal), 3–4; *Final Report*, IV: 21 August–18 September, 1; Cates, "My First," 24; Harry Horsman to author, letter of 23 January 1997 in author's possession. On 15 August, Vandegrift ordered Cates to extend this line an additional 1,500 yards inland, using Cresswell's 1st Battalion, 1st Marines, but the task had progressed little by 20 August.

19. Ibid. Quote is from Tregaskis, *Guadalcanal Diary*, 136.

20. *Final Report*, III, Annex E (Operations Journal), 3–4; *Final Report*, IV, 1; Cates, "My First," 24; George McMillan, *The Old Breed: A History of the First Marine Division in World War II* (Washington, D.C.: Infantry Journal Press, 1949), 61; Frank, *Guadalcanal*, 150–1; Horsman to author letter of 23 January 1997.

21. Quote is from Winston Churchill, *The Hinge of Fate*, vol. IV of *The Second World War* (Boston: Houghton Mifflin, 1951), 92.

22. U.S. War Department, *Handbook on Japanese Military Forces,* (Washington, D.C.: U.S. War Department, 1944), 8–9.

23. Department of the Army, *Fighting on Guadalcanal*, 14, 23. Quote is from *Fighting on Guadalcanal*, 23.

24. A. J. Barker, *The Japanese Army Handbook, 1939–1945* (London: Ian Allan, 1979), 115; U.S. War Department, *Handbook on Japanese Military Forces*, 5–6.

25. Miller, *Guadalcanal*, 310–1; Department of the Army, *Fighting on Guadalcanal*, 12. Quote is by Gerald Thomas, in *Fighting on Guadalcanal*, 40.

26. Quote by Col. Amor Sims, 7th Marines, in Department of the Army, *Fighting on Guadalcanal*, 20.

27. Headquarters, U.S. Army Forces, Far East and 8th Army Military History Section (Japanese Research Division), *Japanese Night Combat*, Part I (Washington, D.C.: U.S. Army Forces, 1954), 81–4; Department of the Army, *Fighting on Guadalcanal*, 5, 7, 12. Quote is by Cpl. J. S. Stankus, 5th Marines, in *Fighting on Guadalcanal*, 5.

28. *Senshi Sosho*, 14:308–9; Hiroshi Kamei, *Guadalcanal Chronicle* (n.p., n.d.); Okada, "Remembrance," 2. The order of march presented in the text differs slightly from Okada's account. I have used the order as out-

lined in Kamei because it corresponds with the Japanese order of attack.

29. Ibid. Quote is from Gordon Prange, *Miracle at Midway* (New York: McGraw-Hill, 1982), 35.

30. U.S. War Department, *Handbook on Japanese Military Forces*, 97–8; Headquarters, U.S. Army Forces, *Japanese Night Combat*, I, 123; Masanobu Tsuji, *Singapore: The Japanese Version* (New York: St. Martin's Press, 1960), 330–1. Translation as rendered in John Toland, *The Rising Sun: The Decline and Fall of the Japanese Empire, 1936–1945* (New York: Random House, 1970), 455–6.

31. Headquarters, U.S. Army Forces, *Japanese Night Combat*, I, 50–3.

32. Ibid., 81–2.

33. Data on Japanese weapons comes from U.S. War Department, *Handbook on Japanese Military Forces;* and Barker, *Japanese Army Handbook*. Quote is from Headquarters, U.S. Army Forces, *Japanese Night Combat*, I, 123.

34. Ibid.

35. Ibid.

36. *Final Report*, III, 3, 9; Vandegrift and Asprey, *Once a Marine*, 139; Merillat, *Guadalcanal Remembered*, 102–3; Twining, *No Bended Knee*, 84.

Chapter 4

1. Anthony Conti, "Just Before the Tenaru," *Guadalcanal Echoes* (November–December 1997), 26.

2. John L. Joseph to author, letter of 5 September 1999 in author's possession.

3. *Final Report*, IV, Annex G, 1; Okaka, "Remembrance," 2, 13.

4. Roger Butterfield, *Al Schmid: Marine* (New York:

Norton, 1944), 98–9; Okada, "Remembrance," 13.

5. Butterfield, *Al Schmid*, 98–103. Schmid would ultimately regain partial sight in one eye.

6. *Final Report*, IV, Annex G, 6–7.

7. George Codrea to Horsman, letter of 22 April 1990 in author's possession, 1; Robert Leckie, *Challenge for the Pacific* (Garden City, N.Y.: Doubleday, 1965), 124; Hammel, *Guadalcanal*, 170. The fact that the Japanese believed the wire was electrified is stated in the captured document "Observation of American Forces," written by Lieutenant Colonel Matsumoto, William Whyte Papers, Box 1, Personal Papers Section, MCHC.

8. Leckie, *Challenge for the Pacific*, 124; Hammel, *Guadalcanal*, 170–1.

9. *Final Report*, IV, Annex G, 1, 3; *Senshi Sosho*, 14:310; *Senshi Sosho*, 28:108; Donahue, "Guadalcanal Journal," 10.

10. Codrea to author, letter of 18 October 1999 in author's possession; Codrea to Horsman letter of 22 April 1990.

11. Ibid.

12. James Wilson, "Scared as Hell at the Tenaru," *Guadalcanal Echoes* (August–September 1999), Supplements E and H.

13. *Final Report*, IV, Annex E, 1; Okada, "Remembrance," 13; Griffith, *The Battle for Guadalcanal*, 84; Merillat, *The Island*, 70. Quote is from Cates, "My First," 24.

14. Thomas, "Of Coconuts," 33–4.

15. Quotes are from Horsman to author letter of 23 January 1997; and Tom Bartlett, "A Japanese Warrior's Final Journey," *Leatherneck* (August 1985), 40.

16. Okada, "Remembrance," 13.

17. Horsman to author letter of 23 January 1997; Donahue, "Guadalcanal Journal," 11; Tregaskis, *Guadalcanal Diary*, 138–9; Harry Horsman to author, letter of 14 September 1999 in author's possession.

18. *Final Report*, IV, Annex G, 7; Codrea to Horsman letter of 22 April 1990; Donahue, "Guadalcanal Journal," 10.

19. Clemens, *Alone on Guadalcanal*, 209–10; Harry Horsman, "Chewed Through His Ropes?" *Guadalcanal Echoes* (October 1989), 4.

20. Okada, "Remembrance," 13.

21. *Final Report*, III, 2; Cates, "My First," 26–7; Tregaskis, *Guadalcanal Diary*, 130–2; Vandegrift and Asprey, *Once a Marine*, 141–2. Quote is from Tregaskis, *Guadalcanal Diary*, 130. Some Japanese accounts state that tanks directly supported Cresswell's advance from the south, but Americans who fought in the battle state that the only tanks that "supported" Cresswell crossed the sand spit.

22. *Final Report*, III, 2–3. Quote is from *Final Report*, 2.

23. Forty, *U.S. Army Handbook*.

24. Tregaskis, *Guadalcanal Diary*, 142.

25. Ibid. Quote is from Cates, "My First," 28.

26. Tregaskis, *Guadalcanal Diary*, 142–3; Okada, "Remembrance," 2. Quote is from Vandegrift to Thomas Holcomb, letter of 22 August 1942, Vandegrift Personal Papers, MCHC; Pedro Del Valle, "Marine Field Artillery on Guadalcanal," *Field Artillery Journal* (October 1943), 728.

27. *Final Report*, IV, 3; Tregaskis, *Guadalcanal Diary*, 139, 145–6; Cates, "My First," 29; Thomas, "Of Coconuts," 34; Hammel, *Guadalcanal*, 175.

28. Ibid.

29. Tregaskis, *Guadalcanal Diary*, 148; Jack Clark, "Beachmaster," *Guadalcanal Echoes* (August–September 1996), 30. Quote is from Tregaskis, *Guadalcanal Diary*, 148.

30. Cates, "My First," 29; Vandegrift to Holcomb letter of 22 August 1942.

31. *Final Report*, IV, Annex G, 2; Okada, "Remembrance," 2, 13; Thomas, "Of Coconuts," 35; Griffith, *The Battle for Guadalcanal*, 86–7. American casualty figures for the Battle of the Tenaru are as follows:

	Killed	Wounded
2d Battalion, 1st Marines	28	44
1st Battalion, 1st Marines	7	13
Weapons Company, 1st Marines	1	0
HQ Company, 1st Marines	0	3
1st Special Weapons Battalion	2	14
1st Tank Battalion	0	1
HQ, 1st Marine Division	0	3
Total	38	78

32. *Final Report*, IV, Annex G, 4.

33. Dennis E. Byrd, "One Day in Hell," *Guadalcanal Echoes* (May–June 1999), 29. Byrd cites a 1985 letter written by Andy Poliny.

34. Tanaka, "The Struggle for Guadalcanal," 164.

35. Cates, "My First," 30.

36. Kamei, "Island of Homesickness," 16. Superior Private Isamu Mashiko lived a charmed life on Guadalcanal. He was also a survivor of the ill-fated Shibuya patrol.

37. *Senshi Sosho*, 14:310; Kamei, "Island of Homesickness," 24.

38. Kamei, "Island of Homesickness," 24.

39. Ibid.

40. Kamei, "Island of Homesickness," 24; ATIS #28, Seventeenth Army Intelligence Summary, 25 August 1942, 64.

Chapter 5

1. *Final Report*, IV, Annex I, 1; Clark, "Beachmaster," 30.

2. *Final Report*, IV, Annex I, 2; Annex G (History of the 1st Marines), 3.

3. Miller, *Guadalcanal*, 86–7; Griffith, *The Battle for Guadalcanal*, 97.

4. Vandegrift to Holcomb letter of 22 August 1942.

5. Vandegrift and Asprey, *Once a Marine*, 144; Frank, *Guadalcanal*, 165.

6. *Final Report*, IV, Annex F (History of the 5th Marines), 2; Tregaskis, *Guadalcanal Diary*, 153–4; Clark, "Beachmaster," 30.

7. *Final Report*, IV, Annex F, 2; ATIS #28, Seventeenth Army Intelligence Summary, 25 August 1942, 65; Tregaskis, *Guadalcanal Diary*, 154–8; Frank, *Guadalcanal*, 176–7.

8. Frank, *Guadalcanal*, 165–88. For additional accounts of the Battle of the Eastern Solomons, see John B. Lundstrom, *The First Team and the Guadalcanal Campaign: Naval Fighter Combat from August to November 1942* (Annapolis, Md.: Naval Institute Press, 1994); Dull, *A Battle History of the Imperial Japanese Navy;* and Samuel Eliot Morison, *The Struggle for Guadalcanal*, repr. ed., vol. V of *History of United States Naval Operations in World War II* (Boston: Little, Brown, 1966).

9. *Senshi Sosho*, 49:586–7; Tanaka, "The Struggle

for Guadalcanal," 167–9; Frank, *Guadalcanal*, 190.

10. Guadalcanal Base Force to 11th Air Flotilla, 231030 August 1942, SRN-1620-1621, RG-457, NARA. American radio intelligence units intercepted this message on 23 August but did not decode and translate it until 2 September.

11. Saburo and Coox, *Kogun*, 227; Imoto to Griffith letter of 14 February 1962; Kiyotake Kawaguchi, "Struggles of the Kawaguchi Detachment," 8, partial translation (hereafter cited as Kawaguchi Memoir), Samuel B. Griffith Personal Papers, MCHC, 8; Toland, *The Rising Sun*, 396–7, 497–500. Kawaguchi was born on 3 December 1892 and died 16 May 1961.

12. Headquarters, U.S. Army Forces, Far East and Eighth Army Military History Section, Japanese Monograph #26, *Borneo Operations*, 4–5; Tsuji, *Singapore*, 40, 57. Quote is from *Singapore*, 57. Japanese infantry divisions underwent organizational changes from square formations (two brigades with two regiments apiece) to triangular formations (one infantry force commander with three regiments) around 1940. Before this reorganization took place in the 18th Division, Kawaguchi's 35th Brigade was composed of both the 124th and 114th Infantry Regiments. The latter unit was retained by the 18th Division to form its third infantry regiment. Although the Kawaguchi Detachment was sometimes known as the 35th Infantry Brigade early in the war, it was really no more than a reinforced regiment until Guadalcanal.

13. Miller, *Guadalcanal*, 112; Intelligence Center, Pacific Oceans Area, *Japanese Land Forces #6*, 12–14.

14. *Senshi Sosho*, 14:304.

15. Kawaguchi Memoir, 9.

16. *Senshi Sosho*, 14:305–6; Kawaguchi Memoir, 9.

17. *Senshi Sosho*, 14:385–7.

18. Ibid., 388–9.

19. Ibid., 390.

20. Vandegrift to Holcomb letter of 22 August 1942; after-action report "1st Battalion, 5th Marines, Operations in Kokumbona, 27–28 August 1942," File A15-1.5, Box 6, RG-127, NARA; Col. Robert S. Amery (ret.) to author, letter of 3 September 1999 in author's possession. Quote is from William Hawkins to Hammel, letter of 28 May 1963, Eric Hammel Personal Papers, Box 6, MCHC.

21. *Final Report*, IV, 4; Annex F, 2.

22. *Final Report*, IV, Annex F, 1–2; Annex E (Artillery), 1–2; Hawkins to Hammel letter of 28 May 1963.

23. Hawkins to Hammel letter of 28 May 1963; Amery to author letter of 3 September 1999; James Tredup, "From the Diary of James Tredup, A Co. Exec on Guadalcanal," *Guadalcanal Echoes* (August–September 1999), 10; Thomas, "Of Coconuts," 39.

24. *Final Report*, IV, Annex F, 2–3; Hawkins to Hammel letter of 28 May 1963; "1st Battalion, 5th Marines Operations in Kokumbona, 27–28 August 1942."

25. *Final Report*, IV, Annex F, 3; Tredup, "From the Diary of James Tredup," 10.

26. *Final Report*, IV, Annex F, 3.

27. *Final Report*, IV, Annex F, 3; *Senshi Sosho*, 14:459–60; Tredup, "From the Diary of James Tredup," 10.

28. Thomas, "Of Coconuts," 40.

29. Diary of Lieutenant Kashii, intelligence officer in the 124th Infantry Regiment, SOPAC-CIC: Item 575, M-2 019483, Oka Intelligence Summary #40, 6 September

1942, William Whyte Personal Papers, Folder 1, Box 1, MCHC.

30. *Final Report,* IV, Annex I (Daily Operations Journal), 8; *Dictionary of American Fighting Ships,* vol. VIII, 365–6; *Senshi Sosho,* 83:41–2.

31. *Final Report,* IV, Annex I, 7–9; Garrett, "A Marine Diary," 12.

32. *Final Report,* V, Annex T, 3, 5–6; Miller, *Guadalcanal,* 225–7. Quote is from RM3 Rene White, "Acorn Red One," *Guadalcanal Echoes* (May–June 1999), 18.

33. Department of the Army, *Fighting on Guadalcanal,* 1, 3. Quote is from *Fighting on Guadalcanal,* 1.

34. Amery to author letter of 21 July 1999; Leckie, *Challenge in the Pacific,* 119.

35. Robert Shedd, letter to the editor, *Guadalcanal Echoes* (July 1992), 26.

36. *Senshi Sosho,* 83:45–50; Merillat, *The Island,* 158; Frank, *Guadalcanal,* 197–8; Garrett, "A Marine Diary," entries for 29 August 1942, 12.

37. Haertlein, "Some Things Were Funny," 5.

38. Morison, *The Struggle for Guadalcanal,* 75–6; Charles Updegraph, *Special Marine Units of World War II* (n.p., n.d.), 72. Transplanting these units was made possible by the landing of elements of the 5th Defense Battalion at Tulagi. One five-inch coastal battery of the 3d Defense Battalion, however, remained at Tulagi.

39. Twining, *No Bended Knee,* 89–90; McCain's written opinions on the importance of Guadalcanal and immediate air reinforcements are found in his message COMAIRSOPAC to CINCPAC 310402 Aug 42, COMSOPAC War Diary, NHC, 81–2.

40. Roy Geiger Biographical File, Reference Section, MCHC.

Chapter 6

1. Tanaka, "The Struggle for Guadalcanal," 169–70.
2. *Senshi Sosho*, 14:391.
3. *Senshi Sosho, Nanto Homen kaigun sakusen, 2, Gato Tesshu Mae, Boieicho Boei kenshujo, Senshishitsu*, Asagumo Shinbun Sha, 5 August 1975, War History Series, *Southeast Area Naval Operations, Part II, Up to the Withdrawal from Guadalcanal*, vol. 83 (Tokyo: Defense Agency, Defense Research Institute, Office of War History, 1975), 24–7; *Senshi Sosho*, 14:391–3; Frank, *Guadalcanal*, 200.
4. *Senshi Sosho*, 14:391–2.
5. Ibid.
6. *Senshi Sosho*, 14:393–4; Tanaka, "The Struggle for Guadalcanal," 172–4.
7. Kawaguchi Memoir, 10; Tanaka, "The Struggle for Guadalcanal," 174–5.
8. Kawaguchi Memoir, 10; *Senshi Sosho*, 14:395.
9. *Senshi Sosho*, 14:397; Toland, *The Rising Sun*, 462.
10. *Senshi Sosho*, 14:397.
11. Proclamation of commander of Seventeenth Army, 28 August 1942, Combat Intelligence Center, South Pacific Force, SOPAC 0324; M-2 015338, William Whyte Personal Papers, Folder 7, Box 10, MCHC.
12. *Senshi Sosho*, 83:33; *Senshi Sosho*, 14:392–3; Tregaskis, *Guadalcanal Diary*, 178–9; ATIS #28, Seventeenth Army Intelligence Summary for 29 August 1942, 68. According to the Kawaguchi Detachment Operation Order A No. 9, the disposition of the 31 August reinforcement run was as follows:

Umikaze	Detachment Headquarters	120
	Guard Company	30

Fubuki	3d Machine Gun Company	120
	Part of III/124 Hqs	20
	Part of the 15th Engineer Regt.	10
Murakumo	6th Independent Radio Unit	28
	Special Radio Squad	6
	67th Line of Comm. Hospital Unit	55
	Part of the 15th Engineer Regt.	40
Hatsuyuki	Part of the III/124 Headquarters	21
	11th Company, III/124	110
	Part of the Regtl. Comm. Unit	12
Kawakaze	12th Company, III/124	120
	Part of the III/124 Gun Platoon	25
Amagiri	9th Company, III/124	110
	III/124 Trench Mortar Unit	40
Kagero	10th Company, III/124	120
	III/124 Gun Platoon	25
	Part of the 15th Engineer Regt.	10

Note: *Suzukaze* was added to the reinforcement run at the last minute. The units landed by it are not known.

13. Griffith, *The Battle for Guadalcanal,* 104; *Final Report,* IV, Annex I, 7.

14. Gerald Thomas Biographical File, Reference Section, MCHC; see also the superb biography by Allan R. Millett, *In Many a Strife: General Gerald C. Thomas and the U.S. Marine Corps, 1917–1956* (Annapolis, Md.: Naval Institute Press, 1993). Thomas was born on 29 October 1894 and died on 7 April 1984.

15. *Final Report,* IV, Annex I, 7; Jon T. Hoffman, *Once a Legend: "Red Mike" Edson of the Marine Raiders* (Novato, Calif.: Presidio Press, 1994), 185. Hoffman's biography on Edson is highly recommended.

16. Merritt Edson Biographical File, Reference Sec-

tion, MCHC. Quotes on Edson are from Hoffman, *Once a Legend*, ix, 213. Edson was born on 25 April 1897 and died on 14 August 1955; Hoffman, letter of 4 September 2001.

17. Updegraph, *U.S. Marine Corps Special Units of World War II*; Hoffman, *Once a Legend*, 131.

18. Frank Guidone, "September 9, 1942—Bloody Ridge Combat Area," *Guadalcanal Echoes* (May–June 1999), 13.

19. Hoffman, *Once a Legend*, 139–41. The weapons allowance of the Raider battalions included the .55-cal. Boys A.T. rifles, but the cumbersome weapons were rarely employed.

20. Robert H. Williams to Hammel, letter of 1 July 1963, Eric Hammel Personal Papers, File 3B47, Box 6, MCHC.

21. Updegraph, *U.S. Marine Corps Special Units of World War II*.

22. Griffith, *The Battle for Guadalcanal*, 104–5; *Final Report*, IV, Annex I (Daily Journal), 11; Hoffman, *Once a Legend*, 186.

23. Griffith, *The Battle for Guadalcanal*, 104–5; Frank, *Guadalcanal*, 202, 212; Hoffman, *Once a Legend*, 186.

24. *Senshi Sosho*, 14:406–7.

25. *Senshi Sosho*, 14:406; Frank, *Guadalcanal*, 25–6.

26. *Senshi Sosho*, 14:407. Diary of Lieutenant Kashii, entries for 4–5 September 1942; ATIS #28, Seventeenth Army Intelligence Reports, 73.

27. Ibid.

28. Ibid.

29. *Senshi Sosho*, 14:409–10; Diary of Lieutenant Kashii, entries for 5–6 September 1942.

30. *Senshi Sosho*, 14:410, 458; Diary of Lieutenant Kashii, entries for 9 September 1942.

31. Kawaguchi Memoir, 13.

32. *Senshi Sosho*, 83:52–4; *Senshi Sosho*, 14:452; Diary of First Lieutenant Matsumoto, USAFISA, G-2 Report 69, Item 1322, 1, William Whyte Personal Papers, Folder 1, Box 1, MCHC.

33. *Senshi Sosho*, 14:440–2; *Translation of Captured Documents on Guadalcanal*, Info Bulletin #18, Item 261, William Whyte Personal Papers, Folder 15, Box 1, MCHC. The men of the Kuma Battalion came from Asahigawa, Hokkaido. The battalion was named after the ferocious brown bears that inhabited northern Hokkaido.

34. Diary of First Lieutenant Matsumoto, 2.

35. *Senshi Sosho*, 83:54–5; *Senshi Sosho*, 14:404.

36. *Senshi Sosho*, 14:442–3.

37. Headquarters, U.S. Army Forces, *Japanese Night Combat*, III, 538.

38. Ibid.

39. *Senshi Sosho*, 14:444.

40. Inui, Genjirou, "My Guadalcanal, I," http://www.gnt.net/~/jribe/Genjirou/genjirou.htm, 31.

41. Kawaguchi Detachment Combat Order 21A, 7 September 1942, Tetere 1300, Samuel B. Griffith Personal Papers Section, MCHC.

42. Ibid.

43. Kawaguchi Memoir, 18–19.

44. Inui, "My Guadalcanal, I," 29–30, 32. The Pak 35/36 antitank guns were captured from Chiang Kai-shek's Chinese forces.

45. *Senshi Sosho*, 14:446; Kawaguchi Memoir, 13–4;

Headquarters, U.S. Army Forces, *Japanese Night Combat*, III, 541.

46. Toland, *The Rising Sun*, 468.

Chapter 7

1. *Report on the Tasimboco* [sic] *Raid by Raider Battalion and 1st Parachute Battalion on 8 September, 1942*, File A36-1, Box 6, RG-127, NARA (hereafter cited as *Report on the Tasimboko Raid*); Griffith, *The Battle for Guadalcanal*, 107; *Dictionary of American Fighting Ships*, vol. IV, 218.

2. *Senshi Sosho*, 14:404–5. The exact strength of the Japanese force defending Tasimboko is not known.

3. Diary of Lieutenant Kashii, entries for 8 September 1942. Quote is by Capt. John Antonelli, commander of Company A Raiders, 1st Raider Battalion Personal Papers, MCHC.

4. *Final Report*, IV, Annex I, 17; *Report on the Tasimboko Raid*, 3; Tregaskis, *Guadalcanal Diary*, 206. The original draft of this chapter stated that the two antitank guns at Taivu Point were of 47mm caliber rather than 37mm, since the only antitank gun in the Japanese arsenal fitting the description provided by Tregaskis was the Model 1 (1941) 47mm gun. With the discovery of Inui's diary, however, this writer learned that these guns were not of Japanese manufacture but German. Inui reveals that the six guns in his unit, the 8th Independent Antitank Company, were German Pak 35/36 guns of 37mm caliber and had formerly belonged to Chiang Kai-shek's Chinese Army.

5. Fred Serral, "A TBX Team on the Tasimboko Raid," 1st Raider Battalion Personal Papers, Tasimboko Raid File, Box 1, MCHC; Hoffman, *Once a Legend*, 189.

6. Tregaskis, *Guadalcanal Diary*, 208–9; author un-

known, "Tasimboko Raid," 1st Raider Battalion Personal Papers, Tasimboko Raid File, Box 1, MCHC.

7. *Final Report,* IV, Annex I, 18.

8. *Report on the Tasimboko Raid,* 2–3.

9. Tregaskis, *Guadalcanal Diary,* 209.

10. Ibid., 210.

11. Ibid., 211–2. John Sweeney to author, letter of 17 April 1997; Oscar F. Peatross, *Bless 'em All: The Raider Marines of World War II* (Irvine, Calif.: Review Publications, 1996), 95.

12. Peatross, *Bless 'em All,* 96.

13. Tregaskis, *Guadalcanal Diary,* 211.

14. Ibid., 212; *Final Report,* IV, Annex I, 18.

15. *Final Report,* IV, Annex I, 18.

16. Ibid.

17. Tregaskis, *Guadalcanal Diary,* 213–4; Griffith, *The Battle for Guadalcanal,* 109; *Report on the Tasimboko Raid,* 3–4.

18. Ibid.; author unknown, "Tasimboko Raid," 3–4.

19. Ibid.

20. Ibid.

21. Quote is from Samuel B. Griffith interview (November 1968), Oral History Section, MCHC, 5; Hoffman, *Once a Legend,* 191.

22. Tregaskis, *Guadalcanal Diary,* 213; Toland, *The Rising Sun,* 465–6.

23. Serral, "A TBX Team on the Tasimboko Raid."

24. Griffith interview, 108; Thomas, "Of Coconuts," 43; Griffith, *The Battle for Guadalcanal,* 109–10. Quote is from McMillan, *The Old Breed,* 71.

25. Twining, *No Bended Knee,* 88; Vandegrift and Asprey, *Once a Marine,* 151.

26. *Senshi Sosho,* 14:448; Kawaguchi Memoir, 14.

27. *Senshi Sosho*, 14:448, 450–1; ATIS #28, Seventeenth Army Intelligence Report, 14 September 1942, 87.

28. Ibid.

29. Headquarters, U.S. Army Forces, *Japanese Night Combat*, III, 541–57.

30. *Senshi Sosho*, 14:454.

31. Kawaguchi Memoir, 15.

32. *Senshi Sosho*, 14:453–4.

33. Ibid., 452–3.

34. Ibid., 454–5. *Final Report*, IV, Annex G, 3.

35. Ibid., 455. Quote is from Inui, "My Guadalcanal, I," 32.

36. Ibid., 457.

37. Diary of Lieutenant Kashii, entries for 11 September 1942; *Senshi Sosho*, 14:460.

38. *Senshi Sosho*, 14:460–1. According to this reference, Oka's attack order had the 124th Regimental Machine Gun Company attached to the Maizuru Battalion for the main attack, but it remained under Oka's direct command.

Chapter 8

1. Griffith, *The Battle for Guadalcanal*, 110.

2. Griffith interview, 96–7; Guidone, "September 9, 1942—Bloody Ridge Combat Area," 13. Basic sources for the Battle of Edson's Ridge on the U.S. side are *Operations of the 1st Parachute Battalion, 13–14 September 1942*, dated 15 October 1942 (hereafter cited as *Report of the 1st Parachute Battalion*), File A36-3, Box 7, RG-127, NARA; and *Report of the Operations of the 1st Raider Battalion, 12–14 September 1942*, dated 21 September 1942 (hereafter cited as *Report of the 1st Raider Battalion*), 1st

Raider Battalion Personal Papers, Edson's Ridge File, Box 1, MCHC.

3. Thomas, "Of Coconuts," 45; Merillat, *The Island*, 93.

4. Peatross, *Bless 'em All*, 98.

5. According to official muster rolls, the Raiders mustered 870 men on 1 September; the Parachutists, 374. Battle wounds, illness, and disease took a heavy toll on both battalions.

6. *Report of the 1st Raider Battalion*, 1.

7. *Report of the 1st Raider Battalion*, 1; John Zimmerman notes on interview with Maj. Houston Stiff, Maj. John B. Sweeney, Maj. Richard S. Johnson, Maj. William E. Sperling, Platoon Sgt. Pete Pettus, 4 February 1949, MCHC. The deployment of the Raiders and Parachutists listed here for 12 September differs from previous accounts, including the official histories. The author's primary source is Edson's official after-action report written one week after the fighting and which is presumed to be the best.

8. *Final Report*, IV, 6–7; Hoffman, *Once a Legend*, 194.

9. *Report of the 1st Raider Battalion*, 1; Guidone, "September 9, 1942—Bloody Ridge Combat Area," 14; Peatross, *Bless 'em All*, 102. Eyewitnesses dispute the number of wounded caused by the air raid. Accounts vary from seven to fifteen.

10. Guidone, "September 9, 1942—Bloody Ridge Combat Area," 14.

11. Twining, *No Bended Knee*, 95–6.

12. Ibid.

13. CINCPAC Intelligence Bulletins, 7, 10, and 12 September 1942, SRSN-013, RG-457, NARA; CNO Intelligence Summary, 12 September 1942, SRNS 0152,

RG-457, NARA; Eighth Fleet to Guadalcanal Base Force ULTRA intercept, 102040 SEP 42, deciphered and translated 110940 SEP 42, SRN 001656, RG-457, NARA. Vandegrift received Nimitz's warning on the possible use of paratroopers, as Richard Tregaskis mentions the paratrooper rumor in *Guadalcanal Diary*, 228.

14. Lundstrom, *The First Team and the Guadalcanal Campaign*, 193–200; First Lieutenant Matsumoto's Diary, 5; Tregaskis, *Guadalcanal Diary*, 220–1.

15. Merillat, *Guadalcanal Remembered*, 133–5; Vandegrift and Asprey, *Once a Marine*, 152–3.

16. Griffith interview, 96–7; *Report of the 1st Raider Battalion*, 1; Guidone, "September 9, 1942—Bloody Ridge Combat Area," 13.

17. Peatross, *Bless 'em All*, 102; Guidone, "September 9, 1942—Bloody Ridge Combat Area," 13.

18. Kawaguchi Memoir, 19.

19. *Senshi Sosho*, 14:462–3.

20. Ibid., 464–5; First Lieutenant Matsumoto's Diary, 6.

21. John Mielke, "A Missing Piece of Edson's History," *The Dope Sheet* (Summer 1995), 1, 3.

22. *Report of the 1st Raider Battalion*, 1; Peatross, *Bless 'em All*, 102.

23. Ibid.

24. Merillat, *Guadalcanal Remembered*, 133; Tregaskis, *Guadalcanal Diary*, 224. Kawaguchi's artillery unit consisted of four regimental guns of the 28th Infantry and two of the 124th Infantry. The four Japanese warships conducted a second bombardment at 0005, 13 September for 45 minutes.

25. *Report of the 1st Raider Battalion*, 1.

26. John Sweeney Ridge Memoir (unpublished), 72.

27. Joseph Alexander, *Edson's Raiders* (Edson's Raiders Association, 1999), 152–4

28. Ibid.

29. Merillat, *Guadalcanal Remembered*, 95; Griffith, *The Battle for Guadalcanal*, 116; Mielke, "A Missing Piece of Edson's History," 3.

30. Mielke, "A Missing Piece of Edson's History," 3.

31. Robert Youngdeer to William Bartsch, letter of 24 September 1991.

32. First Raider Battalion muster roll for September 1942.

33. Diary of First Lieutenant Matsumoto, 6.

34. *Senshi Sosho*, 14:464–5

35. Ibid.

36. Kawaguchi Memoir, 21; *Senshi Sosho*, 14:467.

37. *Senshi Sosho*, 14:463–4, 467.

38. Diary of Lieutenant Kashii, entries for 13 September 1942.

39. *Senshi Sosho*, 14:464, 467.

40. *Report of the 1st Parachute Battalion*, 1–2; Griffith, *The Battle for Guadalcanal*, 116–7; Merillat, *The Island*, 96; Guidone, "September 9, 1942—Bloody Ridge Combat Area," 14.

41. *Senshi Sosho*, 14:475–7; *Senshi Sosho*, 83:108.

42. Benis Frank, "Gerald C. Thomas Interview" (Washington, D.C.: Marine Corps Historical Center, 1966), 362–3; Twining, "Head for the Hills!," 48–9.

43. Twining, *No Bended Knee*, 97–8. Controversy swirls around the existence of Ghormley's handwritten note. Neither Vandegrift nor Thomas mentions it in their writings, but Merrill Twining, an impeccable source who eventually achieved the rank of a full general, insists that it existed. Evidence of the note's existence is compelling.

First, Ghormley's top-secret letter does not seem as dire as Vandegrift and Thomas recalled it. This suggests, at least to this author, the possibility that Vandegrift and Thomas were combining the seriousness of the top-secret letter and Ghormley's note. Moreover, Thomas recalls placing the letter in his shirt pocket, a serious breech of security, but tucking away a handwritten note of such content is understandable. The failure of such a note to survive the campaign would not be surprising. This author believes it is a strong possibility that the failure of both Vandegrift and Thomas to mention it in their writings was a move to spare Ghormley further humiliation rather than a statement of its nonexistence. Finally, those who pine for the need of documentary evidence of Ghormley's handwritten communication should note that the top-secret letter also no longer exists.

44. Thomas, "Of Coconuts," 46–7.

45. Peatross, *Bless 'em All*, 103.

46. *Report of the 1st Parachute Battalion*, 2–3; *Report of the 1st Raider Battalion*, 2; *Final Report*, IV, Annex C (Engineer Activities Guadalcanal), 2–3; Merillat, *The Island*, 96–7.

47. Peatross, *Bless 'em All*, 103–4.

48. *Report of the 1st Parachute Battalion*, 2–3.

49. Peatross, *Bless 'em All*, 104.

50. *Final Report*, IV, 8; McMillan, *The Old Breed*, 75; Griffith, *The Battle for Guadalcanal*, 116.

51. *Final Report*, IV, Annex E (artillery), 2.

52. Elton Whisenhunt, "A Personal Memoir," *Guadalcanal Echoes* (August–September 1997), 11.

53. *Senshi Sosho*, 14:468; First Lieutenant Matsumoto's Diary, 6.

54. *Senshi Sosho*, 14:468.

55. Kawaguchi Memoir, 16; Toland, *Rising Sun*, 469–70.

56. *Senshi Sosho*, 14:470.

Chapter 9

1. *Report of the 1st Marine Raider Battalion*, 2; *Senshi Sosho*, 14:471; Merillat, *The Island*, 97; First Lieutenant Matsumoto's Diary, 7. Quote is from Peatross, *Bless 'em All*, 104.

2. Merillat, *The Island*, 97; First Lieutenant Matsumoto's Diary, 7.

3. *Report of the 1st Parachute Battalion*, 3–4.

4. *Report of the 1st Parachute Battalion*, 4; *Final Report*, IV, Annex E, 2.

5. *Report of the 1st Parachute Battalion*, 4–6; *Senshi Sosho*, 14:472–3.

6. Ibid.

7. Merillat, *The Island*, 98.

8. *Report of the 1st Parachute Battalion*, 4–5.

9. Ibid., 5–6.

10. *Report of the 1st Parachute Battalion*, Enclosure D, 1–2; Whisenhunt, "A Personal Memoir," 11.

11. Pedro Del Valle, "Marine Field Artillery on Guadalcanal," *Field Artillery Journal* (October 1943), 728–9; Hammel, *Guadalcanal*, 228.

12. *Senshi Sosho*, 14:472–3.

13. Toland, *Rising Sun*, 475.

14. Kamei, *Guadalcanal Chronicle, II*, 67–8.

15. Tregaskis, *Guadalcanal Diary*, 226–7; Merillat, *The Island*, 98.

16. *Report of the 1st Raider Battalion*, 2; William J. Owens, *Green Hell: The Battle for Guadalcanal* (Central Point, Ore.: Hellgate Press, 1999), 115–6.

17. *Report of the 1st Parachute Battalion*, 6.

18. Peatross, *Bless 'em All*, 105.

19. Houston Stiff to William Bartsch, letter of September 1991; Peatross, *Bless 'em All*, 109.

20. Peatross, *Bless 'em All*, 108.

21. *Final Report*, IV, Annex E, 2–3; Del Valle, "Marine Field Artillery on Guadalcanal," 729; Merillat, *The Island*, 99. Quotes are from Tregaskis, *Guadalcanal Diary*, 228.

22. *Report of the 1st Parachute Battalion*, 8.

23. Ibid., 6–7.

24. Tregaskis, *Guadalcanal Diary*, 228–9; George Wiggins to Griffith, letter of 11 February 1982, published in *Guadalcanal Echoes* (April 1991), 32; Merillat, *The Island*, 100–1; Hoffman, *Once a Legend*, 205. Another marine of the 1st Marines Weapons Company accompanied Wiggins on the munitions trip but bailed out after encountering sniper fire on the ridge.

25. Peatross, *Bless 'em All*, 109.

26. Griffith, *The Battle for Guadalcanal*, 119; Tregaskis, *Guadalcanal Diary*, 238; George Doying, "Do or Die Men," *Leatherneck* (March 1944), 17. Quote is from Twining, *No Bended Knee*, 100.

27. Stiff to Bartsch letter of September 1991.

28. John L. Zimmerman, *The Guadalcanal Campaign* (Washington, D.C.: Historical Division, Headquarters, U.S. Marine Corps, 1949), 89. Quote is from Thomas, "Of Coconuts," 48.

29. *Senshi Sosho*, 14:472–3; *Final Report*, IV, Annex C, 3.

30. Shohei Haga, "The Aoba Battalion's Plunge Through to the Airfield," *Nama Guadalcanal War History* (n.p., n.d.), 240–55.

31. Carlo Fulgenzi, unpublished *Reader's Digest* manuscript, August 1957.

32. Kamei, *Guadalcanal Chronicle*, 53–4.

33. Tregaskis, *Guadalcanal Diary*, 230–1; Lundstrom, *The First Team and the Guadalcanal Campaign*, 214; Thomas, "Of Coconuts," 48.

34. Kawaguchi Memoir, 22; *Senshi Sosho*, 14:474–5.

35. Tregaskis, *Guadalcanal Diary*, 234–5; Whisenhunt, "A Personal Memoir," 11.

36. Merillat, *The Island*, 99–100; Tregaskis, *Guadalcanal Diary*, 230–2.

37. Edward Fee to author, letter of 18 September 1999 in author's possession.

38. *Report of the 1st Parachute Battalion*, 8; *Report of the 1st Raider Battalion*, 3.

39. Composition of the Kuma Battalion was based on the document "Translation Document Found on Guadalcanal," Item #253, 1st MAC translation M-2-014112, William Whyte Personal Papers, Folder 16, Box 1, MCHC; William Bartsch, "Crucial Battle Ignored," *Guadalcanal Echoes* (November–December 1998), 10, Bartsch's article is the most accurate and detailed article on this battle.

40. *Final Report*, IV, 11–2; Merillat, *The Island*, 102; Bartsch, "Crucial Battle Ignored," 23.

41. *Senshi Sosho*, 14:470; *Final Report*, IV, Annex G (History of the 1st Marines), 5; *Final Report*, IV, 12; Bartsch, "Crucial Battle Ignored," 24; Merillat, *The Island*, 102–3.

42. Merillat, *The Island*, 102–3; Bartsch, "Crucial Battle Ignored," 24; *Senshi Sosho*, 14:470–1.

43. *Final Report*, IV, Annex G (History of the 1st Marines), 5–6; Bartsch, "Crucial Battle Ignored," 24–5; Merillat, *The Island*, 103.

44. Merillat, *The Island*, 103.

45. Ibid. Quote is from Inui, "My Guadalcanal, I," 37.

46. Japanese Anti-Tank Tactics and Weapons, 4–5, File C15-3, Box 8, RG-127, NARA; Merillat, *The Island*, 103.

47. Bartsch, "Crucial Battle Ignored," *Guadalcanal Echoes* (February–March 1999), 6.

48. Merillat, *The Island*, 103–4; *Final Report*, IV, Annex G, 6.

49. Diary of Lieutenant Kashii, entries for 13 September 1942, William Whyte Personal Papers, Folder 5, Box 1, MCHC; *Senshi Sosho*, 14:474.

50. *Senshi Sosho*, 14:474.

51. Ore Marion, "L Company's Ridge," *Guadalcanal Echoes* (May–June 1998), 19; Merillat, *The Island*, 104.

52. Marion, "L Company's Ridge," 19; Ore Marion to author, letter of 12 July 1999 in author's possession; Diary of Lieutenant Kashii, entries for 14 September 1942.

53. Ibid.

54. *Senshi Sosho*, 14:474; Kamei, *Guadalcanal Chronicle*, 78–9; Marion to author letter of 12 July 1999.

55. Ibid.

56. *Senshi Sosho*, 14:474; Merillat, *The Island*, 104; Marion, "L Company's Ridge," 19; Kamei, *Guadalcanal Chronicle*.

57. Diary of Lieutenant Kashii, entries for 13 and 14 September 1942; *Senshi Sosho*, 14:474.

58. *Senshi Sosho*, 14:35–6, 502. Use of the official Japanese casualty report for Edson's Ridge is of a mixed value, because it covers the period 13 August–2 October. This time frame includes a subsequent battle in late September. The report also understates the losses in the 2d Battalion, 4th Regiment.

59. *Senshi Sosho*, 14:471; Kawaguchi Memoir, 25. Ac-

tually, Kawaguchi believed that Watanabe's battalion did not fight at all that night, but this was later proven untrue.

60. *Report of the 1st Raider Battalion*, 3; *Report of the 1st Parachute Battalion*, 8; Griffith, *The Battle for Guadalcanal*, 121; Merillat, *The Island*, 105.

61. A total of 878 rounds of 75mm shells were expended in support of the western and eastern flanks.

62. *Report of the 1st Parachute Battalion*, 7.

63. Quote is from Sun-tzu, *The Art of War*, edited by James Clavell (New York: Delacorte Press, 1983), 27.

64. Diary of Lieutenant Kashii, entries for 14 September 1942; Kawaguchi Memoir, 25–6.

65. Headquarters, U.S. Army Forces, *Japanese Night Combat*, III, 551–2.

66. Marion to author letter of 12 July 1999.

67. *Senshi Sosho*, 14:480–2. Quote is from *U.S. Strategic Bombing Survey (USSBS) Interrogations*, I, interview with IJN Captain Watanabe, 68.

68. Quote is from Vandegrift draft oral history, MCHC, 798.

Chapter 10

1. *Senshi Sosho*, 14:474–5, 500–3.

2. *Final Report*, IV, Annex G, 6; Hammel, *Guadalcanal*, 235–6. Annex G states that losses totaled eighteen, but survivors of the ambush insist that twenty-four perished.

3. Tregaskis, *Guadalcanal Diary*, 248–9.

4. Diary of First Lieutenant Matsumoto, 5, 9.

5. Diary of First Lieutenant Matsumoto, 9–10; Diary of Lieutenant Kashii, entry for 21 September 1942; *Senshi Sosho*, 14:504.

6. Diary of First Lieutenant Matsumoto, 9.

7. Ibid., 10.

8. *Senshi Sosho*, 14:504–5, 507.

9. *Senshi Sosho*, 14:478–80.

10. Ibid. Quote is from page 479.

11. Ibid., 480, 499; *Senshi Sosho*, 83:137.

12. *Senshi Sosho*, 14:523–4.

13. Ibid., 505–6.

14. Ibid., 448–51; 505–7.

15. *Final Report*, IV, Annex I, 25–6.

16. *Final Report*, IV, Annex I, 28; *Final Report*, Phase V, Annex W, 1–2; COMAPHIBFORSOPAC, Rpt Opn for Reinf of Guadalcanal by 7th Marines, Incl F. Quote is from Twining, *No Bended Knee*, 104.

17. Lewis Puller biographical information comes from the Puller Biographical File, Reference Section, MCHC. Edson quote is from Burke Davis, *Marine!: The Life of Lt. Gen. Lewis B. (Chesty) Puller* (Boston: Little, Brown), 108; Frank, "Gerald C. Thomas Interview." Puller was born on 26 June 1889 and died on 11 October 1971.

18. *Final Report*, V, 1–2; *Final Report*, IV, Annex A.

19. *Final Report*, V, 3–4.

20. Ibid., 4–5.

21. Vandegrift and Asprey, *Once a Marine*, 161; Frank, "Gerald C. Thomas Interview"; Vandegrift to Admiral Turner, letter of 24 September 1942, Vandegrift Personal Papers, File 32, Box 3, MCHC.

22. Ibid. Quote is from Vandegrift to Richmond K. Turner, letter of 24 September 1942.

23. *Final Report*, IV, 14; Merillat, *The Island*, 117–8. Quote is from Thomas, "Of Coconuts," 50.

24. *Senshi Sosho*, 14:507.

25. Ibid., 508.

26. Ibid.

27. Ibid.

28. *Final Report,* V, 5.

29. Ibid. Vandegrift to Turner, letter of 26 September 1942.

30. *Final Report,* V, 5; Vandegrift to Turner letter of 24 September 1942; Diary of Lieutenant Kashii, entry for 22 September 1942.

31. Diary of Lieutenant Kashii, entries for 21, 22, and 23 September 1942. Quote is from Twining, *No Bended Knee,* 109.

32. Maj. Charles W. Kelly, *Narrative Report of the Second Battle of the Matanikau* (hereafter cited as Kelly, *Narrative Report*), 1st Battalion, 7th Marines, Summary of Operations on Guadalcanal, AS1-1, Box 6, RG-127, NARA, 1; Davis, *Marine!,* 118–9; Diary of Lieutenant Kashii, entry for 24 September 1942.

33. Joseph Gobel, "Memories of Guadalcanal," *Guadalcanal Echoes* (August–September 1999), 6.

34. Davis, *Marine!,* 119; Kelly, *Narrative Report,* 1; Gobel, "Memories of Guadalcanal," 6. Kelly, in what is apparently the only "official" report of the battle, states that seven marines died in this skirmish, but Gobel, who helped bury the dead, insists that thirteen perished; Hoffman, letter of 4 September 2001.

35. Kelly, *Narrative Report,* 2; Hoffman, *Once a Legend,* 216.

36. Kelly, *Narrative Report,* 2; Diary of Lieutenant Kashii, entries for 26 September 1942; *Senshi Sosho,* 14:510.

37. Kelly, *Narrative Report,* 2–3.

38. Diary of Lieutenant Kashii, entries for 26 and 27 September 1942; Griffith, *The Battle for Guadalcanal,* 135–6; *Senshi Sosho,* 14:510.

39. *Final Report*, V, 7; Griffith, *The Battle for Guadalcanal*, 136.

40. Diary of Lieutenant Kashii, entries for 27 September 1942; Kelly, *Narrative Report*, 3; *Senshi Sosho*, 14:510.

41. Kelly, *Narrative Report*, 4–5.

42. Ibid.

43. Twining, *No Bended Knee*, 110–1; Frank, *Guadalcanal*, 272.

44. Kelly, *Narrative Report*, 5. Quote is from Davis, *Marine!*, 121. In a letter to this author, dated 24 November 1999, Richard B. Frank offers compelling evidence that it was the U.S. destroyer *Monssen*, not the *Ballard*, that assisted the marines.

45. Gobel, "Memories of Guadalcanal," 13.

46. Kelly, *Narrative Report*, 5–6; *Senshi Sosho*, 14:511.

47. Diary of Lieutenant Kashii, entries for 27 September 1942; Kelly, *Narrative Report*, 6–7.

48. Gobel, "Memories of Guadalcanal," Supplement C.

49. Diary of Lieutenant Kashii, entries for 27 September; Kelly, *Narrative Report*, 7; 2d Battalion, 5th Marines, Record of Events for 27 September 1942, 3–4; ATIS #28, Seventeenth Army Intelligence Report #40 for 27–30 September 1942, 102.

50. Hoffman, *Once a Legend*, 218.

51. Ibid.

52. Ibid.

53. *Final Report*, V, 9.

54. Ibid.

55. Griffith, *The Battle for Guadalcanal*, 140–1; Vandegrift and Asprey, *Once a Marine*, 171; Merillat, *Guadalcanal Remembered*, 158–9; Hoffman, *Once a Legend*, 220.

Index